D1566763

IN SEARCH OF GAUGUIN

IN SEARCH OF GAUGUIN

JEAN-LUC COATALEM

TRANSLATED BY LIZ HERON

Weidenfeld & Nicolson
LONDON

First published in France in 2001 by Éditions Grasset & Fasquelle
as *Je suis dans les mers du Sud*

First published in Great Britain in 2004 by Weidenfeld and Nicolson

This book is supported by the French Ministry for Foreign
Affairs, as part of the Burgess programme headed for the French
Embassy in London by the Institut Français du Royaume-Uni.

Liberté • Égalité • Fraternité
RÉPUBLIQUE FRANÇAISE

A CIP catalogue record for this book
is available from the British Library.

ISBN 0 297 82968 8

Typeset by Selwood Systems, Midsomer Norton
Printed by Butler & Tanner Ltd, Frome and London

Weidenfeld & Nicolson
The Orion Publishing Group Ltd
Orion House
5 Upper Saint Martin's Lane
London, WC2H 9EA

'Is our need for demons then so great?'

HENRI MICHAUX, *Un Barbare en Asie*

ACKNOWLEDGEMENTS

The author would like to extend warm thanks for their help and support to: Maeva Salmon ('Maison de Tahiti et de ses îles'), Gilles Artur (musée Gauguin, Papeari), Brenda Chin Foo (musée Gauguin, Papeari), Françoise Fiacre ('Iles du Monde'), Serge Gatinel (Hotel Hanakee, Hiva Oa), Manuel Carcassonne (Grasset), Eve Sivadjian, Marcelino Truong and, in particular, Olivier Frébourg.

Acknowledgement is also made to the following works, which have been indispensable guides and companions at every stage of the journey: Pierre Leprohon's *Gauguin* (Gründ 1975), Bengt Danielsson's *Gauguin à Tahiti et aux îles Marquises* (Editions du Pacifique 1975), and David Sweetman's *Les Vies de Gauguin* (Belfond 1995).

PROLOGUE

I got into my car, threw a travel bag on the seat along with a thermos flask of coffee, and left the twelfth arrondissement to head for the ring road and out of Paris. It was six in the morning and sleet was slanting down over the capital. Through the rise and fall of the windscreen wipers, the headlights shed dense yellow trails. I had hardly glanced at the road map; how could I go wrong? I was travelling against the oncoming traffic, on my way to Holland to see a Tahitian painting, a painting by Gauguin. I felt giddy with excitement, like a kid playing truant, a convict getting lucky over mixed-up cell numbers, or better still, a hole in the wall. This cold front across Europe would offer me anonymity and let me travel incognito. It would screen my escape, it would give me an edge, concentrate my attention; it would bring me back to myself, to my longing for Gauguin.

I would drive along motorways lined with signposts brittle like glass, moonscape petrol stations, trees as grimly stark as ideograms. A road that went straight on for six hours, maybe seven, through Mons, Brussels, Antwerp, Breda, Utrecht, Ede, Otterlo; in the land of polders and windmills. Sometimes, in the distance, through the mist, whose curling outlines were etched across a rice-paper sky, there was the breath of a farm horse over hard ground, the flight of a straggling bird ... There I was, alone with my notebook and a biography of the painter by Pierre Leprohon set on the front passenger seat. As a bookmark, I had a photocopy of a poem by Nicolas Bouvier: 'the small cigars tied with red thread, they cost just five annas a bunch, where are we going tomorrow?'

Oise, Somme, Pas de Calais and Belgium crossed, Holland reached. At Utrecht there's a turning for Ede, Otterlo – unlikely destinations in this snow which was falling thickly, or through thin nasty black sheets of rain, or else downy flakes dropping onto the papery glass of the windscreen, between white felt bushes and exclamatory trees. Two hundred and fifty miles clocked up, north all the way. Either side of the car, the air was becoming solid; the cold was gripping Europe in its jaws. I picked up speed through this suspended stage set blanked out by the fog, between shuttered hamlets, phantom towns hovering in the distance, their electric wires vibrating in the cold, a network of exposed nerves. Soon, on the other side of some invisible frontier, everything would stop, myself included, petrified, I imagined, in the ultimate kingdom of ice.

What was it that drove me on through this now abstract landscape? Just an old photograph, of an Anglo-Polynesian woman called Helena Suhas. This original print had been bought at auction in Paris a few years earlier when a Victor Segalen collection was up for sale with some pre-1900 documents thrown in. Was she some mystery *vahine* (common parlance for a Polynesian woman)? The photograph was deemed to be of limited interest. However, she had known Paul Gauguin and, it seems, he had done a small portrait of her son on canvas. Nobody wanted this photograph. There were far more interesting things among what was left of the collection, and wealthy collectors, dealers and museums concentrated on the drawings and the last remaining possessions of the master of Hiva Oa. My younger brother raised his hand; the hammer fell and the Tahitian woman's photograph was ours for one thousand five hundred and fifty francs. We took it away knowing nothing about her, a little of her life in our lives.

It is a sepia photograph mounted on stiff card, four inches by five and a half, printed around the end of the nineteenth century, and in good condition. There would have been another copy of this photograph that belonged to Gauguin's friend, the painter Georges Daniel de Monfreid. Rigidly posed, to allow for the poor sensitivity of photographic plates, the *vahine* sits in three-quarter left profile; her face is round but fine-featured. She is twenty-five or so, with a faraway, dreamy air of melancholy. Her hands are demurely crossed on the muslin missionary dress, and a shining plait of hair hangs smoothly from her shoulder to the crook of her arm. Adorning her left wrist is a silver bracelet, two gardenia blooms are at her ear, and she wears a glass earring, a transparent diamond shape. An artificial lawn can be glimpsed in the background, a hazy hint of sky.

Scouring biographies of the painter, I had learned a little more about her. Her maiden name was Burns, and she was the daughter of an Englishman and a native woman related to the royal family. Her name changed to Suhas when she married Jean-Jacques Suhas, a 'bacteriological' nurse assigned to the colonial hospital in Papeete. A minor character in Gauguin's story, of course, but one linked to his Polynesian exile, and directly to that 1892 work, *Atiti, the Dead Child*. This lifeless child was Helena's son.

On his arrival in Tahiti, in 1891, the painter had lived near Papeete Cathedral, in lodgings next door to the Suhas. In the early weeks of his stay, they had helped him to find his way around and, on more than one occasion, they had lent him money. Aristide, known as 'Atiti', was the only child this couple had, sole offspring of Helena, the *vahine* in the photograph, and the male nurse. With his own five children left behind in Denmark, Gauguin had become fond of the youngster. After moving away to the coast road, the following year he paid them a visit on 5 March. Some hours before, Atiti had fallen victim to a bout of enteritis, and Gauguin arrived in the midst of the family tragedy. Dressed in his best clothes, the child lay on his deathbed. Touched by the grief of the parents and probably seeing it as a way of repaying his debt to them, the painter took out his charcoals, cut a ten- by twelve-inch rectangle out of some sacking, sketched the corpse and laid on his colours: red-brown, yellow, white and dark blue, making an instant portrait of the small dead body, which held a rosary in its hands, its hair upon the pillow greasy with cold sweat. He then presented this work to the Suhas. But on the canvas, his face streaked with the olive-green light of the curtains, his features marred by heat and death, their adorable little boy had become a scary apelike creature, a swollen-necked gnome, mummified by paint.

'He's all yellow! He looks Chinese!' the mother screams, wrenching away the unspeakable painting.

Helena gives way to hysterical sobbing. Jean-Jacques puts the painting in a corner and brings the painter some rum ... What becomes of the canvas? No one knows. It disappears without trace for fifty years and crops up again in Europe after the Second World War, to be bought by the Kröller-Müller Museum.

After a network of cycle tracks, I found Otterlo's first red-brick houses. It was a small and unassuming Protestant town, inhabited by a number of Dutch giants muffled up in anoraks. The temperature was minus eight. A glossy coating of icing sugar rounded off the picture.

On the left, a sign indicated the way in to the Hoge Veluwe National Park. I drove on slowly as I covered these last few miles. It was a Monday afternoon and, with temperatures this low, not many visitors had ventured out here. An unctuous silence seemed to make its way down from the trees onto the pathways of the vast park. The Kröller-Müller Museum finally appeared as I turned a corner. Standing in a clearing, the building of glass and beige-coloured stone, designed by Henry van de Velde, looked half-modernist, half-Assyrian temple, with its clever fitting together of blocks and bays, the unreal light cutting right through before spreading out around it.

I had made up my mind to be methodical, to take notes, make a sketch of Atiti, the little captive Pharaoh in this maze, lying in his painting for all eternity. But my heart was beating fast. Then, among scores of admirable van Goghs at which I did not cast a single glance, I finally unearthed it fixed on a wall between a Renoir and a Monet landscape. Atiti, at last! Aristide Suhas in a yellow frame, in the 'Tahitian manner', catalogue number W452, labelled with the laconic epitaph: *Portret von Atiti, 1892, oil on canvas, purchase 1951.* Yes, filling the whole canvas was the corpse my thoughts had dwelt on so much, cut off around the navel, the kid with one large ear visible, a yellow complexion verging on green, and heavy brownish–yellow eyelids. His joined hands formed a sludgy mess with an entwined rosary floating about on it. He wore a ridiculous looking baptismal robe, a holy medal around his neck on a crinkled blue ribbon. His head lay on the pillow, the black hair plastered with sweat; a lace sheet was pulled up over his stomach. A frothy bunch of flowers to his left, perfunctory and smothered. A chestnut-brown background with the signature at top right: P Go.

The child was clearly dead and the botched canvas laid bare this tragedy, denounced it, made it theatrical. What a strange notion, painting little Atiti! How could this laid-out body, this exotic wax doll, be kept as a memento? I could understand the Suhas' anger and disappointment. Moving backwards and forwards, shunning the other rooms as I multiplied the angles and viewpoints in this one, I stayed there for at least three-quarters of an hour, taking all my time since I had come from France just for him, for her, her story, their story, broken and in little pieces, but brought to life by the clumsy grace of the painter. And then, in its transparent envelope, I had the photograph of Helena. What was to stop me at some point from bringing the two together, bringing them face to face? This was what I did, ceremoniously, like a sorcerer's apprentice trying out an old formula. Impervious to the surveillance cameras and the attendants, in an act of bravado, I laid it right against the canvas, with the photographed face up against the painted face, so that they could be as one, look at each other again, be face to face once more, the mother and the child, the child and the mother. There was nothing morbid in this gesture, no, just a feeling of vindication, appeasement, the conviction of something lasting, of a spark renewed. Only then did I retreat, clutching this invisible treasure, a shrinking of time, a combining of fates, hemispheres, affections and chance.

Outside, I immediately felt defenceless and feverish. From the Batavian sky, snow was falling again, but softly and lightly. Onwards! It was time to make tracks. I only had to fill up my tank, buy some mineral water and sandwiches, leave behind the wooded acres of Hoge Veluwe Park, and Otterlo, head due west beyond the wheezing windmills, and I would discover the litany of the ocean, the vastness of the sky.

In no time I was on the motorway, ploughing through the bad weather. Darkness came rolling in, catching me like a sudden tide, so I made a halt at Scheveningen, an out-of-season resort. The casino, the trams, the hotels with their salt-eroded carpets, the rundown villas with their close-mown gardens, the brasseries serving beer, fish and foaming hot chocolate, gave an antiquated air to this strip of seaside.

Late in the afternoon, I took a ground-floor room in a 1930s-style hotel whose bow windows looked out onto the open sea. In the distance, a twinkling line of tankers glided towards France. The lamplight-studded promenade resembled a smeared canvas. It would snow tomorrow over the North Sea.

Coat collar turned up, I walked aimlessly about the dismal quay-sides, had a quick dinner, drank a bottle of riesling and staggered back to my room with the wind biting at my back. The television glowed soundlessly as my thoughts returned to Helena Suhas and the sepia photograph, to Atiti Suhas, my Aristide, a travelling companion I would never have imagined, and to the island of Tahiti, where I had spent my childhood.

That night, I drafted the first few lines of what was to become a book about Paul Gauguin. What was he in flight from, such a long way from his own people, a deliberate outsider in far-flung Polynesia? What had he become? What had he left behind in Europe that made him so beside himself with emotion that he dashed off this painting of a waxen-faced yellow corpse?

In other words, where were *we* going tomorrow?

I already knew Paul Gauguin. I loved his zigzag course across the globe, the way he turned his back on everything; I loved his lofty, primitive works hanging in the Jeu de Paume, then later in the Musée d'Orsay. He had become the favourite painter on the walls of my own personal museum, and behind his ferocious appetite for the world of Elsewhere I had glimpsed a desperate headlong flight. By coincidence, his landscapes, whether real or imagined or sometimes chimerical, were the same as mine: Tahiti, where I had been a child; Madagascar, where he had wanted to settle and where I had got through the Seventies; and the former Indochina, where my grandfather was stationed between 1927 and 1930, and which Gauguin had long dreamed of, picturing himself reborn in the Orient. Not forgetting Brittany, of course, even though, unlike him, the one I inherited is more seagoing Atlantic than inland. The Crozon peninsula, in Finistère, 'the head of a barking dog', as Alexandre Vialatte described it. Baie de Douarnenez, Anse de Morgat, île de l'Aber, Pointe de Saint-Hernot, the terrifying Cap de la Chèvre . . . a tracery of rocks, a maze of creeks where we amateurs plied our rundown sailing boat. From here, from this *finis terrae*, this end of the earth, a mass of cindery heaths covered in gorse and heather, all the ships sailed, all the desires for adventure were born. An extremity of Europe, a sandstone trident pounded by the currents of Iroise Bay, the peninsula was a cruciform tongue darting out to the west, into the blue.

At Morgat, once a tuna-fishing port, we still have our family home, a big slate and granite farmhouse built in the eighteenth century, with a barn and a stable adjoining. Around squat dry-stone-walled fields, the five or six *pen-ty* of Penfrat overlap with one another, huddled up into their fenced-in gardens, beside their millstones and their wells. A way of trapping and thereby defying the wind and storms, the rainy sadness of the winters, the solitude of those long nourished on black bread and sardines. There was a makeshift harbour, too small, but we clung to it with peasant pride and a sailor's determination to hold his course. On the front lawn I planted three palm trees, *Trachycarpus fortunei*. This is a mountain species that comes originally from Asia, and can still stoically survive at a temperature of minus twenty degrees, stoutly growing along the Mediterranean coast and all the way up to Scotland. They are quite happy among my hydrangea shrubs, swaying in the salt-soaked air between two upturned dinghies. Their dark green tufts of foliage and their shaggy trunks, the long-haired covering resembling a winter coat, give our hamlet a misleading air of 'back to Africa'.

Sometimes when I am in the library, rereading Alain Gerbault's books or old prizegiving albums, or Jules Verne or Robert Louis Stevenson, I look out of the window at those three hairy comrades as they rustle, magnetised by the breath of the tides. They too speak to me of Polynesia, and of their cousins, the *Pelagodoxa henryana*, on the other side of the world, on the bounds of that ocean which is never-ending even though it alters its name, sheltering all the exiles of the southern hemisphere under their palms. And of those sun-filled archipelagoes of my childhood, those visions of sands and lagoons where I was so happy, so carefree: in a word, so lucky. And also of the painter Paul Eugène Henri Gauguin, who made his escape there to give meaning to his painting, which is to say his life.

On the north coast of the peninsula, the manor house of the symbolist poet Saint-Pol Roux, who died in 1940, stands likewise at 'that end of the earth which is the sky's beginning'. It juts out over the sea, perched upon its precipice, with an escort of one hundred and forty-three quartzite standing stones which are so many totems marking out equinoxes and solstices. . . Pen-Hir point, Pen-Hat ridge. At dusk, the tawny light fires these remnants, which may well be haunted. Broken balconies, caved-in stairways, decapitated turrets – this edifice was destroyed during the bombing raids over Brest in 1944, its fallen fragments eaten up by the heathland. In the summers as a teenager I liked to roam around the shattered remains, while the

Iroise heaved among the rocks. On the tip of the continent of Europe, fastened to its topmost edge, the manor house of Coecilian dominated everything: the fishing fleet, the buildings of the Naval Academy, the Brest Channel, the Tas de Pois promontory, a convex ocean ploughed by cormorants, the infinite sea and sky. The artist is a sorcerer, a medium, a magus, intoned this white-bearded poet who looked like King Lear. He was a man who was new because he was of another time, for he could remake fire by striking flint, and his 'sun envisioned surpasses the sun that is real'. Gauguin was to retain this lesson. And indeed, on his death, the large woodcarvings from his hut in the Marquesas were brought back to Europe by the indefatigable Victor Segalen, to adorn the walls of Coecilian. These panels, touched by the foreign and unknown, in exile sang the same mystery, the same anxious *joie de vivre*, from a glittering bay at Hiva-Oa to this spur of Breton sandstone.

Then Gauguin had also made me travel into the very heart of his life's adventure. At every stage, I had tried to see his paintings, and was prepared to turn my work upside-down to do this. Mine was the jubilation of an entomologist entering a specimen in his notebook. I was delighted by the Wildenstein classification, which covered more than six hundred and fifty items. Drawn up by Georges Wildenstein and published in 1964, this catalogue lists the entirety of the painter's recognised works. It gives each of them a number, in chronological order of production, preceded by the letter W. For me it had become a kind of game played out on the map of the world. There were canvases with Wildenstein numbers all over the place: twenty-four in St Petersburg, eight in Tokyo, three in Munich, six in Oslo, one in Hawaii, two in Cairo, a score or so in Copenhagen. I would have liked to go and feast my eyes on them one at a time, doing nothing else for several months. So, five years ago, when I was on a reporting assignment in the United States, I managed to extend my stay in Chicago by seventy-two hours, so that I could take a good look at *Merahi metua no Teha'amana* (*Ancestors of Tehamana*), W497, a painting of the young Tahitian woman Teha'amana. Gauguin's first love, once the light of the tropics had been reached and embraced – or at any rate his fantasy, his Eve, his girlfriend. What was my excuse? An interview with Cassius Clay! The boxer had a suite at the Palmerston

House, on Monroe Street, and a number of articles had come out greeting the publication of his autobiography. My editor in Paris got carried away. A Muhammad Ali scoop! My additional expenses would be covered ... The meeting was feasible, though of course I still had to fit myself in somewhere between the various bookshop signings, a gossip columnist, a smart Michigan Avenue restaurant, a TV spot. For the whole day, I followed the black giant at a distance. He had Parkinson's disease and trembled like a leaf, and with his two limousines and his bodyguards, the living legend resembled a nice, complicated big kid out sleepwalking ... I hung on, hung about, then got tired of it. Maybe tomorrow? No, the King would be in Detroit on his next promotional stop. On the telephone, then? Without fail ... But what did it matter, now that I had gained three days here by delaying my flight? And as I charged down the Magnificent Mile, I could only keep thinking of the opening hours at the Art Institute and the ten Gauguin canvases inside it. W300, W387, 439, 486, 513, etc. As for Cassius, I'd forgotten him. W497, an 1893 vintage, outdid the champ! I had ejected him from the ring of my preoccupations.

There was another time, in South America, at Asunción, the capital of Paraguay. For sixty solid days I was meant to be at the beck and call of the French embassy's cultural services, having agreed to this in Paris. However, it was August and the river capital was empty; there was no one behind the whitewashed hacienda walls. Nobody cared whether they heard me droning on about Flaubert or Chateaubriand. They had all gone off to Punta del Este for a dip in the Atlantic.

I sought no better excuse to desert. I knocked my ennui on the head and made a getaway over the frontier into Argentina so that I could feast my eyes at last on the genuine *Vahine no te miti*, *Woman of the Sea*, a Maori-Breton painting in green, yellow and blue, number W465.

As if gasping its last, a McDonnell Douglas with stoved-in seats heaved itself into the listless sky, where it managed to stay airborne by balancing one wing over the other, and made a terrible landing near the River Plate ... I threw myself into a taxi and headed for the Museo Nacional on Avenida del Libertador. Among the Goyas, the Manets and Picassos, there was a Gauguin canvas that had been waiting for me since 1892. And because I stayed in front of it for so long, observing in such detail its blues and its yellows, its warm browns and oranges, I wound up attracting the attendants' notice and very nearly had to explain myself. What did I have to explain? That I had come all the way from a neighbouring country just for the sake of this painting, which was inspired by Ingres' *Valpinçon Bather*? That in the heart of rainy Europe, this splendid human animal with her harmonies of sand and sea had made me dream? I loved this sculptural water-sprite, her splayed leg, her naked buttocks on the sand, the slope of her skin in a drift of gardenias, her sarong the colour of night, the concordance between the ear and the shell, a spiky murex, and the leaf from the tree painted to look like a grateful hand.

Yes, like the others, she was a part of these works which were mine and which, across oceans and centuries, waited to surrender to me: tacit, innate complicity, simple yet perfect aesthetic happiness, weaving together the threads of our real lives. In the footsteps of Gauguin, through his prism, I would find only myself, and him once more. Our two commingled lives. Archipelagoes caressed by the same currents.

CHAPTER 2

August 1849, the Strait of Magellan, between Patagonia and Tierra
del Fuego. The *Albert* is a two-masted brig, a shoddy merchant ship
which, after fitting up at Le Havre, is sailing to Callao, in Peru. On
board are a journalist and his wife: a seemingly ordinary couple,
accompanied by their young children, Paul and Marie. As soon as
they can, they go up on the bridge to stretch their legs, admire the
coastline, breathe in this icy air. They count the ashy-plumed sea
birds. Just now, three albatrosses flew around the masts, beady-eyed.

The crossing is interminable. After the Atlantic, the *Albert* sailed
along the Patagonian coast of Argentina, then left Cape Virgin to
starboard to head into the Strait of Magellan. This final cleft in the
American continent before Tierra del Fuego is a natural channel
which makes it possible to avoid Cape Horn and sail up the west
coast of Chile in the shelter of inland waterways. The ship makes
slow progress coasting past these fiords sheared by glaciers. The first
narrows, the second narrows, Isabel Island, the Bay of Futility, the
Cape of Anxiety. Once through this slender cordon, where the ocean
becomes no more than a blue vein connecting the two worlds, life
begins again to the west, on the far side of the globe, in the cor-
rugations of the Pacific waves. For everyone on board, passengers and
crew, this is a physical sensation. A release.

Paul's father, Clovis Gauguin, is a socialist, a committed Repub-
lican, and a former political writer on the progressive paper *Le
National*, which was edited by Thiers and Marrast. In Lima he plans
to found a newspaper. He is in flight from the disappointed hopes of
the 1848 revolution, the downfall of liberal ideas and the rise of Louis
Napoleon Bonaparte, who was elected president in the previous

December. Having fiercely supported the opposing candidate, Louis Cavaignac, Clovis decided to pack his bags. Peru would be the next stop; there, things might take a turn for the better. But, shut up in his cabin, brooding on his defeat and in suffocating despair, Clovis seems in a very weakened state. He suffers from heart disease. He is thirty-five years old, in a state of nervous illness and at the end of his tether. He has had a violent clash with the ship's captain, who has been running after his wife, and he has nearly come to blows with this man.

Why Peru? Because his wife, Aline, née Chazal in 1825, is the daughter of the audacious Flora Tristan, and still has relatives there, the Moscoso family, who are wealthy and very influential. They descend from the first *conquistadores*, with perhaps, Gauguin will later surmise, the blood of some Indian prince also in their veins. Don Pío Tristan y Moscoso, aged eighty and a former minister, still reigns at the centre of this South American clan. He has a title, a house with a staff of servants, and a fortune founded on sugar. Don Pio is the younger brother of Don Mariano, who settled in Europe and had two children with a Frenchwoman whom he subsequently abandoned. Flora, the elder daughter of this union, and Paul's grandmother, was born in Paris in 1803. There is no doubt that her future writings would have shocked this landed aristocracy, starting with her *Peregrinations of a Pariah* (1836), followed by her *London Journals* (1840) and *Union ouvrière* (*Workers' Union*, 1843). But in Gauguin's imagination, Peru remained a land of the fabulous. A blessing of gold and honey.

Off Punta Arenas, which had been founded the year before, a whaling boat is about to put out from the side of the *Albert*. Twelve sailors are at the ready for some hard rowing. The choppy pale-green sea is deep and icy. As far as the eye can see there runs a coastline made jagged by the currents and the backwash – the point where the Cordillera abruptly comes to an end. The wind gusts fitfully, as if someone were coughing and moaning behind the rock masses and the lugubrious shingles, so that the impression is one of desolation. Seals swim in pairs between the two stretches of water, their snouts nuzzling the surface, among bunches of drifting algae. On the shore, by a pebble-beached creek, are clapboard houses, a few lopsided huts, a chapel, two fishing boats and some Alakaluf Indian canoes. A torn flag flaps about. A settlement where the polar air cuts into you like a dagger, a minute scrap of civilisation between branches of water, eroded islets, the immemorial pounding of the ocean and the melting of pale glaciers.

Clovis wants to go and stretch his legs on land, to buy some baubles from the tribes of the Strait, and some provisions to improve on the fare on board. Perhaps there will be sightings of penguins on the rocky banks. He is getting ready, putting on some fur-lined boots, dressing warmly. Muffled up from head to toe, his children and his wife are already in the whaling boat. He hurries to join them, despite the fatigue that grips him in the fore and aft gangway, dulling his senses and seeping into the very marrow of his bones like the Antarctic cold, freezing him, as if he were becoming porous and the landscape were entering his being. Then, just as he is about to step onto the accommodation ladder, all of a sudden he collapses. It's a ruptured aneurysm, and Clovis Gauguin dies on the deck of the ship. In no time he has turned a mottled blue and his lips are black.

There is no way back! There is not even any question of staying there, in that ghastly channel hammered by dangerous winds, in that nightmare of geography with its stifling, battering despondency. The body is disembarked on a stretcher. A quack and an unshaven Chilean non-commissioned officer certify the death. What is to be done? Poor Clovis is buried with great haste. A hole, five planks, a clumsy cross; the ground is brittle and stony. Port Famine. Mist floats like a shroud between two sinister trees.

'I cannot delay sailing,' the captain explains. 'This is a commercial line; timetables and connections must be observed. Either you stay here or you come with us.'

Already, the anchors are being hauled in. The *Albert* resumes its course in this labyrinth which is several hundred miles long and where, in the depths of tiny coves, giant tree trunks rot along with dozens of wrecks. Clarence Island, the island of Santa Inés, the island of Desolation, the Gulf of Trinity, Port Eden. On the ship's deck, where touching steel burns his fingers with the cold, Paul has become an orphan. The second-class cabin is empty on the evening of 30 October 1849. Aline is sobbing on the divan, wrapped up in a blanket, her hair wild about her face like a madwoman's. She has torn her dress. And she has not answered the steward who came to give her his condolences, bringing tea with milk and cakes for the children. They are still too small to understand: Papa has stayed at Port Famine beside the raging ocean. There is nothing to be seen through the porthole now. This is the New World, say the sailors on watch. For the Gauguins, it is a rebirth that begins with death.

A month later, of course, arrival in Lima will be miraculous. For the widow and her two orphans in flight from Europe, from poverty and grief, it will mean guaranteed help and protection. After disembarking at Callao, the Gauguins take the first diligence for Lima. There, in this tropical Granada, they fall into the arms of Don Pio, who is overwhelmed and embraces his children from the Old Continent. They are the descendants of his beloved brother, Don Mariano. Besides, the twenty-four-year-old Aline bears a likeness to him.

The colonial palace in Calle de Gallos dates from the time of the *conquistadores*, the Pizarro brothers. Three internal courtyards, terraced roofs, an extravagant dining room, vast bedrooms with wrought-iron balconies, tiled floors imported from Italy, even in the corridors. Succulent food, fine wines from Spain, the cries of tamed birds in the patios decorated with mosaics and potted trees. Cousins everywhere, who are noisy and talkative, and white-pyjamaed servants by the dozen whose bare feet slip noiselessly along the flagstones. There is drinking, laughing and singing and a fondness for outings in the glossy barouche, with an escort of stiff-backed horsemen, under the sugar palms along the banks of the Apurimac River. At dusk, in a purple light which fires the mountains and powders the adobe houses, the temperature is as warm as in paradise. 'All of this brought us an extended family, and in the midst of it my mother was truly as spoiled as a child,' the painter would later acknowledge.

The Gauguins learn Spanish, yield to local custom, play the game, pray as required in the Baroque churches where the gaudy saints are baby-faced. Guano magnates who made their fortunes in five years, and thirty-year-old generals in toytown uniforms hover around the Frenchwoman who is Paris personified. Aline is invited to balls, to parties, to horse racing in the *campo*, to candlelit dinners at the haciendas. She sleeps alone, badly, under a mosquito net. The lesson is clear for anyone willing to learn it and forget everything else. 'How graceful and pretty my mother was when she dressed as the ladies of Lima did, with the silk mantilla covering her face and leaving only one eye visible; this eye so soft and imperious, so pure and caressing . . .' And the octogenarian patriarch with his overlong kisses is in love with her too. He is more and more importunate. Half consenting, Aline is a prisoner, incapable of rebelling against this easy luxury which goes to her head and crushes her. The penniless widow of a socialist, the daughter of a revolutionary, she is powerless above all to refuse this love, this attention, this happiness, these gowns and perfumes. She receives an income of 5000 piastres every month. The protection of the noble family is total and unassailable. Such is the grandeur and splendour of the Moscosos.

Pampered, waited on and entertained, the French family rediscovers an appetite for life in 'this delicious country where it never rains'. For Gauguin this exotic childhood will always remain an enchantment, a revenge, 'a perpetual fairytale'. Life has been able to regain its rights, like a diverted river back on its sandy bed. He will speak of remembering a Chinese servant, a black maid, the taste of sugar cane on his teeth, the sun stretched out like a wild beast across the red plains, massive silver figurines from the kingdoms of the Andes, Chimú funeral masks, luminescently painted mochica earthenware, Paracas *fardos* which preserve the bodies of children in the foetal position, mummified with vicuna wool. Encouraged by her uncle, Aline will start a collection of pre-Inca art. These primitive statuettes and ceramics will come to haunt the artist: out of the darkness of time, enigmatic Indian faces loomed over him, their eyes hollow, their lips sealed upon their unspeakable secret.

The Gauguins were not to return to Europe until 1855. Paul was then seven and a half. The South American sun had cauterised everything. Among these rich half-Indian descendants of *conquistadores*, these forgotten dynasties, in the exuberance of a savage natural world, where nothing can lie and nothing causes pain, being himself was enough to ensure the protection of some guardian figure. Everything had been given and received on the other side of the world, in the shadow of the Andes, in a land which resembled a dream. Gauguin will never forget it.

CHAPTER 3

Aged thirty-three, in 1881, Gauguin was an unlikely golden boy. This was a time of great ferment, and France under the third Republic, with MacMahon, Jules Ferry and Gambetta in government, was supremely confident. In an extremely favourable social and financial climate where there was a solid respect for the law, technology and industry were developing hell for leather. Abroad, diplomatic successes and military conquests followed thick and fast, and the colonial empire was rapidly expanding, from Indochina to Madagascar, in the wake of Algeria, Tunisia and the Sudan. Beating such a drum to the rhythm of a triumphant modernity, France, at the heart of Europe, imbued these undeveloped territories across the globe with what it saw as its great civilising influence and humanitarian mission. On every latitude the tricolour flag united ambitions, captains and capital. The sciences were not being left behind. Nor was art. Zola, Daudet and Vallès were famous. The towering figure of the aged Victor Hugo presided. Loti and Maupassant were fashionable. As for painting, in the embers of an Impressionism striving for its second wind after the first exhibitions of 1874 and 1876, hundreds of canvases blazing with light were being painted by Monet, Pissarro, Sisley, Signac, Morisot, Guillaumin, Cassatt and Renoir, as well as Cézanne, Manet and Degas. Breached from official art and the academy, this grouping of talents and ambitions was plagued by internal conflict, and was yet to find its audience. The disagreements of the former and the gradual rallying of the latter marked each of the eight Impressionist exhibitions, the last of which took place in 1886. By then a new generation, impelled by its momentum, was feeling its way in their wake: Van Gogh, Seurat and Toulouse-Lautrec. But the majority of these artists were still starving.

In 1878, Claude Monet's pictures went for thirty-five francs and Pissarro's for between seven and ten francs.

How did it come about that the erstwhile Peruvian orphan, who knocked around the oceans of the world between 1865 and 1871 as a merchant seaman on the *Luzitano* and the *Chili*, turned into the bourgeois of rue Vivienne who took cabs and dined out in top hat and bespoke tailoring? It was his protector and guardian, Gustave Arosa, originally from South America, who pushed Paul to go into business as soon as he left the Navy. He himself was a redoubtable financier, a wheeler-dealer both on the stock exchange and in the world of painting, and like his brother Achille, he was a collector who knew what to look for. Secretly, this solid, bearded personage had succumbed to the charm of Aline, Paul's mother. Though the love affair was not conducted openly, it was intense and feeling was mutual, for on his mistress's death in 1867, Arosa became Aline's legatee and the guardian of her children. In fidelity to these commitments, Gustave looked out for his wards, and in 1872 he found Paul a position at the Bertin agency in rue Laffitte, where the director was a relative. In 1879 Gauguin then went to work for Bourdon the banker, in rue Le Peletier, and, a year later, for Thomereau in rue de Richelieu.

Paul excelled at business. He was shrewd and intelligent. His colleagues were wary of him; he was too distant and ironical. And there was his past as a seafarer who had sailed round the world, on four or five trips, even as far as the Antarctic Circle; a privileged childhood in Peru, and a secret protector. But the clients appreciated his brisk, no-nonsense way of doing things. He himself began playing the stock market and made a few killings during the economic boom. As a matter of inclination rather than speculation, following his mentor's example he invested this money in paintings that were to be the start of a collection. Taking confident financial gambles, he could boast of earning several tens of thousands of francs a year, at a time when by comparison a factory worker would be paid scarcely a hundred francs a month. Monsieur Gauguin was doing very well for himself. Oriental carpets, fine furniture and ornaments.

In 1876, Paul already owned works by Manet, Renoir and Sisley, and a number by Cezanne and Daumier. He had ready cash and a good nose. His colleague at Bertin's, Emile Schuffenecker, 'good old Schuff', was like him consumed by the idea of painting. Together they attended Colarossi's academy and walked around museums, first and foremost the Louvre, where they made copies of the masters.

Gauguin admired the classics, venerating Cranach, Titian and Holbein. While he had a passion for Delacroix, he was also wild about the ancient art of India and Egypt, 'the nourishment and vital force of primitive art', and of the Middle Ages, which he studied 'at night and on holidays'. The young lion also visited the galleries of the dealers located near the stock exchange: Carpentier, Petit, Durand-Ruel. Every Sunday, in the manner of the 'Barbizon School', the two friends took a train to the suburbs and went off with their charcoals and brushes to work from life in the woods, in sunny clearings and on grassy river banks. In the evening, by the fireside, Gauguin would draw for hours with febrile intensity until he was bleary-eyed.

Before long, Achille Antoine Arosa introduced him to Pissarro, who was to take him under his wing as 'a temporary adopted son', as the historian Françoise Cachin puts it. He was certainly tentative and conventional at the start: landscapes, still lives, portraits. From *Wild Flowers in a Blue Vase* (W19) to *Apple Trees at the Hermitage, near Pontoise* (W33) ... But Gauguin took heed of every piece of advice, applied it to the letter and made it bear fruit. He bought the works he wanted to take as models and scrupulously copied them. As a young man he made progress because he put all his fervour and ambition into it. And he became an 'Impressionist' even if the subtleties of this movement were not his own. Already in rebellion, he felt that he had to go beyond this stage. 'The struggle had to be waged body and soul against all schools, all of them without distinction ...' It was the modernity of the idea that seduced him, the boldness of the theories rather than the outcome. He loved the unmuddied tones, the definite forms, the scope of the compositions. His entry into the group, which split in 1880, would be as discreet as it was tactical. For him it was both a guild and a springboard. For them, he represented a strong advocate and ready cash. He joined them in 1879, despite the fact he could barely stand some members, one of those being Claude Monet.

Meanwhile, he had got married, to Mette-Sophie Gad, a tall young Danish woman who was lively and alert, who loved France, restaurants, balls and the Paris department stores. Mette spoke good French. She was the daughter of a judge, and had been a governess in the house of a high-ranking politician, Jakob Estrup, Prime Minister of Denmark. She had acquaintances and influential connections in the aristocracy. In Paris, her practicality was turned to account in acting as chaperone to the daughter of a wealthy industrialist, Marie Heegaard. They were in the circle of the Arosa family and on one of their visits Mette met the young Gauguin. She was a Lutheran, a little on the stout side, as solid as a church pew, and she fell for the charm of the businessman, 'who looks like a hidalgo but has a steady profession.' After an earlier disappointment in love, this would be her compensation as a woman. Gauguin seemed like the ideal candidate: comfortably off, amusing and original, but not too original. The wedding took place in November 1873 and the couple started married life in place Saint-Georges, then moved to a house in rue des Four-neaux, where the ceramicist Bouillot would initiate Paul into his techniques. In 1875, at number 54 rue de Chaillot, their apartment consisted of 'an antechamber, a dining room, three bedrooms with fireplaces, a study, a drawing room, a kitchen.' Then came the children, with Emil in 1874, Aline in 1877, Clovis in 1879 and Jean-René in 1881. And the first serious pictures arrived too: four in 1874, seven in 1875, ten in 1879. By now there was at least one masterpiece, tender and premonitory, in 1881 – W52, *Young Girl Dreaming*: his daughter Aline, her hair short, lying in a boat-shaped cot, pictured from the back, her white nightdress riding on her thighs, her face turned to a green wall where exotic birds that could be Baudelairean hummingbirds flit about the wallpaper, like the creatures of a day-dream – and near the bed with its scrolls of wrought iron we have that elf in red, a puppet bought for a few pence, a little ghost that seems to haunt the sleep and the warm flesh of children.

Under Pissarro's guidance, Gauguin learned fast, retaining what he studied, from him and in the work of others too. He had the capacity to analyse and come to his own conclusions. He spent his free time with his mentor, at Pontoise and Osny, sometimes together with Cézanne, whose work was to mark him deeply. His colour 'is grave like the character of Orientals,' Gauguin observed. He liked Cézanne's 'heavy tranquillity'. Each of them understood that Impressionism was a dead-end, an over-clever optical game. It was important to move on to something else, without thereby forsaking the expression of sensation.

Paul was headstrong, and he had gained confidence. His strength was not as a draughtsman, but as a colourist with a talent for composition. And since he bought up so many of his colleagues' pictures, he knew the art world well and if need be played the go-between, receiving commission. His collection became his war chest, the other side of the bureaucratic life which he despised, a phenomenal breath of fresh air.

Although he got on with Degas, who was to defend him until his dying day, there were other artists, Renoir among them, who found the Peruvian somewhat irritating and too much of a dilettante. Wasn't he just a banker turning out some slapdash art and slumming it with them? A Sunday painter who knuckled down and went back to the office on Mondays. A dauber who liked a bit of excitement and then took a cab home to the family and some piano-playing. But this bourgeois had ready money and whenever he did well on the stock exchange he invested. In 1881 alone he acquired two Renoirs, a Manet, a Brown and two Jongkinds ... For him, painting was the true value. He could spend up to fifteen thousand francs a year on pictures. Whenever there was a picture he liked, he really burned to have it. Manet noted that at times the young man in the frock coat could also act 'the dictator'. By now he was something of a presence; he let nothing stand in his way and was unconcerned by what anyone thought. With his easel planted on the banks of sleepy rivers, on quaysides, in undergrowth, or in the middle of market gardens, the former naval topman got on with his work, hunched over his colours and listening to nothing but his own mad craving. 'The only way of reaching up to God is to do as our divine master does, and create.'

Still under Pissarro's protection, he took part in the fourth Impressionist exhibition in 1879, then was invited to participate in the fifth, the following year, at rue des Pyramides, when the split in the group was confirmed. He was to hang his works again in the sixth, at Nadar's studio, in 1881, and would finally exhibit in the seventh, in 1882, at the rue Saint-Honoré. In 1880, in the columns of *L'Art moderne*, Joris-Karl Huysmans referred to Gauguin's *Study of a Nude, Suzanne Sewing* (W39) in these terms: 'Of the contemporary painters who have worked with the nude, none has struck such a vehement chord with reality.' This was a halfway success. The gallery owner Durand-Ruel finally took an interest in him and, in 1881, bought four of his works for the sum of one thousand seven hundred francs. So there he was, recognised as a painter! Exhibiting with them and bought by the dealers. In short, what Mette saw as the hobby of a husband worn out by the vagaries of the stock exchange became transformed into an unappeasable hunger; an illumination, the conviction of a superior artist. Paul moved up to the second slope of the mountain, touched by the light. He was to sacrifice everything to it, her included.

The elements of the drama were in place. Likewise the divergent, diagonal trajectories, set in motion overnight when, in January 1882, the Bank of Lyon and the Union Générale collapsed under the weight of speculation and scandal. Bankruptcies followed thick and fast, in a domino effect. Shares plunged. The stock market was sinking and there was turmoil throughout the world of finance. This was a crash! Savers and investors were panicking. Some of the demonstrations on the street turned into a riot. Troops were sent in, and in left-wing milieux, members of anarchist groups were arrested. Was the French State incapable of taking action? 'This time, the issue is the public's faith; the national wealth has to be defended against a stampede of selling, against panic in the market,' screamed *Le Figaro*.

Gauguin wavered in the face of this débâcle. Business dried up, transactions ground to a halt. Shareholders were petrified. The whole thing had been hot air, tinkering with accounts, nothing but a mirage! What is more, Gauguin had made some bad investments on his own account. He had put nothing into gold, unlike Schuffenecker, who had given up the job and made up his mind to devote himself to his art. And what about Gauguin: would *he* be able to live off this painting which at last was about to bring him dividends of admiration and interest? He played for time, looking for other ways out. Pisarro prudently made no attempt to push Gauguin, the family man, along that route. The climate was disastrous. Painters had been indirectly affected by the slump. Nonetheless, at the age of thirty-five, Gauguin handed in his resignation. Unless, that is, he was dismissed. Things remain unclear on this score. In January 1883, he was free at last, though not entirely by his own volition. He had finished with regular employment. He would be an artist.

'From now on, I shall paint every day,' he announced boastfully to his wife, who was pregnant with their fifth child, Paul-Rollon, known as Pola.

Mette was appalled. Hadn't she entered the state of matrimony with a banker who collected rare breeds of roses and Persian carpets? Wasn't this a case of dishonest trading? 'You don't love art. What do you love then? Money,' her husband would later write in a letter to her. It was the ruination of their bourgeois family. All along Paul had been hiding the soul of a circus performer; now he was trampling on her dreams as a woman, a wife and a mother. He wrote to Pisarro: 'My head is too full of worrying about the future of my art for me to make a good business worker ... In short, come what may, I must find my life in painting ...' The reply came: 'After thirty years as a painter, I am still struggling to make ends meet. Young artists should bear this in mind. It is our fate!'

It was too late, there was no turning back, a new life was beginning, one that was both carefree and anxious. Gauguin was out and about, with his fellow-artists; often he didn't go home. He saw only one solution: to cut expenditure to a minimum, weather the storm, wait for business to pick up and for his art to find an opening. To forget cabs, balls and restaurants, to stay at home in the room that had been converted into a studio, and to paint, paint, paint like a man possessed, a man accursed and drunk with happiness. Mette was trapped. Money continued to melt away, with nothing coming in, only outgoings. Her husband's plans had fallen through. The powerful Gustave Arosa was dead. They had to leave Paris and bury themselves in the provinces; in 1884, they moved to Rouen, near Pisarro.

In the direst of straits, Mette-Sophie tackled this man who was now a stranger to her. Fearful of the future, she hardened her attitude. The Danish pragmatist in her ridiculed the painter and his calling, denigrated the collector who was now finding it hard to sell off any masterpieces, and repudiated the lover. 'My wife has become unbearable here, she can only see how bad things are, how black the future looks ... My small nest egg is sorely depleted and there is just enough to live on for six months at the most,' Gauguin tells Pisarro.

Paul envisaged divorce, as did his wife. In the meantime, he turned out pictures: twenty-three landscapes, four still lives, some seascapes and portraits; nearly forty works in the course of the year. As he tried to escape from Mette's gloomy sermonising, his thoughts wandered; he ran through the list of friends, acquaintances and brokers. In despondency, he even tried to get another job. In vain. This was a rout, and it was every man for himself. With his paintings under his arm, Gauguin travelled up and down to Paris. 'I have just approached a great many people, and everywhere I get the same answer, that business is going badly ...'

Relations with Pisarro became tense. Manet had died. There were no Impressionist group exhibitions in 1883 or 1884. Durand-Ruel, on whom he was relying, had enormous problems: 'The fellow is struggling hard to stay afloat.' Schuff had lost his nerve and was back in the fold; he would teach drawing at Vanves.

Adding up the price of bread and milk, Gauguin would finally take heed of his wife's entreaties: 'She is ill-suited to poverty.' The solution was to go home to Denmark with her. Since he was incapable of supporting a family, since he lacked the means to keep them in France. Like his father taking ship for a mythical Peru, he now had to go and place himself under the protection of in-laws, relatives and allies.

In August 1884, Mette and two of the children travelled by steamboat to see the lie of the land. Then she came back to fetch her husband. At least she would be able to give French lessons and do translations. Confronted with his wife's obstinacy, Paul vacillated. 'I am taking the children and the furniture ...' Schuff came up with the money for the removal. Gauguin followed, a vague contract for work as a company representative in his pocket. In November they came face to face with the Danish clan, meeting the ironic smiles of the in-laws who had never accepted the unorthodox marriage, who had never liked this jumped-up, dark-skinned South Seas sailor, this stock-exchange circus turn. In Copenhagen-on-ice, Paul the dauber, the Levantine, the penniless Peruvian, kept a low profile in front of his mother-in-law, Madame Gad, in among the well polished furniture, the ticking clocks, the Victorian sofas and chandeliers. A modern painter? Was he joking?

Mette would not forgive him the humiliation of this forced return.

CHAPTER 4

Gauguin was to leave his children in Denmark: Emil, Aline, Clovis, Jean-René, Pola. An act of desertion. The first time in June 1885, then, for good, in 1891, after some summary toing and froing whose reasons and urgency he kept to himself. We can call it an amicable separation. This was Mette's painful victory: Paul going back to his own country, the French in France and the Danes in the kingdom of Denmark. They would write. Since the Parisian was an artist and wanted to paint, let him paint, far away.

Earlier, though, in the long straight avenues of this capital city whose canals reflect the image of its brick buildings endlessly, with scarcely a ripple, Paul had made great exertions. Between November 1884 and June 1885 he tried to redeem himself by becoming the representative of a Roubaix firm, Dillies and Co, specialising in 'waterproof and non-perishable tarpaulins' imported for sale to industrial concerns, railways and shipping. Speaking not a word of Danish, he soon wore himself out dealing with the express letters, invoices, customs charges, the travelling back and forth and the handling of requests for advances and samples. Through his connections he wangled two or three contracts: 'I've had a visit from an admiral who is a distant relative and the administrator of supplies for the Arsenal. He has given me an order for 125 yards of superior quality A-category black tarpaulins,' he announced to his employers.

Business did not flourish. When he left the anterooms where his patience with waiting had run out, he gave up pieces from his precious collection to put food on the table for his children. A Manet for a thousand francs ... In five months, Gauguin had pocketed a mere seventy-eight francs from his confounded industrialists. 'I confess that

29

I am weary of all of these errands and interviews that promise much, but later give me no more than a glimpse of what I need to earn my bread.' And he had not forsaken painting (forty-two works in 1884, forty-nine in 1885) nor the aim of exhibiting and selling it. 'Here my art torments me more than ever.' He exhibited with other artists in Copenhagen. His 'ghastly painting', as Mette puts it, is judged disconcerting. The press makes fun of it. The couple move house, leaving the seven rooms at Gammel Konjeveg, where the rent is too high, for a more modest apartment at number 51 Norregade, in the centre of the city. Mette was furious. Gauguin had given himself six months. The Frenchman was no longer at all 'funny'.

When I got to Copenhagen, here too I kept on discovering traces of the painter. And at the start, I kept taking myself off to places where he lived, lurking around houses, sitting on benches nearby. With a map of the city, a hired bike, gleaming black, and a list of addresses in my notebook, I was all set. Nansensgade, Vendersgade, Norre Sogade, Vester Sogade, Vesterport ... It was November, cold, and as I pedalled between the tramlines and the silvery canals I was glad I wasn't on foot. I liked the seaport. I felt at ease in this maritime atmosphere where the ships' horns of ferries bound for Sweden reverberated among the churches and equestrian statues. On the first evening, settled into the Kong Arthur Hotel, in the west of the city, I made an initial discovery that bowled me over: page 564 of the 1999 telephone directory for Copenhagen. I had not doubted that there would still be individuals with Mette's maiden name, Gad, but there were also eleven entries for the name Gauguin. His descendants. The grandsons and granddaughters of his children. So here was a Jacob Gauguin, at 26 Jydeholm; a Maria Gauguin at 93 Prinsesseg; a Bente at 22 Guldagerv and a Bitten at 3 Hostrups Have. There was an eerie Mette Gauguin at 80 Aldesborg; an amusing Pil & Marcelino Gauguin – very Pizzaland – at 16 Gartnerg; and, on the Concordiav, a PM Gauguin krim.insp (criminal inspector?).

I dithered about calling them, maybe picking out two or three, for instance the cop or the pizza vendors, and telling them about my project, asking them what they knew, describing how their great-grandfather had become my secret companion, my invisible other half. But no sooner had I torn out this page 564 (may I be forgiven a venial sin) and folded it up in my wallet, than I gave up the idea. What was the point of telephoning them? None of them had known the painter. Gauguin had stayed for only a few months. Only the youngest of his children, Pola, who died in 1961, had been close to him, from 1883 to 1885, then in 1891, when he was seven years old. Moreover, he stuck firmly to a narrowly familial perspective, as witnessed by his *Paul Gauguin, mon père*. His book begins with these hateful words: 'I am the son of Paul Gauguin and a mother brought up in a good bourgeois family . . .'

In my view, these Danes had betrayed the painter. None of them had understood him. Their ancestors had let him go, while they kept the pictures they would later sell. The Gad clan had got rid of him as if he were some filthy cur to be chased out of the farmyard. 'The most total isolation . . . I am a worthless animal,' Gauguin wrote. Was it now time for them to swagger about claiming to have his blood in their veins?

As you go up Norregade on the odd-numbered side, you go straight from number 49 to number 53. The building seemed to be the one on the corner with avenue Norre Volgade, adjoining the baleful Orsteds Park. Unless the streets had been re-numbered over time? A fine-looking, clean, white building of five storeys. Two shops took up the ground floor: a record store (*Rille Dille Kassik*) on Norregade, and a very well-stocked grocery shop called *7 Eleven*, with its entrance on the avenue. I copied down the tenants' names on the electric doorbells: P. Albersten, E. Ferm, T. Lessey, and Paresh Desai.

Under the eaves of this building which showed no overt sign of any history, Paul Gauguin had suicide in mind. He warmed his artist's soul to this idea. 'Every day, I wonder whether I shouldn't go up to the attic and put a rope around my neck. It's painting that holds me back . . . There is only one thing I can do, and that is paint.' However, he knew he was right: his subjectivity would be stronger than anything else. 'If we are nothing, then what is all the fuss about?' Isolated, barricaded inside, a prisoner under a square of empty sky, his chair drawn beneath the skylight, this was where he began theorising about 'sensation'. This would become the *Notes synthétiques*, sixty pages of jotted-down reflections on art, an attempt to explore the Impressionist movement and its work.

Would he be the solitary herald of painting? An unwitting avant-garde? What awareness did he have that others did not yet conceive of? He explained this in his letters: 'Some tones are noble, others commonplace; there are tranquil, consoling harmonies, and others which excite you by their boldness ... A strong feeling can be translated immediately; dream on it and seek its simplest form...'

Shipwrecked upon a flat ocean, he set himself an iron discipline. In his cubbyhole, every day he painted, from memory, French scenes such as *The Road to Rouen*; and self-portraits; the faces of his children, Aline and Clovis. When he was short of the money to buy the tubes of paint he wanted, he drew in pencil, rubbing things out and starting again, concentrating on what he wanted to convey, no longer seeking to represent reality but to transmit the idea of it which he perceived and received, the jolt of it, the naked evidence. Then he understood that 'colour is a kind of music.' And that art, cast into this current, this flux, this kaleidoscope of events and matter, could only be the outcome of a reality sublimated by an imagination. The sign and the signature of a presence in the world, its echo.

Yes, he made them leave the luxurious Gammel Kongevej, which was too close to the park and castle of Frederiksberg, to come back to the centre of the city and this gloomy apartment. The official reason was that Mette's pupils from the Foreign Ministry who came to learn French would not have to travel halfway across the royal city. One after the other, these gentlemen would come into the drawing room and set a Manila envelope containing a few Kroners on the side table. A second life was set in motion, with Mette-Sophie at its centre, its engine. A Mette who had swallowed her tears, who had had to forget the social play-acting that so intoxicated her, the happiness glimpsed and trampled upon. 'Poverty has completely soured her, especially in her wounded vanity (everyone knows everyone else in this country), and I have to suffer all her reproaches,' he acknowledged.

During the day, when he was not traipsing around after some hypothetical appointment, the Inca was relegated to his attic prison. 'The most total isolation. Of course, as far as the family is concerned, I am a monster because I don't earn any money. These days only successful men are respected.' His presence repelled these austere and puritanical Danes. He was a nuisance to Mette, who had to translate everything for him and to whom he owed every meal he ate. 'I haven't a penny, and I am thoroughly fed up with it.' His brother-in-law and sister-in-law openly ridiculed him. His role was that of a half-wit, a husband in name only who didn't speak a single word of their language! And a more dangerous one than they had bargained for: he attended neither church nor chapel. Was he an anarchist? He was banned from the marriage bed and slept in the drawing room, on a fold-out armchair. There was not much likelihood of this autistic Latin impregnating Scandinavia. 'I deeply detest Denmark. Its climate, its inhabitants . . .'

Taking notes and making sketches, I loitered around their first home, which was rather elegant and somewhat British, in the Park district, on Gammel Kongevej. A tall, wide building with blackened bricks, surmounted by a pinnacle-like green dome, and freshened up with newly-painted white bow windows. This residential suburb had preserved something of its Victorian character, with its wooded side paths, the spots of colour lent by dark pink and faded yellow villas, sedate behind their gloomy gardens. Next door, a pastry shop offered cakes with whipped cream, *flodeskumskage*, *spandauer* and *makronsnitte*, macaroons filled with raspberry. Now there were traffic lights, a video-rental store, all Hollywood and kung-fu, and Saab cars parked one behind the other like variously hued greenflies. It was Sunday. I looked at number 105. On the frontage overlooking the street, one of the doors still looked as it would have done in those days, heavy and elaborately worked. Another had been removed and replaced by a security grille where bikes were tethered. On the left, a small concrete-surfaced yard was plunged in semi-darkness. Near the dustbins, empty aquavit bottles were neatly arrayed. I ventured into the threadbare hallway, making for the first floor, my hand on the banister, holding my breath and listening for any sound that might come from the landing, where light flared in from the fanlights. A woman's perfume hung in the air, French . . .

The ground floor, where the Gauguins lived, took up the corner between the street and the side path. It was now occupied by the Oriental Market, a sumptuous store that had set out its November bargains. But, apart from this nod to far-off days, there was nothing left. The western facade even sported an incongruous and intriguing sign: 'Hauschborg 1907.' What if I were mistaken and this wasn't the right building? I was like a sorcerer without any power. None of this gripped me as I had been gripped the night before in the Central Station, where lost footsteps had come and gone. Below me were the rails of shining steel that headed towards the south, and I imagined, almost saw like an apparition, my Gauguin with his return ticket in his pocket, holding his luggage and hugging his children, who were clad in their worsted wool overcoats. And Mette's strained face under her fur toque, the painter's clammy hand, the abruptness of their breathing; a family broken and dispersed by time, their words already meaningless, not connecting, attaching to nothing, were foreign languages, the children between them like drifting lifeboats buffeted by monstrous currents, living-dead who were going to grow up, kisses pressed against scarves, Aline's shivery body pressed against his, sweet little Aline who dreamed of hummingbirds, the only one who would have liked to be going with him.

'I am astonished when I think now of how foreign my father seemed to me then, in his way of doing things and his language. I was incapable of grasping the fact that this was my father,' Pola explained when recalling 1891. It was hard to endure this family betrayal. 'A monster of egotism,' brooded Gauguin's wife. For the rest of his life Gauguin would carry the burden of it with him. At the hour of his death, in 1903, the yellowing photo of his five little ones would still be pinned to the wall of his *fare* at Hiva Oa. This is the dark, shameful underside that shadows the blossoming of his life's work. A desertion which gnawed at him like a cancer.

By way of Platanvej and Roskidevej, I reached Frederiksberg Park. There's a lake, winding paths, an Italianate palace. With a cap on his head and muffled up in woollens, Gauguin painted clumsy skaters on the frozen-over water. This canvas stayed in Denmark, together with the Pisarros and Cézannes from his private collection: what the painter left behind, what the husband sent back, what the father pledged. Along with others, this work with the skaters is kept in the Carlsberg Glyptotek. There, behind an internal garden with giant palms, his surviving works are like so many tropical fragments transplanted to the Baltic. They are exhibited on the second floor, above a room dedicated to Degas, in a special well-lit space, with ceramic and carved-wood pieces. There are twenty-three paintings, six of them from Tahiti (among them *Vahine no te tiare*, *Woman with a Flower*, 1891, W420), one from Martinique (*By the Seashore*, W217), and four from Brittany. Canvases sent by slow mail from Brittany or Tahiti, that Mette would dispose of without much conviction on the Scandinavian market to raise money for the rent. Vivid landscapes for Danish kroners. An elsewhere for the here and now. A dream for the sake of reality.

'I detest Denmark,' he would say again and again in his correspondence. The feeling was certainly mutual. After the failure of his small exhibition at the 'Friends of Art' in May 1885, Gauguin locked himself into a dark silence. 'Feeling that one is an imperfect element, but an element nonetheless, means finding doors closed everywhere. The fact that we are the martyrs of painting has to be savoured . . .'

Paul went back to France in June, for fear of being embittered and becoming stuck in Denmark. Getting out before being thrown out. Free, and relieved too. Blinded by his new freedom as an artist, but socially excluded. 'He leaves so that he can make his way, she stays in her native country to preserve what there is . . . Was he to betray his duty to his family or betray himself?' Pola wondered. With him Paul took one of the children, six-year-old Clovis, the least favoured. He took him as a hostage, as a promise of return, as a prolongation of the family fiction. 'This was something he discovered painfully for himself: the law of bourgeois society knows no pity, and it judges personal value through the lens of economics; in these terms, he was cast out. This was something he had already suspected in France, but in Denmark it had been explained to him with such starkness and simplicity,' his son lucidly acknowledged. When the genius is cut out, he becomes a pariah.

In Paris, Gauguin stayed with friends, presumed on hospitality, cadged from acquaintances. In a freezing hovel, Clovis contracted smallpox. To save him from death in this garret, to pay for fuel, charcuterie and bread, medicine and some blankets, his father worked nights as a bill sticker at the Gare du Nord for three weeks. The boy was looked after. In the end his mother came to reclaim him. Gauguin was beaten: 'Your family must be pleased at its triumph over the whole of our line. You're all Danish now!'

He could go off and disappear, to Brittany for example; he could curl up in a hole. He had no profession, no wife, no children, no home, no job, no savings. He would just grant them, and be granted, that return trip in March 1891, five or six days to see his children again and find they no longer spoke French. Aline had become a young lady, Emil a hulking lad, set to be over six feet, a colossus. In the apartment, which he left at night, Gauguin silently contemplated these alien children and the severe, short-haired Danish woman, brusque in her movements, as they stared at him with glass-coloured eyes, embarrassed smiles on their altered faces as they now failed to understand him when he spoke to them. 'A martyr of painting' would be his vocation, his ego as an artist against the world and time. He would have to paint against the servants of the void, the merchants who are satisfied with emptiness. Painting to give and to catch up, like self-damnation and self-redemption; his own life against their death.

CHAPTER 5

'Paris is a desert for a poor man; I must leave,' he kept telling Mette in 1887. Between borrowing money and sporadic sales, he shuffled between Dieppe and Paris, Paris and Pont-Aven, alone. 'It is an artist's duty to work and become better ... Nevertheless, I am not succeeding.' To hold on without doing anything else but painting; always painting, fast, very fast, with a fluid, renewed energy, as if he were responding to some higher voice, this was his obsession, his creed. First in Brittany, where sometimes those in need could live on credit: 'Painting pictures and living on little. Brittany is still the best place for a man to live cheaply.' A landscape of gorse-covered moors, with ploughmen whose hair makes them look like Indians, women in lace coifs that give them dignity, timidly standing back at the bend in a road, and children fighting in the undergrowth. And in the slate-roofed hamlets, flocks of low houses that smell of cider, a simple way of life that at times is rife with legends and revenants.

This Brittany of the hinterland, the *Argoat*, a land of woods and rivers, differs somewhat from my own preferred *Armor*, which faces the Atlantic elements and is wracked by matter. And it is odd that the former sailor should have preferred hillsides and valleys, fields and meadows, to the savage spectacle of the coastline, seagoing Brittany's bedrock, where the ocean is ripped along the jagged contours of prongs and spurs. Even at Le Pouldu, his coastal landscapes are few and far between. Two or three women bathers. An austere beach scene, or else a woman collecting seaweed. You will scarcely find any fisherman and sailing boats, but instead little farmhouses amid the flowers, along with cows, carts and peasants. The Inca's brush renders a silent Brittany of religious belief, where girls dance in a ring, where haymaking is done bare-breasted in the green light, where the standing stones change colour hard by magic streams. There is no wife awaiting a sardine fisherman's return at the end of a jetty, with hands stained like old apples behind her back. No shipwrecks, no cargoes, no currents that carry you off to cast you up on far-flung islets; no, Gauguin's Brittany remains a tranquil garden, a haven for sea-drenched shadows, a medieval paradise of torrents and mossy rocks. It is a soft-hued, milky-skied land of content, guarded by forests and spells. On canvases bathed in watery light, the dry-stone walls have kept their warmth and the animals returning to the farms nose about in sunken lanes. With slate and heather all around, this is the timeless antechamber of a world reconciled with itself. It verges on invention.

Between Pont-Aven and Le Pouldu, further south, he was to stay in Brittany five times, for periods of varying length: in 1886, 1888, 1889, 1890 and 1894. There, surrounded by painters who admired and were in awe of him, he felt less isolated. Who were these companions? Ferdinand du Puigaudeau, Henri Delavallée and Henri Moret. Fresh minds, young talent; beginners with varying fortunes. None of them was over thirty. First and foremost, at the Inca's feet, there was Charles Laval. Gauguin, who was always addressed with the formal *vous*, would be their master, their melancholy totem, by turns taciturn and full of laughter, brutal and tender. He observed that the bolder and more eccentric he was, the more he was respected. The more he imposed himself the more imposing he became. 'Work freely and furiously.' Van Gogh records a conversation where Emile Bernard talked about Gauguin: 'He says that he regards him as so great an artist that he is almost afraid of him, and that he sees everything that he, Bernard, does as inadequate by comparison with Gauguin.'

Pont-Aven was a pleasant place. The train from Paris Saint-Lazare, which passed through Lorient and Quimperlé, meant a journey of only a few hours. English and American artists were wild about it. Its mundane attraction was that you could find a month's full board, lodging with someone like Marie-Jeanne Gloanec, including hot meals and red wine, for just seventy-five francs ... What joy!

Gauguin already had a reputation here, because he had exhibited with the Impressionists, in France and in Denmark. He was somebody; his work had been reviewed by several critics, and he had sold a handful of pictures to dealers like Durand-Ruel. The former seaman and ex-banker who cut loose had come from South America, and was known to be a fine swordsman and an expert boxer. He had a big mouth, he was a hard-hitter and he didn't suffer fools gladly, starting with the friends of Monsieur Maupassant the elder who turned out 'pretentious' stuff. Photography with colour laid on top! What a travesty! Art is subjective, a thing of the mind, pure creativity. A heartfelt duel between matter and consciousness.

Meanwhile, Paul worked hard. His progress was indisputable. His touch was lighter, his brush strokes confident. His technique was improving. 'I use only the colours of the prism, juxtaposing and combining them as little as possible so as to achieve maximum luminosity,' he explains. As for drawing, he says: 'I do it as simply as possible and synthesise it.' This was a long way from the dark woods of Barbizon or the Impressionists on the banks of the Seine. 'Here, I work a great deal and with success; I am respected as the best painter in Pont-Aven.' Yet, when he saw Georges Seurat's canvases, particularly *La Grande Jatte* (1886), Gauguin realised that he had no monopoly on audacity and modernity. His progress was too halting to make him a leader. Georges Seurat had taken the lead with pointillism, the latest offshoot of Impressionism, and Signac and Pissarro were swept up in it, supported by writers such as Gustave Kahn and Jean Aljabert. As a matter of strategy, he drew closer to Degas and Guillaumin. For the time being, he had to play on a different terrain, to find another way of painting and seeing: his own. Openly, he couldn't care less about 'the dotters'.

What if he were to go back across the ocean? Suppose that by taking himself far away, a family reflex, he were to gain the upper hand? The more he surprised, the more he would be talked about, the more he would sell, and, released from contingencies, he would be free to paint. 'I cannot go on with this deadly existence that saps my strength, and I will try everything so that my conscience is clear.' But his energy was undermined by a lack of money. Most of his possessions were with the pawnbroker. Whenever the Inca went back to Paris, he lived in a 'little hovel'. At one point he was quite destitute and had nothing to eat for three days. He lived from hand to mouth on the little bits of money Schuff doled out. The solution, he reflected, would be to emigrate to some part of the world where the cost of living was lower. He could choose the 'wandering, unpaid life' that Arthur Rimbaud had hoped for in 1880, in Abyssinia, the Congo and Somalia. He could go to Tonkin or Madagascar. Unless he settled for Panama, given that his brother-in-law, Juan Uribe, his older sister Marie's Chilean husband, was there. Acting on his intuition, Gauguin made up his mind to go overseas. Wasn't there a little island off the canal they're digging, called Taboga, which was 'free and fertile and almost uninhabited'? He imagined living off fruit and fish, wearing hardly any clothes, on a virgin island where, under a changeless sun, he would only have to help himself from the trees, or hunt in the thickets. Taboga it was to be. 'I shall take my colours and my brushes, and I shall reinvigorate myself far away from everyone . . .'

Constructing countless schemes, picturing an operetta land where things were paid for with worthless trinkets, he packed his bags. Goodbye Brittany! What did he have to lose except his garret and his debts? For Gauguin, this was less a matter of exoticism than of saving money; not geography, but market economics. This was the wily stockbroker speaking, his rationale that of income rather than inclination. So he booked his passage from Saint-Nazaire; third-class on the *Canada*, a steamer of the Compagnie Générale Transatlantique bound for the French West Indies, which had been colonies since the seventeenth century. And if anyone else had a taste for adventure they could bring along their palettes and paints.

Gauguin borrowed the seven hundred and fifty francs for the ticket. 'I am going to live like a savage,' he writes, striking a blow at his wife. They had got themselves letters of introduction for the companies on the Canal. Who was to go with him: Bernard, Puigaudeau, or Schuff? All three found excuses at the last moment. Only Laval would accompany him.

It is 10 April 1887. Paul and Charles laugh heartily as they lean on the ship's rail, puffing at their pipes. The ample sea is beautiful, its blueness unstinting. One by one, the tugboats detach themselves from the hull, and pale currents criss-cross the horizon. They say farewell to old Europe. The New World is going to save them, they think.

CHAPTER 6

It all went wrong too soon. They were not to reach the lost island where Paul aimed to live just as he pleased. When they arrived, Uribe's help proved not to amount to much, and at Taboga there would be no land for sale or rent. There were problems with the administration, disagreements with the Indians. And worst of all, on this enchanted island the Company had set up a recreation centre. This was no promised land, but an island an hour and a half off the coast that had become an expensive suburb, a retreat for European managers and technicians who wanted to relax. Prices had shot up and the atmosphere was repulsive. 'There is no way of building a hut and living off fruit; if you try, they come down on you and treat you like a thief!' Laval had contracted malaria. They forgot about Taboga and went back to the mainland to lick their wounds.

The only answer for these vagabonds was to get themselves hired as labourers by the Panama Canal Company. Work had begun in 1881 on the initiative of Ferdinand de Lesseps, on a stretch of one hundred and thirty miles and six locks. Work was to end in 1888, followed by the liquidation of the Company and, in 1892, a financial and political scandal which would shake France. For our travellers, the reality would be digging up the ground with pickaxes, pushing wheel-barrows, obeying the foreman's orders and a lot of shouting. This was gruelling work in a scorching heat that would take its toll on the workers, like some ancient monster exacting tribute. The feet and yards dug out were added up, the dead subtracted from the running total. Gauguin was as strong as a horse, so needs must, for he was unwilling to turn out 'bourgeois' portraits for the sake of making do – unlike Laval in his state of weakness. In one of his letters he writes: 'You think I am settled on the island, but you are wrong! The digging of the Canal across the Isthmus has made life impossible even in the most deserted spots . . .'

It was Gauguin's turn to fall ill. 'I had such terrible burning pains in my chest that I suffered from nervous fits and cried out terribly . . .' Laval threatened to kill himself. 'We are in a ghastly mess!' In the end, they headed back to Martinique, the jewel of the empire, rich with sugar, cotton and coffee. Settled on the northwest coast, at Anse-Turin, the two men regained hope. 'We are in a native hut and, compared with the Isthmus, this is a paradise. We are twenty-five minutes from the town; below us is the sea, fringed with coconut palms, and above us there are fruit trees of every kind . . .'

Here was generous, luxuriant nature; lush landscapes and bodies at ease. Could this be the dream come true? Certainly, they were living on the margins, in an abandoned house remote from the colonial community. In the midst of blacks, Chinese and Indians and mixtures of these races, among agricultural labourers and planters, they were immersed in the bustling life of the villages, the markets, the world of fishermen and peasants. But at least there was regular mail, bringing money and news – Schuff, who was fighting their corner, had managed to place Gauguin's ceramics. Galvanised into action, they began painting again. 'Below us there is the sea with a beach where we can bathe, and either side there are coconut palms and other fruit trees which are perfect for any landscape artist . . .'

But the Inca's health, like that of his companion, was still fragile; he suffered from dysentery and fevers. A doctor advised him to go home without delay. So, after having painted a dozen canvases and piled up a multitude of sketches, Gauguin made a hurried departure. This haste was impelled the more by an extremely worrying silence from Mette. What if she had died? What would he do about the children? He took ship for home, either with the help of a remittance from Schuff or a passage as a member of the crew. This was a bitter leave-taking, for Laval, too frail to travel, was left behind. He was to make the journey back three months later.

In November 1887, Gauguin was in Paris, 'in the midwinter snow', struggling along the boulevards where cabs passed him gleaming like hearses. What a contrast with his life of recent months. Now, dysentery-ridden and with skin tanned like old leather, he had his sun-fired canvases under his arm as he tried to find a place for himself. Schuff was giving him a roof over his head, feeding him and lending him his studio. The Inca suffered from 'unbearable stomach pains' and holed up there like a wounded animal. His debts had piled up, and, from her 'sad, fog-bound country', Mette was demanding money. Her family had left her to her own devices. Dillies and Co also wanted the return of their advances to Gauguin from the time when he was negotiating contracts for them. Bouillot and Chaplet, on whom he had been counting for work or for commissions, had vanished into the countryside. Had everything gone wrong? No, for in these six months his work had taken a new turn and found its own immediacy. His palette had brightened and been freed: reds, hard blues, greens and violets are applied in flattened blocks of colour. He had broken with the shimmer of Impressionism, that manner of painting for the shortsighted, and initiated a style that is his, a potent style straight out of the paint tubes. He was aware of this: 'my painting has never been so light, nor so lucid.' This phase has proved to be of great significance: 'Only there have I truly felt I was myself, and it is in what I have brought back that anyone must search if they wish to know who I am, even more than in my Brittany works,' he acknowledged in a letter to Charles Morice. In his search to give fuller expression to figures and poses, his drawing has become plainer. Half-naked, hieratic bodies; thick vegetation; strange, sensual beauties; heavy, round fruits; towering trees with decorative foliage; the impassivity of saturated skies, the depth of oceans: *Beside the Huts*, W221, *Tropical Vegetation*, W232, *Mango Pickers*, W224, or the two superb *Seashore* paintings, W217 and W218. These are lustful, timeless paintings, irradiated by some great heat. Captivated, he would call this 'the land of the Creole gods'.

Now nearly forty, with this 'stunning' work Gauguin had just become aware that, apart from any economic issues, he needed to reconnect with that primitive world he had known as a child in the streets of Lima, and which he pretended to remember. For him, the truth was there, on the other side of the world, in the embrace of new meridians. In Panama and in Martinique, 'practically back from the grave', he had become a new man, guided by that 'always unappeased hunger for art'. His future as a man lay there, his posterity as a painter. His strength would come from his difference, whenever he showed himself to be driven and whole, a playful pagan, bewitched and open to sensations, however abstract these might be. As if under the effect of some chemical solution, the Peruvian savage had re-emerged in the sun of the West Indies. As he explained to his wife: 'Ever since I left, little by little I have closed my tender heart, in order to preserve my moral courage . . . You must remember that there are two natures within me: one that is Indian and one that is oversensitive. The oversensitive one has disappeared, which allows the Indian to go forward with sureness and resolve . . .'

He would burn his last bridges. The elsewhere, he was convinced, would be his redemption. The other within him had just been born.

CHAPTER 7

In 1887, the dealer Theo Van Gogh, then thirty years old and his brother Vincent's double, was running a gallery on the boulevard Montmartre for the firm of Boussod & Valadon. In parallel with more classical interests, he defended the Impressionist and Neo-Impressionist movements.

For his part, Vincent attempted to rally around himself a circle of painters that included Louis Anquetin, Emile Bernard and Toulouse-Lautrec. He exhibited with them in a Clichy restaurant late in 1887. These are the mockingly self-styled 'petit boulevard impressionists'. They shared no common theories, only a fondness for Japanese prints, a use of the decorative, and pure, strongly contoured colour. This did not mean opposition to the so-called pointillism of the Neo-impressionists Seurat and Signac; rather a wish to do something different, to come up with something new. A purer oxygen.

After meeting Vincent in 1886, Gauguin was to become a weighty ally in the outlining of a movement. Vincent made some first tentative moves towards winning over the as yet unsusceptible Paul, and in the end the two brothers paid him a visit. The dealer admired the Inca's work and the Anse-Turin paintings opened the way; he bought three of them for nine hundred francs. 'Theo bought a large painting of his of negresses dressed in pink, blue, orange and yellow cotton under tamarind, coconut and banana trees, with the sea in the distance. Somewhat like the description of Otaheite in *The Marriage of Loti*,' Vincent later wrote, referring to one of these, probably W224, *Mango Pickers*. Theo offered to put on his first solo exhibition, planned for January 1988: two mezzanine rooms for his Breton and Martinique works along with his ceramics. Gauguin couldn't have hoped for more.

'Little by little, he'll have his clients polish us off,' Gauguin noted optimistically, delighted at having found the very dealer he had been waiting for since the start of his career: an honest gallery keeper with a passion for modern painting, who was willing to subsidise him. The exhibition was to have scant success, with press reviews only by Félix Fénéon and Paul Adam. But the dealer had something else in mind right from the start: for Gauguin to join Vincent in Arles, in his 'provincial Japan'.

Why shouldn't they work together to found an 'atelier du Midi', an open studio for artists in the south, gathering around them the vital forces of Post-Impressionism? Was it too much to imagine Laval, Moret, Chamaillard and Bernard together? It would save on expenses, be an impetus to everyone's creativity and would stimulate its own market. It would also subdue Vincent, who could get rather out of hand. 'When it comes to several painters living together, I have to make it plain that we'll need an abbot to take charge and it should unquestionably be Gauguin,' Vincent announced in September 1888.

The Inca balked at this. Swearing only by the great Paul, Vincent insisted: 'You know that my brother and I have a very high regard for your painting and that it is our great wish to see you free of anxiety.' Meaning free of financial anxiety. Though Gauguin might have the soul of a leader, he still wanted to be independent, and Vincent was too unpredictable.

'I was aware that Gauguin had travelled but I didn't know that he had been a real seafarer, a real mariner up in the crow's nest. It gives me an extraordinary respect for him . . . If comparisons can be made, he has something in common with Loti's Icelandic fishermen.' Van Gogh was seeking a mentor, a companion, and in some way another brother to quieten the ghost who tormented him, that elder brother born exactly a year before him, on 30 March 1852, who did not survive and whose names he bore: Vincent Wilhelm Van Gogh, born on the same day and in the same month as himself! Vincent's painting is stigmatised by the hollow presence of this corpse that haunted him: those black imprints on ripened wheat, those billiard halls painted like tombs in a green otherworldly light, the wooden box with his name on it behind an empty straw-bottomed chair, where a pipe is smoking away. Over and over in his works we find the sign, the signs, of something that cuts through everything, like water flowing underground. 'What I want to express in my figures and my landscapes is a tragic sorrow,' Vincent wrote. In all his relationships with other people there are the sequels to that missing one which calls out and asks its questions through him: the voice of the unconsoled and unconsolable dead child.

'Would you like to share my house here?' he pleaded. Although Gauguin was keen to cash in on Theo's sales, he had no intention of mothering Vincent. Psychological support was not his strong point. He was too selfish, too consumed by his own fire, and he did not have it in him.

One February morning, Gauguin headed west again and settled into the Pension Gloanec. 'I am on the verge of becoming known and I must make one more supreme effort for my painting, so I am going to Pont-Aven in Brittany for six months to paint pictures,' he explained to Mette. She had suggested that he meet her at the seaside in Denmark and see the children again. He refused. He had to work on transforming a rough and give Theo the canvases he was waiting for. In June, the dealer offered a monthly advance based on Vincent's: 150 francs a month for twelve paintings to be delivered within a year. This was also a way of tying Gauguin down.

In the course of their triangular correspondence, Vincent, in Arles, made no bones about telling him: 'My brother can't send money to you in Brittany as well as to me in Provence.' And he urged Theo: 'Above all Gauguin must come here, for the sake of my finances and yours. Above all.' In short, it was essential that 'the little Bonaparte tiger of Impressionism', as he was to call Gauguin after the drama of cutting off his ear, should come to the south. It would suit everybody. 'I find my own artistic ideas excessively commonplace in comparison with yours,' Vincent observed in a letter to Gauguin. But at Pont-Aven, Gauguin met up with his companions of old, in particular his dear Laval, back from Martinique. Why should he take on the incomprehensible Van Gogh down in Arles?

In Brittany the gang was anarchic and eccentric, emphatically male. They drank, brawled and teased the servant girls. But they worked at their painting above all else. The original crowd had been joined by some younger painters: Moret, Delavallée, Jourdan, Sérusier and

Chamaillard, who wanted to make progress under the iron rod of the master. Passing through, Signac remarked ironically that Pont-Aven took itself for a new Athens: 'Everywhere there are painters, clad in velvet, drunken and loutish. The tobacconist has a palette for a shop sign – it says Artists' Materials, in English; the servant girls at the inn have very painterly ribbons in their coifs and must be syphilitic...'

Was this some kind of Arcadia? It seems so: there was work and plenty of talk, walks in the fresh air, dips in the river, fishing parties and drinking, casual affairs in a room above the post office ... In *A Painter's Pilgrimage Through Fifty Years* (published in 1939) a Scot, A. S. Hartrick, described one scene when Gauguin appeared:

> Perhaps the most vivid memory I have of him is of a blazing hot day when I was painting some distance down the river Rance, and I saw a boat rowed by two Bretons coming slowly up the river; it contained his pupil P., Madame X., her five small children with their *bonne*, and, just astern, Gauguin, naked save for a pair of slips, holding onto a rope, was being towed along on his back, like a dead porpoise, but evidently enjoying himself hugely.

In August 1888, Gauguin laid out his principles: 'Do not paint too much from nature. Art is an abstraction; take it from nature by dreaming in front of it and giving more thought to the creative act which will result.' The Inca was taking giant steps. There were seventy-four works that year, and seventy-one in 1889. In his wake and by his side, the young Emile Bernard was also making progress, and was proud of his canvas *Breton Women in the Green Meadow*, which made such an impression on Gauguin. His answer to it was *Vision after the Sermon (Jacob Wrestling with the Angel)*, W245, a key work, in which the planes of dream and reality merge and become telescoped into a single space.

He wrote to Schuff, stuck in Paris, worn out by the quarrels with his wife – whom Gauguin happened to find very attractive: 'This year I have sacrificed everything, execution and colour, for the sake of style, because I wanted to set myself to do something different from what I already know. I think of it as a transformation which has not yet borne fruit but will do so ...' In a letter to Vincent, describing the *Vision*, he goes into more detail: 'In the figures I think I have achieved a great simplicity which is rustic and superstitious.' He observed: 'For me, in this painting the landscape and the struggle exist only in the imagination of the people praying.'

Together, their tentative ideas were to outline and release a new current: the abandonment of classical perspective, the superimposition of planes, and *cloisonnisme*. He knew this, foresaw it: art is only addition, a fusion of the real and the imaginary, of the seen and the felt, of emotion and reasoning. He suggested instead of articulating, interpreting the spirit and the essence of things: a synthesis. And leaving country fairs where young girls in peasant coifs had danced to the sound of Breton bagpipes and bombards, it was the dull and muffled reverberation of their clogs on the sunken roads that he sought in his painting: the solemn song of the world. Sometimes when their hearts beat too loudly, Brittany seemed too narrow to contain them . . .

CHAPTER 8

Was it to be Tonkin? Or back to Martinique? 'Theo hopes to sell all my pictures. If I have that good fortune, I shall go to Martinique; I am sure that I can do some good work there now ...' Or to Oceania, where he had already been offered the lure of a post as 'a cultural worker'? But first of all he had to satisfy his dealer and take himself off to Arles. Not for the sake of the climate, 'the Greek beauty of the women', or Vincent's presence, but to avoid getting on the wrong side of Theo. Prudence had resigned him to it. Gauguin also knew how to calculate and plan ahead. He judged that the inconvenience of this cohabitation would be compensated for by the cash in hand. In Arles, working methodically on a full stomach, he would prepare all the better for his future abroad.

'Van Gogh has just bought 300-francs-worth of ceramics from me. What's more I'm leaving for Arles at the end of the month ... From now on he's going to provide me with a small monthly allowance,' Gauguin told his friend Schuff with boastful optimism in October of that year. Arles certainly did not attract him. Besides, after all the arguments, it was Theo who had paid for his train ticket. By now, Gauguin only went where he would find credit or illusions: Pont-Aven and Arles for financial reasons; Copenhagen and Taboga to make good, chasing notions and schemes. Time after time, hard-pressed and driven by the need to be himself, he sought out some fresh impetus from a group, an ally or a country. What else could he do, once he had made up his mind to live from his painting and do nothing but that?

As for the mythic pairing of Paul and Vincent, it never came to anything. In the two months between 21 October and 24 December

1888 it was over and done with. 'I had an instinctive feeling that things would not be quite right . . .' This was no idyll in the manner of Verlaine and Rimbaud, runaways in the London fog, or Flaubert trailing through the deserts and romantic ruins of the Middle East with the brotherly companionship of du Camp. No, because if painters respect one another they will have nothing in common. Apart from the Japanese influence, a way of mixing flat colours and gradations, of playing with framing and recession, they did not admire the same masters, nor did they think of their art in the same terms. Gauguin noted that Vincent 'admires Daudet, Daubigny, Ziem and the great Théodore Rousseau, all of whom leave me cold. Whereas he hates Ingres, Raphael and Degas, all of whom I admire.'

In this would-be Provencal Japan, one of them saw a Daumier while the other would be referring to Puvis de Chavannes. The only catalyst in their semi-destitution was Theo, the protector, with his monthly allowances, his gallery and his clientele. The two men remained on a formal footing; they did not want the same thing. Their philosophies and sensibilities were in opposition. 'He is a romantic and I am something of a primitive,' Gauguin observed, judging that Vincent 'flounders about'. The Dutchman was all for expressiveness, vibrancy and humility, aiming to convey 'the terrible passions of humanity'; the Inca was looking for a freshness of composition, a new starkness, a poetic language, an imagined world. Their trajectories intersected like those of meteors. Vincent's epileptic fits, his alcoholism and his nightmares, drove him to create canvases whose harshness conveyed his unhappiness and distress, and thereby the fragility of his human presence. 'Victory does not matter to me at all, and in painting my only aim is to get through life . . .' This former evangelical preacher was an anguished mystic, a sinner in search of a consoling God, for whom the Christ figure was an 'artist among the greatest of all artists, scorning marble and clay and colour, and working in living flesh.'

Paul, on the other hand, thought ahead and was determined to win. In the first place, without mentioning it to Theo, he was wary of Vincent: how could he make an impact on the market alongside a painter who was regarded as demented? Artistically, the Inca was caught up in a pantheist dream. He was feeling his way towards distant shores where a childlike savagery would prevail in a re-found Eden that would finally allow him to breathe. He was motivated by revenge and prepared to come to blows with this society which he despised, prepared to lash out bloodily at critics, collectors, scrimpers. 'We have to let him wage his battle; he'll win it anyway,' Vincent recognised.

Living side by side in the Yellow House, for a time these two strove for compatibility. One painted from life, the other what was in his head. Vincent made an effort to tidy up; Gauguin saw to the cooking, old seafarer that he was. They kept a shared kitty in a biscuit tin. When the need arose, the rules were slackened. But Gauguin was the dominant one and never thought twice about giving Vincent lessons 'to put him straight'. 'Gauguin gives me the courage to imagine, and imagined things undoubtedly take on a more mysterious character,' Vincent confessed, even while fully engaged in his art.

This, then, was the blueprint for the 'Atelier du Sud'. On the programme was painting, reading, discussions at the Alcazar where they drank too much absinthe, the 85-per-cent-proof green fairy that rots the brain, and recreation at the licensed brothel run by Madame Virginie. 'Personal hygiene, regular sex, and getting on with one's own work, are all a man needs to keep going,' Gauguin wrote to Schuff. They had been forming some cordial acquaintances in the town: the postman Roulin, Madame Ginoux, and an officer in the Zouaves, second lieutenant Milliet, back from a tour of duty in Asia. This soldier, who had known the thrill of the Orient and the poetry of pearl-sheened paddy fields, had become a friend. In his extravagant red and blue uniform, he regaled his attentive audience with stories of Tonkin and Africa. The exotic! Wasn't this what the world was called when it had the beat of something wholly unknown and thrilling? Gauguin listened open-mouthed. He gave Milliet a drawing in exchange for an illustrated edition of *Madame Chrysanthème*, Loti's Japanese novel, which was revered by Vincent.

Racked by metaphysical questions and made fearful by the solitude of these last years, Vincent was also a great reader. He bombarded his co-tenant with books from his library: Tolstoy, Dostoevsky, Zola, Renan, and Daudet's *Tartarin of Tarascon*, 'which had made him believe in the Midi as an extraordinary place', and more Loti, his Tahitian *Marriage*, as well as philosophical studies, articles on Buddhism, and a work on the Marquise Islands, written and illustrated by Max Radiguet, a Breton from Landerneau. This was *Les Derniers Sauvages*, which came out in *La Revue des Deux Mondes* in 1861 and was subsequently published by Hetzel.

All this reading and the conversations with the Zouave, who was unfailingly attired in his fez and Turkish trousers, set the Inca dreaming again. His 'terrible itching for strange places' beset him again. He constructed hypotheses. 'I told the Zouave about you and I think that in Africa you will have quite an easy life that will also be very helpful to your art,' Gauguin told Emile Bernard, who was also eager to travel. And supposing he himself were to settle in Asia?

Vincent panicked. Arles, this fine town which he likened to the beauty of Japan for its 'limpid atmosphere and array of bright colours' – the splendid yellows and the earth that turned blue at twilight – was not enough for his august fellow-painter. Gauguin, the one-time sea dog who had sailed the world over, saw it as too narrow a theatre. On an outing to Montpellier, when Gauguin was in rapture over Delacroix's *Women of Algiers* at the Fabre Museum, Vincent realised that he was going to leave, and everything became uncertain. The great Paul's thoughts were on departure, not on him or Theo, who was giving his last drop of blood to support the two painters financially; not on their shared future or this brotherhood they had. The tension rose. Why should Gauguin betray the trust of the Van Goghs, betray their Mediterranean phalanstery and his twinship with Vincent?

In a fog of preoccupation, Vincent looked at another of Delacroix's paintings, a portrait of the museum's benefactor, Bruyas, and described it to Theo thus: 'He is a gentleman with a beard and red hair who bears an extraordinary resemblance to you and to me ... the portrait resembles you and me like another brother.' Then, in the Arlesian women painted by Gauguin (*Old Women of Arles / Garden at Arles*, W300) he thinks he sees veiled Moorish women. And, not without a certain perspicacity, in *Café at Arles* (W305), behind Madame Ginoux and her bottle of soda water, near Milliet and Roulin the postman, he discerned kimono-clad Japanese women in the back room. Didn't these give away a secret? Gauguin was going to abandon him like everyone else and meet up with the Zouave in the Casbah. He was getting out.

Paul tried to calm things down. Theo's monthly payments had set him back on his feet. He had repaid his debts to Schuff and even sent 200 francs to Mette. There was a point when he had thoughts about a return ticket to Copenhagen. Despite Vincent's agenda, he would have liked to stay on in Arles, but what could he do about this situation? He was neither a doctor nor a relative. How was he to respond when Vincent told him: 'Even if I know them, the people I see seem to me to come from very far away and to be quite different from how they are'? Was this oversensitivity, over-emotionalism, or epilepsy? Vincent was prey to 'appalling fits of terror', visual, auditory and schizophrenic hallucinations. Was this madness, as people were wont to say about him? What was the name for this melancholy that seized him with such 'great force' and gave him 'a horror of life'?

Perturbed and unstable, affected by too much absinthe, Vincent took to sleepwalking, wandering threateningly around Gauguin's bed.

Gauguin woke up with a start. 'What's wrong?' he asked anxiously.

The other man dissolved into the shadows, only the whites of his eyes to be seen, then sank into a heavy slumber. How long had he been staring at him in the dark, just inches away from his face, their breaths hovering together?

Gauguin confided in Schuff: 'My situation here is quite awful ... Anyway, I'm staying, but I'll just be biding my time.' In the Yellow House, with cloudbursts overhead, the two men paced around one another like electrified tigers. 'He was becoming very odd, but I was wary of him.' On one occasion they painted together at the Alyscamps, the Roman necropolis, on 'that melancholy pathway of cypresses edged with a succession of ancient empty sarcophagi, broken and covered with moss'. But as the Inca observed: 'Vincent and I are generally not much in agreement, especially over painting.'

The arguments became fiercer. The weather, torrential downpours, didn't help. Trapped in the house, where the tension was becoming extreme, Gauguin stayed indoors all the time and began work on a portrait of Vincent, his *Portrait of Vincent Van Gogh Painting Sunflowers* (W296). The result horrified his companion, who paced about scratching the walls like a man buried alive: 'It's me all right, but it's me after I've gone mad!'

A fight broke out between them and Vincent threw his glass of absinthe at Paul. Gauguin informed Theo: 'I would be obliged if you would send me part of the money for the sale of the paintings. All things considered, I have no option but to return to Paris. Vincent and I are quite unable to go on living in each other's company without awkwardness since our temperaments are not compatible.' Then he changed his mind. Hearing about this a few days later, and beside himself, Vincent ran up to him in the street 'with fast, jerky little steps', and attacked him with a razor. The Inca pushed him away and, unwilling to go back to the Yellow House, holed up in a hotel for the night.

This was late December. What followed is well known from what Gauguin has described: the violent crisis of the next few hours when Vincent took the razor to himself and cut off the lobe of his left ear, offering it like a Christmas present wrapped in newspaper to a prostitute called Rachel, because Gauguin wasn't there to receive it. A false brother who had deceived him, betrayed him, who had perhaps accused the two Van Goghs of using him, keeping him there with monthly payments as a kind of minder for the sick man. 'We did not exploit him; on the contrary it was important to us to safeguard his life, his means of working and . . . his honesty,' Vincent would later argue.

A laconic report of the melodrama appeared in *Le Forum républicain*: 'Last Sunday, at half past eleven in the evening, a painter by the name of Vincent Vaugogh (*sic*), a native of Holland, appeared at the brothel licensed as No 1, asked to see a woman by the name of Rachel and gave her his ear, with the words: "Keep this object with the utmost care." Then he disappeared. Informed of this event, which could only be the action of a poor lunatic, the police went next morning to his house and found him lying in bed showing scarcely any sign of life. This unfortunate has been urgently admitted to the hospital . . .'

After being questioned then released by the police superintendent, Gauguin sent a telegram to Vincent's brother. Theo arrived post-haste and took over. Gauguin went into hiding: 'Seeing me could be fatal for him.' A doctor took Vincent away – 'His mind was beginning to wander' – and he was admitted to hospital. 'Rage, indignation and grief too,' Gauguin explained. The register states: 'Vincent Van Gogh, landscape painter, aged 35, bachelor, son of the late Theodorus Van

Gogh and the late Anna Carbentus, Zundert (Holland), deliberate severing of one ear.'

Poor Vincent, who struggled so much, a poor sick man with his head bandaged. Theo spent a few hours with him, made sure he would be taken care of, and left 100 francs for when he got out of hospital, before going back to Paris along with Gauguin. They were both in shock. The severed ear – the bleeding ear lobe cut off with the razor – haunted them. In his hurry, the Inca had forgotten his sketchbooks and his fencing mask. Only Brittany would blot out this black sun, expunge this sadness and waste. Out of the train window, swaying along as he lay on the wooden seat, his bundle of clothes wedged behind his neck, the painter watched as night cast a veil of frost over the Rhone. The dark valley, glimmers of light, plumes of smoke from the chimneys. It was Christmas 1888. Where were his children, and what Nordic song would those beloved little Danes be singing around some decorated fir tree? Gauguin couldn't sleep; living made him feel cold.

On the platform at the Gare de Lyon, dulled by the bad night he had spent, Theo said goodbye. This whole dreadful story was not his fault, yet his gaze was different in the pale dawn. Gauguin thinks back to the bloodied towels in the Yellow House, the coagulated traces of blood all the way up the stairs, where Vincent had rubbed his head against the wall and left carmine swirls across the plaster. A magnified canvas of their lives. Nothing would ever be the same, ever again.

CHAPTER 9

The polychrome statue of Christ which had so beguiled Gauguin and which he painted in 1889 as *Yellow Christ* (W327) was still in the Tremalo Chapel at Pont-Aven, a half-mile or so outside the town. It was June when I went there, along the roadway lined with beech trees, the cornfields behind them rippling like a swelling sea. On the end wall of this solitary 16th-century chapel which resembled a ship under repair, the ivory-skinned Jesus in his loincloth still watched the passing of the years and the curious, his tortured arms stiff, his legs stretched as if on a rack, slow runnels of flaking blood scoring his thigh.

What a strange totem to hold sway over human time. It was both Papuan and medieval, having something about it of the primitive fetish object and of the owl nailed to a barn door. Yet, in his Calvary, this crucified man was not alone. On the worm-eaten beams, apostles, angels and monsters grimaced or went into ecstasies around him, like so many Oceanic *tupapau*. An entire kingdom of fantastical animals, devouring dragons and beatific saints had come to life under the chisel of these naive sculptors, probably to commiserate and keep him company. And in their midst this effigy with his Inuit looks, his small eyes, his triangular chin coming to a bearded point – an effigy half dead and half alive – was the very spitting image of Paul Gauguin. Indeed, this man, divine and emaciated, a bough of grace and pain, prefigured that man who would be known as Koké-des-Marquises, naked in his Tahitian loincloth, scarily thin, nailed to his boards, to his morphine, to his incomprehensible art. A dazzling premonition which he was to place in his canvas among yellow hills and red trees, a salting of unhappiness, of fate, with him still, and he always as actor and material: Paul Gauguin. The *Yellow Christ*, the *Green Christ* inspired by the Nizon calvary (W328), the red-brown Christ known as *Christ in the Garden of Olives* (W326) – each time, the Peruvian, a reader of Renan, who saw in the Christ a divine man, stages himself in the agonies of death and is aware of bearing the burden of his vocation, his inspired mission: 'This is my own portrait I have made. But it also stands for the crushing of an ideal, a sorrow as divine as it is human. Jesus forsaken,' he would explain with reference to *Christ in the Garden of Olives*. 'A potent synthesis of grief,' as one journalist would observe.

Further down was the river and the chaos of Aven. Round slick shale rocks made a polite pretence of being stranded mammals. Here was a tamed and peaceful garden, Bois d'Amour, the Grove of Love, a world suspended, fashioned from water and echoes, from shade, reflections and sonorities. It was close by that the famous lesson had been given to Paul Sérusier, the painting known as *The Talisman*, in September 1888; an almost abstract work, the gospel of modern painting on a heart-rending cigar-box lid. From the inspired master to the pupil, the attentive disciple receiving the precious fluid in the Garden of Eden. Gauguin talked to him, advised and initiated; he was heeded like a Messiah, the Messiah of modern art.

'How do you see those trees?' Gauguin asked Sérusier.

'They're yellow.'

'Well, paint them yellow; and paint those blueish shadows with pure ultramarine. And what about those red leaves? Use vermilion!'

On the strength of this teaching, this freedom of colour and form and the primacy of subjectivity, the movement of the Nabis – 'prophets' in Hebrew – was to have its beginnings. Around Sérusier, to whom the task had fallen, between 1888 in 1900, some dozen artists gathered, including Bonnard, Vuillard, Valloton and Maurice Denis, and the sunlit piece of cardboard would remain their tablet of laws. 'In this way we learned that every work of art was ... the impassioned equivalent of a received sensation.'

Trémalo, Nizon, Bois d'Amour; all these high places of modern painting were now stuck between carparks and motorways. At Pont-Aven, where I returned to have lunch, the pension Gloanec had been turned into a newsagent's. A commemorative plaque adorned its façade. What prestige the past can lend. On the stands packed with the weekend newspapers and magazines, a few art books had been displayed in case any art lovers turned up. So-called galleries devoted to third-rate painters whom the Japanese were buying up at any price until 1990 occupied the ground floor of the Hotel Julia, the one with the 'good landlady', as well as every doorstep in the vicinity. The Rosmadec mill had become a restaurant. Among the hilly alleyways, I wavered between a crêperie called Le Talisman and the Tahiti Restaurant. How long would it be before these traders in the temple, for whom the postcard-sellers meant an income for life, brought us mini-Gauguins under icing-sugar palm trees? A yellow marzipan crucifix? A mini-palette set with candied fruits?

To cheer myself up I visited the museum, which has a lot going for it despite having only a small collection. It was set up in 1985 as a centre for resources on the Brittany painters between 1860 and 1940. Several retrospectives had brought to light the work of Delavallée, Puigaudeau, Schuffenecker and, naturally, Gauguin himself, who had unwittingly become the star of this Pont-Aven school. A world gone without trace, except for the footbridges over the river torrent and the fussy alleyways, which still had some of their bygone charm, with the little gardens and hydrangea-flowered houses harking back to the town the Inca and his comrades would have known. Ruelle Bel-Air, rue Bois d'Amour, place Royale. It would have been nice to come across them, to run into them on the way through some drinking haunt or small square, maybe in the rye fields around the church, their canvases strapped on their backs and wearing sweaters and berets, just as we know them from black-and-white photographs of the day. That mixture of freedom and anxiety in the old countryside, the fields, woods, meadows and river bristling with rocks and mills. Where were the washerwomen, the peasant women in their coifs working the hay like some extraordinary substance, and the cattlemen fighting among themselves in an 'altogether Japanese' manner (*Breton Boys Wrestling*, W273)? Sometimes the sea air mingled with the breath of the forest from which the artists returned mud-bespattered, paint-stained and famished. Pont-Aven in those days seemed outside time, standing still in its 'willow valley', drawing its vigour from old Armorique. On the quaysides of the old harbour at high tide, where sardines and silver-blue mackerel were unloaded, Gauguin in clogs dreamed of sailing away again. 'He was taciturn, austere you might say ... He could have been a Basque, comfortably off, with his own schooner,' one bystander recounted. He was waiting for his time: a theatre on a scale with himself, his Golgotha on the other side of the oceans. 'What I wish for is a corner of myself that is still unknown.'

Down towards Le Pouldu, further south along the coast, is the inlet of Grands-Sables, the mouth of the Laïta. In 1889, Gauguin and Sérusier stopped there for a few weeks. 'I arrived yesterday. The beaches are magnificent and I'm going to be staying here for a fortnight, alone with Gauguin, with no distractions, no worries and no aperitifs,' the young painter wrote enthusiastically.

Along with Meyer de Haan, Van Gogh's friend and compatriot, in the end Gauguin withdrew to this hamlet of seaweed-gatherers some two and a half miles from Clohars-Carnoët. It was quite different from Pont-Aven: just a stretch of heathland, two paths and five houses. There were fields that sloped gently down to the ocean, and sandy beaches with dunes. He was in retreat and forgotten; an ideal. 'Do you want my news?' he asked his wife in June of that year. 'I am by the seaside in a fishermen's inn, and I'm living here like a peasant who calls himself a savage ...' In exchange for lessons 'in Impressionism', Meyer paid for Gauguin's board. 'I bleach some of my own linen in secret; in fact, apart from simple food I am bereft of everything,' he acknowledged, now with not a centime to his name. Not even for tobacco, though he was a heavy smoker. He was prepared to sell his work at any price.

Back behind the wheel of my car, I drove on under lashing rain. Through the rise and fall of the windscreen wipers, big Atlantic rollers were coming in, breaking on the shore in fast succession, like a cavalry charge. Along the paths, walkers caught out by the weather were being whipped by a gale. At last the wind dropped and the rain eased off as shafts of sunlight broke through. The sky was opalescent, the colour of new slate, and the ocean glittered like a silver plate all the way to the horizon.

I parked on the seafront and took a little walk in this new light. Everything shone. The air rushed into my lungs like precious manna; distances seemed to have been eradicated. I felt I could have reached out and touched the white fluff of the clouds which were reappearing, and held between two fingers the houses tucked in among the churned fields. I wondered whether I should go right to the shoreline, among the rocks with their manes of seaweed, to see if I might find some *Breton Eve* or *Woman in the Waves* (W335, W336, W337), of the kind painted by Gauguin, naked sea sprites caressed by the shifting foam.

In the harbour, further over, the last of the rough sea was battering against the moored boats. To the south, lined up along the cliff, half a dozen houses faced down the tenacious remnants of the rain. In one of them, Villa Mauduit, the two artists are about to throw open the salt-eroded windows of the attic. Suddenly they look out on the ocean, the wind and the void ... 'As we work now, we can see storms straight in front of us – for we are right above the sea.'

Not far from there, on the only hilly street, stood an exact reconstruction of the inn kept by Marie Henry, the Buvette de la Plage. This building, a mere ten yards from where the original had been, was occupied by a café-tabac. An orphan from Quimperlé, born in nearby Moëlan-sur-Mer, in her youth Marie had worked in Paris as a chambermaid, saving every last penny so as to acquire some property on the Brittany coast. She was independent and determined, and so beguiling that she was nicknamed Marie Poupée, Marie the Doll. She had a daughter, Léa, whose Asian looks were something of a puzzle, and she brought her up alone, as well as running her establishment with a firm hand. After she became the mistress of Meyer de Haan during Gauguin's time there in 1889, in his wake her two-storey house became a refuge for the Pont-Aven painters. Laval, Bernard, Moret, Roderic O'Conor and Filiger all piled in, either singly or together, for short stays or weeks on end, regarding themselves as 'painting in secret just as the early Christians prayed in secret'. It became a rendezvous for artists of diverse talents and varying success, but with the Inca always as the charismatic central figure. Paul-Emile Colin later wrote that they saw him as 'a Christ whose disciples we were'. A Christ who would fight against the public's indifference and against artistic habits and reflexes. A Christ burned by what he bears and what he is: a freedom and a poetry that are new and irrational.

Van Gogh, now in a period of grace and again in touch with

Gauguin, for whom he still professed 'sincere and deep friendship', would also have liked to be there, joining the apostles of this new faith. He said so when he wrote, concluding his letters with the drawing of a fish, a symbol used by the early Christians. Thoughtfully, the Inca dissuaded him, advising against a visit to this remote heathland: 'I think your idea of coming to Brittany and Le Pouldu would be an excellent one were it feasible. The thing is that de Haan and I are in the middle of nowhere, far from any town and with no means of communication other than a hired carriage. For an invalid who sometimes has need of a doctor it's a risky situation.' Was this the final blow for Vincent, the ultimate abandonment, and if Gauguin had said yes, might this putative stay in Brittany have altered his fate? We can imagine so. Yet Vincent was already out of control; he himself felt that it was too late. A few weeks later, on 27 July 1890, at the end of a walk in the countryside around Auvers-sur-Oise, where he had been brought from Arles by Theo, Vincent returned to his room in the Auberge Ravoux bent double, furtive and hiding the state he was in. With a bullet in his chest, he lay dying in his iron bed. 'He set his easel against a haystack then went behind the chateau and shot himself with a revolver,' wrote Bernard. When Doctor Gachet was called, he gave vent to his helplessness in the face of the haemorrhaging wound. 'In the night he cried out, a very loud cry . . .' Vincent suffered for hours; there was nothing that could have been done.

Vincent's strength failed him on 29 July; he died in his brother's arms, surrounded by his paintings, which formed a kind of 'halo'. Bernard hurried there and found the coffin closed and lying on the billiard table in the inn, with masses of yellow dahlias around it. Van Gogh was buried among the wheat fields. Stunned, Gauguin gritted his teeth. But he knew all too well 'how much the poor fellow suffered in his struggle with madness'. He felt no guilt. What could he be blamed for? Why should he have to carry one more cross? 'He took with him the consolation of never having been abandoned by his brother and of having been understood by a few artists . . .'

In the midst of these young men, at forty-two Gauguin was the elder, the spiritual father and guide. 'The more I go on, the more I am filled with this sense of translating ideas.' Writing to the painter Henri Delavallée, he explained: 'When it comes to drawing, I do it as simply as I can and I synthesise it!' This means a lot of sketches done outside and then systematically recomposed in his room; work in the darkroom of ideas after exposure to reality. 'For each country I am in I need a period of incubation, in order to discover the essence of plants, trees and all of nature.'

How would he define himself? His answer: 'Like an insurgent', half-pirate, half conquistador. In his book, *Diary of an Art Student*, published in 1938, an Englishman called Alfred Thornton left this description after seeing him at Grands-Sables cove: 'Gauguin was evidently possessed of great physical strength, of which he could, but rarely did, make use; his expression was severe and his movements were slow, giving him an imposing manner that kept strangers at a distance. Yet lurking behind was a fiery temperament leading at times to fierce outbursts of wrath ... We felt his power, we did not really understand him ...'

Jacob Meyer de Haan, who had a private income thanks to a family-owned biscuit factory, continued to pay for the maestro's meals so long as Gauguin, Christ-like with his beard and shoulder-length hair, corrected his paintings. 'Up to his ears in debt,' Gauguin agreed, and between June 1889 and the spring of 1891 he managed several trips to Brittany while keeping one foot in the capital, where he busied himself with various projects, notions and wheezes. His aura remained untarnished, but his commercial affairs made no progress whatsoever. 'I show my work at Goupil's in Paris – I'm the only one – and the pictures make a lot of impact, but it's very hard to sell them,' he noted in mid-June of 1889. 'Not a penny in the bank!' He lived on low-level credit, on the backs of others, dispensing promises and lies. 'Everything goes badly and nothing goes well; I am definitely hounded by some misfortune ... Might as well give up the ghost!'

At Le Pouldu, in the clean space of the open air, these talented artists trekked around from morning till night across the fuzz of the heathland, through the fields, the green woods, over the plants and slippery rocks, playing with the tides and the changing light. If it rained they painted the doors and windows of the inn. They teased the local girls and to relax they made music, with Gauguin on the accordion, played games of dominoes and organised singing contests. Or else they shot arrows at cardboard targets as they had seen done at the Universal Exhibition. Hairy and bohemian, they were like real Indians. When the young André Gide was on holiday in the area he happened to dine in the same place on one occasion. Later he wrote (in *Si le grain ne meurt*): 'The three of them were barefoot, superbly slovenly, with booming voices. And throughout the whole of the dinner I sat with bated breath, taking in every word they said, aching to speak to them, to have them know me, to know them.'

There were numerous paintings done by all and sundry in this 'out-of-the-way spot for making art in'. There were some master-pieces, like the Japanese-influenced *Beach at Le Pouldu* (W362), which belonged to Maillol; the hieratic *Seaweed Gatherers* (W349), or the *Breton girls by the Sea* (W340) whose astounding primitive qualities prefigure the Tahitian period. There was also the famous Kersullec exercise, when Gauguin and de Haan each painted a picture with the same subject: a squat farmhouse where Marie used to stock up on eggs and milk for her inn. Gauguin's painting (W394) shows dogs and logs of wood in the foreground; his pupil's has rocks in the foreground. But there is the same peasant woman drawing water from the well, seen from the back, her white coif on her head.

The blue-roofed house was still there. There was wet gravel in the garden, clumps of hydrangeas, deckchairs left out on the lawn. I crept about like a thief, hearing the prattle of unseen children. A cat, black as ink, was eyeing passing birds. I was about to ring the doorbell when a neighbour at her window called me back. She was cooking something on a stove and as she spoke to me she kept half an eye on the food. The smell of crêpe with grilled ham wafted into the alley, to be carried off on the wind.

'The owners have had more than enough of people nosing about, you know, Monsieur. They're eighty years old. The whole village will tell you! Gauguin and his friend painted the outside of the house . . . that's all I know.'

'Do you have a lot of people visiting?'

'No, but their cars are parked in the way and it's awkward when we want to drive out.'

Disconcerted, I turned off towards the shore, along the road where the fishermen's lookout post was. The wind had risen again over this ragged coastline. Occasional houses clung onto it, those *pen-ty* which are squat and solid like little fortresses, pleasing to the painters for the very reason that they are isolated and tenacious. I followed the pale earth of a path that headed straight towards a sea the colour of a stained-glass window. Gauguin and his gang worked away in the salty wind at the foot of the cliff. 'I try to put into these desolate figures the savage I see in them, and who is also in myself.' They were drawn to these stark spaces where work became a hymn to nature and to life.

I took my time walking back, zigzagging. The roar of the ocean intoxicated me; the whole sky sat on its shoulders. And when I chanced upon a wooden gate that creaked over the sloping ground, among the windswept trees resembling one of Christian Dotrement's logograms, I would have liked suddenly to see that man in the nut-brown Inverness cape, his beret pulled down over one eye as he muses about one of his compositions, so that I could simply say: 'Bonjour, Monsieur Gauguin.' Perhaps he would have answered me then, amazed that I knew his name. His hand would have shaken mine under this grey light, the hand of an artist and a seagoing man: short, sinewy and vigorous, as much a sailor's as a painter's.

In Le Pouldu, I stopped at the beach café, which abuts the recon-struction of Marie Henry's house. This café was in fact the original establishment, but retained no trace of it. Alongside, the fake-real inn that was Marie's sported a huge imitation sign across the pediment: 'Buvette de la Plage'. Inside, all the reconstructed rooms displayed objects and furniture of the period; some reproductions of paintings had been added, with no detail overlooked. There was a big slab of Marseilles soap in the bathroom, a tub and a basin, towels, sheets and quilts on the beds, seasoned pipes in the ashtray, a great quantity of books, glasses on the tables. Since everything was so convincingly arranged, it left an impression that one had broken in, taking advantage of Marie and her clients being out. It wasn't so much a museum as an empty house, and the person who lived there would come in at any moment from the kitchen garden or the market, while her tenants would arrive back from the beach.

An art student had the job of taking visitors round and providing a commentary, and she answered the questions asked by some half-dozen people intelligently. For all her enthusiasm about this summer job and her evocations of the painter in these surroundings, she owned to finding Gauguin 'selfish' and 'exploitative'. Quite stung, I spoke out and retorted that he had no choice about it: Gauguin burned himself up, he was the moonstruck priest in the service of the god of Painting. This made the tourists embarrassed; there was some whispering, then the tour continued.

When I got carried away, I took stock of the distance between myself and the visitors to the museum. I wasn't looking for something to fill up the afternoon because there was another rain shower over Grands-Sables. Each time I went into one of the rooms, I was entranced and suffocated in equal measure by every single thing, by every object, by every engraving. I saw everything, I saw nothing any more, everything oppressed me, everything fell short. Once again, everything was still to come.

After the tour, I apologised to the guide, explaining that I was preparing an article on the Pont-Aven school and that essentially Gauguin interested me more than the others. This was a half-lie. Because of it she let me wander round the house and go back upstairs to the attics, where the museum kept its documents. I had Marie Henry's inn all to myself.

I sat for a quarter of an hour on the stairs with my back to the wall, as if I were at the bottom of a pyramid, a tomb raider who had lost his way. In the three first-floor rooms, respectively those of Sérusier, Gauguin, and the room shared by Meyer and Marie, there was a smell of wax and salt. De Haan's bible was open on a stand and a travelling rug had been opened out. There were heavy clogs in a corner and the floor creaked, the wind whistled through the glass of the windows. At any moment Meyer would appear out of nowhere, carroty-haired, excited, with a canvas roughed out in Prussian blue. He was on his way to call his mistress, Marie, who was downstairs serving cider to the seaweed-gatherers. Despite what people might say, they were lovers. Hearing them at night, on the other side of the thin partitions that separated the adjoining rooms, Gauguin, and Filiger too, seethed with the jealousy of the chaste.

Gauguin's room overlooked the garden; I went back into it as if entering a nest of boxes. For a moment I sat down on his bed. A bound copy of the illustrated review *Le Tour du monde* lay open at the pages on Tahiti. Gauguin was reading it furiously just as, pencil in hand, he had perused volume 4 of *Colonies françaises*, which had come out to coincide with the 1889 Exhibition. 'Born beneath a sky that sees no winter, on a soil of wondrous fertility, the Tahitian only has to raise his arm to pluck the fruit of the breadfruit tree and the plantain which form his staple foods. So he never works, and fishing, whereby he varies his diet, is for him a keen source of pleasure ... For the Tahitians, life is a matter of singing and loving ...' Between one drizzle and the next, in the midst of so much silence, these faraway people made him dream.

It was as if Paul were there. Beside the wardrobe whose mirror was specked with rust, beside the broken grey marble pedestal basin, in the shadows, the details, the patterns in the carpet and the yellow wallpaper, in this hollowed space, this trap of time. He was lighting a clay pipe and smoking as he turned the pages, the volume opened out on his knees. 'The moments of doubt, the results that always fall short of what we dream, and the scant encouragement from others; all this contributes to flay us raw.' He mused: 'In the end painting is like man, mortal but alive, always struggling with matter. If I thought about the absolute, I would cease making any effort even to live.'

The fact was that at this time there was yet to be any real boost to his career, even though he had exhibited twelve pictures in Brussels (in February 1889), had taken part in the 'Impressionist and Synthetist group' exhibition at the café Volpini in Paris (in May 1889), and finally stirred some favourable interest at a Copenhagen event (in October 1889). Admittedly, Theo had sold another five or six of his paintings and Gauguin himself had placed some ceramics and statuettes, often sales to artists, but this was no more than getting by. 'Commercially, my art is making hardly any headway. And I have reached an age where I am, so to speak, going downhill, so I see little point in soldiering on without ever coming up trumps. And even if I could make a living in business, I have no wish to do so.'

To stop himself from moping about, he makes quick work of things and goes down to the Buvette to be with his fellow-painters in the dining room, blotting out his worries with laughter and noise. There is sand on the floor, pitchforks are propped against the granite walls, geese are led in by a boy with a stick. Taciturn peasants with lined faces drink bowls of cider. Filiger picks out a mournful tune by Schumann on his mandolin; Meyer plays dominoes with Colin; Sérusier reads Shakespeare, head thrown back to savour the lines. Their canvases are drying and the whole establishment is a cage for wild beasts: walls, windows, doors and wardrobes have been covered in painting. Along the muddy road, a seaweed cart turns off towards the vale of Kersullec. Cows ruminate among abstract hayricks.

'It's a clear night, so tomorrow the weather will be fine,' Marie pronounces as she lights the lamps.

Her guests will paint the breaking waves in the manner of Hokusai, the gentle Japanese. Through the window, a silhouette can be seen stealing onto the beach. It is Gauguin, the beggar king wandering among the rocks. The tide washes away his footprints. When can he leave? And where does he get this endless desire, this unappeased restlessness; 'homesickness without a home', as Nietzsche put it? The signs are that this need for adventure was for him part of the soul's receptiveness, something on a very personal level: the proof that without imagination reality was never enough. And that existence was not solely governed by appearances. Faraway journeyings which are only journeys deep inside oneself, in Victor Segalen's words. 'We dream, and then we settle down to painting.'

CHAPTER 10

'Departure for the tropics assured. Money to follow. Send your entire output. Guaranteed sale.' Theo Van Gogh sent this telegram in October 1890, three months after Vincent's suicide. His own grief and pain ultimately got the better of him and, stricken with paralysis, Theo followed Vincent into madness. He died in hospital at Utrecht on 25 January 1891. The astonishing saga of the Van Gogh brothers was over. This whimsical telegram was as much an exhortation as it was a sob. In the interval, the Boussod–Valadon Gallery cancelled the over-enthusiastic proposal.

'Van Gogh has been stricken with madness and it is a sorry blow for me.' Gauguin was shattered. The only dealer to find buyers for his pictures and to advance him subsidies was finished, and if he was to pursue his destiny he had to put up a fight. He had already seen his own fault-lines in Vincent, his double only weaker.

How else could he resolve things except by going somewhere far away? That 'terrible itching for the unknown' had never left him. 'The future belongs to painters of the tropics which have not yet been painted,' he had told Emile Bernard in 1888. How did he envisage it: was it in Vincent's original terms, which he had taken up and followed in Brittany, as a phalanstery for pirates of modern art? He had to leave, and if possible at the head of a group with himself as guru, as ultimate yardstick, as the vital spirit. It mattered to him as a man as much as an artist that he should have another role on a different scene, and should return to this one with applause; coming home to fame, then perhaps to his wife. Had his father not attempted the same thing by setting sail for Peru in 1849? As Mette had done, after a fashion, by going back to Denmark in 1884, and Arthur Rimbaud, writing to

71

his family in 1886, with the same thoughts in mind: 'I hope ... to take refuge in a few months' time, in the mountains of Abyssinia, which is the African Switzerland, with neither winter nor summer, where one can be free and life costs nothing.' A different country, a second chance, the cards dealt again after the first bad hand.

Who would go with him, and finally escape from the daily round? All of them back out, from lack of money, or lack of courage, or from fear of being in the master's shade. This is to say nothing of Paul's temperament, far from easy-going, always demanding, and quick to turn sour.

Everything comes to grief. Tonkin first of all, the idea that has haunted him since meeting Milliet, the officer of the Zouaves, who had galvanised them with his mirages and his lacquered dragons. 'A good position in Tonkin where I shall work on my painting and save money ... The West is rotten these days and any Herculean spirit can follow Antaeus' example and draw fresh strength by touching the earth in those parts. And a year or two later one comes back from there, a man of some substance,' Gauguin wrote.

Why Asia? Undoubtedly because of the Universal Exhibition in Paris, in May 1889, which had made such an impression on him. This was the main commemorative event for the centenary of the French Revolution, the triumph of this industrial society which had such faith in itself and its technologies. The Eiffel Tower was inaugurated on 31 March, provoking a rapturous reception for its iron poetry, 'the substance of a future art'. There was an ensemble of colonial pavilions, budding gems of empire, and a retrospective of the great French painters, with Gauguin and his mavericks exhibiting on the fringe at the café Volpini. This was the 'Impressionist and Synthetist' group, made up of Van Gogh, Bernard, Guillaumin and Schuffenecker.

It was undoubtedly intended to be an edifying spectacle. The now subjugated world was on show in glass cases, and behind security cordons. Were there not some life-size items from the temple city of Angkor Wat, and likewise Khmer statuary of a religious and erotic nature, somewhere between the sacred and profane? Gauguin had been amazed. With its costumed natives, exotic food and perfumed spices, this was the world's bazaar at close quarters, a rich larder where different races and traditions came together in good harmony. 'In the

Javanese village, there are Hindu dances. The entire art of India is there and the photographs I have of Cambodia bring it back to life.' A huge box of figurines in enamelled lead and living images! Gauguin bought himself a cowboy's Stetson and applauded the Buffalo Bill show. After that he went back to being serious and made copies of apsaras.

So then there was Tonkin, which was part of the Indo-Chinese Union. French troops had occupied Danang in 1858, secured Cochin China and the Poulo Condor archipelago (now Côn Dao) in 1862, then taken Hanoi and the Red River delta between 1873 and 1882, and all of these were brought together under treaties in 1887. France's Asian empire would expand to include, under different statutes, Cochin China, Tonkin and Annam, as well as Laos and Cambodia. The colonial lobby of the parties, the banks and industrialists, goaded on by foreign rivalries, was now at its peak. Between 1880 and 1914, this appetite and influence became as one, in the eyes of opinion, with the expansion of France itself, still bruised by the Franco-Prussian war of 1870. This consensus united left and right through an overriding interest. The stubborn nationalism of the press gave support to a programme which combined politics, economics and humanitarianism. The statesman Jules Ferry deemed that 'Colonial politics is the child of industrial politics.' But what if the only progress lay in making the world a better place, as the Saint-Simonians proposed? Yet, what was being played out under the French triumphalists was plainly a strategic struggle, primarily against Great Britain, or against regional powers in Asia, such as Siam, Japan and China, which was vast. And local populations counted for little; territory was conquered and, sabres and holy water sprinklers in hand, the Europeans threw themselves upon their prey. For once the clerical party and the secular camp were in agreement, accepting overseas what they fought over in France. The same went for higher interests. The ideas of certain intellectuals, such as Arthur de Gobineau, who pronounced that 'no civilisation can exist without the help of the white race' (*Essai sur l'inegalité des races humaines*, 1853–55), produced justifications for this scramble. Here and there, a few discordant voices were to be heard: liberals, Christian Democrats, radicals and humanists. But these were primarily on the grounds of national priorities, or the cost of such hazardous undertakings, or that they meant a shift of attention that was orchestrated by Germany, and rarely on the grounds of foreign peoples' right to decide for themselves. Under pressure from members of Parliament, several cabinets came off badly; Jules Ferry's, for one, was brought down in 1885 after the defeat of French troops at Lang Son. But nothing could stand in the way of this forward march, this fearsome expansion, this greedy seizure of territories and peoples.

As a French citizen, Gauguin approached the authorities inquiring about a situation, a grant, a mission or a post of some kind or other. 'If I do secure anything at all in Tonkin I'll be off there to study the Annamites.' He told Bernard: 'I'm going to try my best to get some kind of situation in Tonkin, and maybe there I'll have the peace to work on some art just as I please.' Disappointment was not long in coming. 'For now the replies are more or less in the negative.'

There was an about turn; he changed direction towards Madagascar, following the promptings of Odilon Redon's wife, who was a native of Réunion. 'She told me that with 5000 francs you can live there for thirty years if you like.' The journey meant a route from the China Sea to the Indian Ocean, from teak pagodas to laterite huts, from lush green deltas to high burnt-out plateaux. Since the Treaty of 1885 the island had been an unofficial protectorate, with a resident in charge of the kingdom's external affairs and guaranteeing military assistance to the Hova dynasty which had been placed under its protection. Though the situation was complex, with the British only waiting for one false move that would let them step in, the resident Le Myre de Vilers proved himself to be able, consolidating and multiplying French interests in the years between 1886 and 1889.

In 1895, armed resistance resulted in Madagascar being annexed by 15,000 bayonets and eight artillery batteries. Britain would not risk redeploying its forces in the area, for they were guarding the island of Zanzibar. Madagascar became French territory in 1896 and Gallieni took charge of the island's fate. In a phrase that has become famous, he turned a 'rebel forest' into a 'tranquil and prosperous colony'. Harbours were dug out, roads made fit for vehicles, schools, general hospitals, maternity hospitals, and refuges for lepers were built. In line with the colonising power's domestic requirements, the cultivation of rice, coffee and hevea was fostered. Colonists were urged to settle.

For Gauguin, this semi-continent 'has more to offer in its range of types, its religion, mysticism and symbolism. There you find Indians from Calcutta, black tribes, Arabs, and Hovas, who are a Polynesian type.' He got carried away by his open-mouthed naiveté. 'I can buy one of the native huts like the ones you saw at the Universal Exhibition. It would cost practically nothing, and I could make it bigger just by chopping down some wood, and turn it into a dwelling that would suit us, with cows, chickens and fruit trees, so these would be our staple food and we would end up living for nothing.'

The more he talked about Madagascar in his letters in the course of 1890, the more he sought to convince himself. 'My departure for Madagascar is irrevocable. I shall buy a mud hut in the countryside and shall extend it myself, planting things and living simply – I'll have a model and everything one needs in order to study. So I shall found the Studio of the Tropics. Anyone who wishes can come and see me.' His arguments had male candidates in mind: 'A Malagasy woman has as good a heart as any Frenchwoman, and is far less calculating.' Sometimes they emphasised virility: 'With five thousand francs you can live there for thirty years if you want. Hunting is easy and will provide your food.'

Young Bernard would go along this time. It was up to him 'to find a way of having the government pay our passage', Gauguin explained. 'You have to write to the Minister for the Navy saying that you want to settle there and are too poor to pay the cost of the sea voyage.'

The pursuit of this idea in the face of any common sense ground to a sudden halt. This was when Doctor Charlopin disappeared. Gauguin had fondly believed that, from the dividends on his patents, this inventor would buy 5000 francs' worth of his paintings before he left for Madagascar. Charlopin was more of a Charlie Chaplin figure, vanishing into thin air along with his promises. At Le Pouldu, Gauguin had even stopped painting. 'I go about like a savage, with long hair, doing nothing. I have made some arrows and I practise shooting them on the sand, the way they did at Buffalo Bill's show. So that's what the so-called Jesus Christ is up to.'

Meanwhile, Bernard had set up a lottery involving the sale of tickets for pictures, with the winner being drawn by lot. Nothing came of it. His enthusiasm was to no avail. 'Getting away, escaping, to the ends of the earth, wherever the devil it might be, so long as it is into the unknown! Leaving behind this abomination of life in Europe, with its boors, its overfed sneerers, the whole pestiferous crew . . . how good it would be to get myself dead drunk on freedom, to be able to look at the sea, to be intoxicated with life.'

Who else was there that he could strike out with? 'I shall put exactly half of my daily bread at your disposal,' the Inca pleaded. Schuff was angry, Laval silent and distant. Filiger was almost down and out. Georges Daniel de Montfreid, a friend of Schuff's whom Gauguin had a liking for because he too had been a seafarer, had fallen in love. Even the faithful de Haan had left him in the lurch by going back to Holland, for fear that his family might cut off the 350 francs he received as an allowance, and for fear that Marie Poupée might keep him at Le Pouldu now that she was pregnant. Gauguin had been counting on him, because of his income.

There were no travelling companions and there was no money. He had to find yet another destination, another scheme to calm down his inner voices and to break the spiral of his poverty. And to set about creative work again on what he felt, what he sensed. 'My answer to commercial art is no, even if it is Impressionist. Deep inside myself I have an inkling of something greater.' Then he imagined Tahiti, the archipelago of the Society Islands, magical places, and he heard murmurs of approval. After all, no one had painted these things yet. 'Each and every island that the lookout sights/is Fate's promise of an Eldorado . . .' wrote Baudelaire. So, it is onwards to Polynesia, like a ship changing course to get the wind in its sails. But Gauguin is all alone in his boat.

'May the day come (and soon perhaps) when I shall go and take refuge in the woods of an island in Oceania, and live with rapture, tranquillity and art.'

Who told him about Tahiti? Was it 'little Bernard', yet again, who lent him a brochure about the 'French settlements in Oceania'? It seems, however, that it was Gauguin's reading Loti's novel, *Le Mariage de Loti*, rather than any colonialist propaganda, that was the trigger. In April 1888, Van Gogh wrote: 'I can easily imagine a painter nowadays doing something similar to what we find pictured in Pierre Loti's book.'

This work was serialised in Juliette Adam's *La Nouvelle Revue* in 1880, with the original title *Rarahu, idylle polynésienne*, then published in volume form by Calmann-Lévy. The story is skimpy: Tristan and Isolde in the tropics, Paul and Virginie in the naturist version. A simple-minded tropical symbiosis of fantasies about *terra ignota*, and living and loving free of constraints. The coming together of a particular period and a particular author, the romantic Orient shifted eastwards to the realm of ghost-islands where there are flower-women and tattooed warriors.

It was a huge success: there were four new editions annually, over eighteen consecutive years. 'Staggering,' was the verdict of Julien Viaud, a naval officer who played some part in writing the book. Viaud was a dwarf, wore make-up, curled his moustache and had an equivocal look in his eye; a very strange kind of sailor, sporting rouge on duty, going about in built-up shoes, boasting that he never read at all and getting through quartermasters and pretty women alike in port and on board ship. His cabin was stuffed with curios, perfume burners and delicate fabrics. He displayed the whims of a pasha, adding a jackal to his collection, a tortoise, cats wearing clothes and coiffures. One might describe him just as a muscular fin-de-siècle 'queen' who happened to pose nude for photographers, but he was more complicated than that, and more exceptional. His private journal, obsessed with the idea of nothingness, is emotionally harrowing, and his accounts of his travels, *Mahé des Indes* for example, are still darkly beautiful.

In Loti the traveller, there is something crepuscular and haunting, something heartrending and thrilling. One night, as his armoured ship cruised through foreign waters, a sailor woke this officer; stiff in his tight gold-buttoned uniform, he threw wreaths of flowers down into the black waves. Loti carried scars and memories in equal measure: his deceased elder brother obsessed him like a *tupapau*, those unappeased spirits of the dead. And even in *Le Mariage de Loti*, we find this Van Gogh theme writ in filigree: where is the dear departed one, Gustave, who, before Pierre, was loved by the Tahitians and 'who had come away from this place with ineffable memories'?

This novel had provincial France enraptured out of its bored existence of hoeing and herding cows. Loti was hailed as a genius. In order to work, exoticism needs a raw light, flagrant emotionalism and fake jewellery in acid-drop colours. This was enough to persuade our Inca. The painter's son, Pola Gauguin, summed up his father's departure in this laconic phrase: '*Le Mariage de Loti* and an enticing official description of the Pacific islands decided him on Tahiti.' This is how Fate moves somewhere between avowed hankerings for escape, sexual fantasy and the lust for revenge.

Who is this paper Eve, Rarahu? A 14-year-old Polynesian child-woman, her body made firm by swimming, her mouth ruby red, her skin copper-hued, her tresses clothing her. On the verdant shores of her island, this princess falls in love with a British officer, Harry Grant, to whom she gives herself; he is rechristened Loti, with the lotus-flower in mind.

'Loti,' asked Rarahu after a long silence, 'what are you thinking about?'

'Many things,' I answered, 'that you could not understand ... I am a child of the old world, born on the other side of the globe, and I am here beside you, and I love you ...'

Everything fell into place. Even these words, in the style of reportage, which must have delighted our traveller-painters: 'Tahiti is one of the few countries where one can safely fall asleep in the woods on a bed of dead leaves and ferns, with a sarong for one's blanket.'

It is mind-boggling that this novelette should have mesmerised major artists of the stature of Gauguin and Van Gogh, enraptured authors such as Daudet and Dumas *fils*, and even as cerebral a writer as Mallarmé who, utterly bowled over by the book, gave his feline verdict: 'It is exquisite, a flavour that is almost beyond the power of literature.'

After the eroticised hankerings for bazaar-style exotica, the European continent became consumed by these myths of South Seas sensuality, with little concern to separate truth from fakery, or the real from the sublimated. Hadn't Bougainville christened this archipelago New Kythera, Kythera being the island of Aphrodite, or Venus as the Romans called her? When it was published in 1771, his *Voyage autour du monde* (*A Voyage Round the World*) fired the imagination and the senses of its readers; if it was to be believed, on the far side of the oceans it was possible to lead an idyllic existence, in a setting made for innocent and happy human beings in their original state. As for native women, in this healthy climate they were inevitably naked, their bodies given freely without shame; they were sisters 'of the Graces unveiled', in the words of the naturalist Commerson. This was a vision of paradise such as those dear to the Enlightenment philosophers and to the Utopians, an Eden unsullied by the foul miasmas of sin. A counterpoint to a European civilisation obsessed with moneymaking and moralising; a sensual and anarchic revenge on industrialisation, it was like a fable writ large.

And then, at latitude 17° south and longitude 159° west, there was finally a protectorate where the coconut groves did not see the usual quota of blood spilt. Although there were missionaries at work by 1834 in the Gambier Archipelago, and six years later in the Marquesas Islands, the French had already made themselves at home in Tahiti by 1842, after evicting the British and their Protestant parsons. In 1847, King Pomare made a treaty that placed Tahiti, Moorea and their dependencies, the islands of the Society Archipelago, under the protection of France. One after the other, the different archipelagoes of Tuamotu, the Austral Islands, the Wallis and Futuna islands, fell into the same lap. As the centre of the 'Etablissements français de l'Océanie', the French operational base, Tahiti, saw an influx of civil servants, soldiers, sailors, merchants, planters and Chinese labourers.

Forty years on, the voluptuousness so celebrated by naval officers was somewhere in between being primitive and under control. It was remote but reachable at the end of a two-month voyage on ships of the national fleet and on merchant navy services. It was wild, indeed, but under the thumb of banks, firms and concessions. It was exotic, but colonised, because kept well in hand by the army and the doctors. It had natives under administration to be painted, and white administrators to whom drawings could be sold, and nature there was generous. 'The breadfruit trees, the wild bananas and so on ... But all this exists in the region of the tropics where there are coconut palms and so on ... To be able to live off this kind of food takes some time to get used to. Ask Laval,' Gauguin thoughtlessly requested. Prices were low, and there were thrills without risks. 'Tahiti is a paradise for Europeans,' he harped on to Bernard at the end of July 1890. 'Don't overlook anything for our departure, which amounts to our freedom.'

Gauguin, daydreaming of a better life, pictured himself compensating for the gaps and the flaws in the life he had through something oneiric and sexual, something alive and free, a romantic balm for his wounds to be found on the other side of the globe. 'I deem my art, which you like, to be no more than a seedling, and I hope to cultivate it out there for my own sake in its primitive and savage state,' he observed to Redon. Even out there, this did not prevent him from bearing in mind earthly needs and constraints. He had become a builder who was prudent in his fiery passions, painstaking in his efforts. 'We shall have six months of hard work; I want to build a fine house that is well-made and durable, I want to sow and plant everything necessary for our food. Later, if there is no money, we shall have enough to feed us without any worries or difficulties.' Nonetheless, the Inca had no intention of staying on for so long: 'I'm not going out there with the idea of staying and never coming back to Europe.' His round-trip voyage to Polynesia was meant to be a transition, a way of bouncing back, a necessary reprieve. A voyage out followed by a return, from which he would learn something. 'I hope that I shall not always be a pariah.'

The government was giving support to migration, and anyone prepared to make good under the tricolour flag was guaranteed the backing of the authorities. There was an Emigration Society to oil the wheels. From Le Pouldu, Gauguin handed out his orders to Bernard: 'They are the ones to ask about whether there is a way of finding a free passage, or some reduction on the steam packets.' Once there, de Haan could start up trading in pearls, 'doing business with merchants in Holland', to boost the finances of the emigrants. If it came to the worst, after a year there was the prospect of a return journey free of charge.

'Don't worry, we'll go!' So it was to be Polynesia, where the light was stronger, where the energy of the world was palpable and shimmering. Nurturing this dream, they began packing their bags and getting ready for the fray, like unruly children. They still needed some money. At Le Pouldu, Gauguin had thought about this long and hard and come up with a solution. He would stake his all, and since he had nothing to lose, the entrepreneur in him would succeed where until now the artist saw no hope. At the Hôtel Drouot salerooms.

CHAPTER 12

It was all a bluff or, to be more accurate, a meticulous and patient operation of infiltration and seduction. Gauguin himself mounted the sale at auction on 23 February 1891, with his friends and disciples pitching in, and it was one of the high points of his life as a painter. Since he had to leave for Tahiti and had not a farthing to his name, he set about creating the solution out of thin air. Between November 1890 and February 1891 he made the preparations for a media coup promoting himself, his extravagant works, his departure for far-flung places and his future legend. He fashioned himself into theatre, played his part, established and sold himself. The erstwhile banker took the destiny of the flashy foreigner in hand.

'Around ten thousand francs. I think that a well-prepared sale of thirty or so pictures from Martinique, Brittany and Arles could bring me that,' he explained, detailing his strategy to Charles Morice, a journalist whom he had tamed. In other words, rather than waiting for someone to come and buy his paintings in a studio he did not have, or for someone to pay for his passage, he turned the situation around: he would make news. His network proved its worth; not just because of good planning, but also because the time was right, his reputation was still rising and a generation of young artists recognised themselves in his strivings. What's more, he had a personality that made an impact in the salons and the studios.

Through Emile Bernard, Albert Aurier introduced him to painters and writers at the café Voltaire or the café François premier; Sérusier was back from Brittany and was publicising him all the time; Maurice Denis likewise. Gauguin was doing the rounds from painters' studios to literary salons, and before long he became part of the *Mercure de*

France set, spending time with Symbolist writers such as Jean Moréas, Francis Viélé-Griffin and Edouard Dujardin, and getting to know other literary figures including Paul Verlaine, Maurice Barrès and Henri de Régnier. His effect on these Parisians among whom he moved ranged from surprise or irritation to fascination. He had been a seaman, crossing oceans all over the world, sailing through the Aegean, the Black Sea, the polar circle; he had been a representative in Copenhagen, a labourer in Panama, he had starved in Martinique. As a stockbroker, he had handled millions of francs on the Paris stock exchange. He had collected the greatest artists and worked with the best: Pissarro, Cézanne and Van Gogh. Degas admired him. He was the grandson of the revolutionary anarchist Flora Tristan, he spat on bourgeois and priests. He also described himself as Peruvian, descended from the Borgia royal family of Aragon, but he lived like a Breton peasant in farmhouse garrets and wore waistcoats stitched with traditional Breton embroidery. He was confident about his rustic art, boxed with style, and was a swordsman the equal of D'Artagnan. This 'tramp steamer captain' was apt to say, sententiously: 'Primitive art proceeds from the spirit and makes use of nature.'

His painting was disturbing and mysterious, therefore modern. He wore clogs, had long hair and theories about pure colour, he knew Japanese art thoroughly and had assimilated its fragmentation, its interplay of surfaces and recomposed perspectives; as an innovator he proclaimed: 'Work freely and madly, and above all do not sweat over a painting; great feeling can be conveyed immediately, dream about it and seek out its simplest form.'

Gauguin could be simultaneously shrewd and sincere; with his hoarse voice, his pale eyes and wrestler's build, he presented himself as a 'primitive aristocrat'. His intellectual theories were as robust as his shoulders. He was a reasoning adventurer and a thinker ever on the move, a barefoot traveller and a prince; he had enough haughtiness and self-assurance to command instinctive respect. This charismatic fellow mocked systems, castes and norms, by having defeated, ignored or transcended them. 'He had a lofty nobility, clearly inborn, and a simplicity which bordered on coarseness,' in the words of Charles Morice, who added: 'Although there might have been other foreigners in the group at whose centre he was, I saw only him and I would go up to the table where perhaps a dozen poets and artists were listening to him speak, and stand there for a long time.'

Also thanks to Morice, he met Stéphane Mallarmé, the translator of Edgar Allan Poe and the leading figure of the Symbolists. Mallarmé was won over and acknowledged Gauguin as one of them, finding in this contemporary's originality a pictorial extension of his own aesthetic ideas. 'Suggestion, this is what the dream is. It is the perfect use of that mystery which constitutes the symbol: gradually evoking an object in order to show a state of mind or, inversely, choosing an object and drawing out a state of mind from it through a series of decipherments,' Mallarmé had written. After Jean Moréas's manifesto in 1886, Edouard Dujardin attempted to theorise symbolism in these terms: 'In painting as much as in literature, the representation of nature is a chimera ... What ought to be expressed is not its image but its character.' He urged exploration of the territories of dreaming and imagination, of the fantastic and the magical, of sleep and of death; in other words the repudiation of a precise, constructed, rational and intelligible world. And with the reek of anarchism about it, the refined despair and sulphurous mystery you find in Puvis de Chavannes, Gustave Moreau or Odilon Redon. Gauguin was not a long way from this.

While Mallarmé was all sensitivity and delicacy, very much in the 'British' mode, Paul Gauguin had the air of a well-muscled seafarer, someone inhabited by the realm of the real but pierced through and through by an endless reverie. They were fascinated by one another. Gauguin's story was 'poignant', cried the poet. The support of the 'delightful Mallarmé' would from then on be unshakeable, Gauguin recognised: 'that hand held out to offer joy and strength ...' Symbolism, as he understood it, was a refusal of mere realism/naturalism and an opening up to the subjective through the plasticity of language. Mystery and mysticism, the essence of the world behind its forms and constraints; colours have a sound, a sense and a destination. The artist does not contemplate, he meditates on the world, then experiences it, speaks it through himself, through his art. It is not a matter of merely conveying a visual impression; this is pushed to the point of experience, of the idea, the essential, its interrogation. Red, blue and green are squeezed out of the paint tube, and the artist must then know how to transmit human passions and make brush strokes that give shape to the questioning of destiny. In October 1888, in a letter to Schuff, Gauguin was already aware that 'This symbolist path is strewn with pitfalls, and I have made only tentative steps upon it, but it is in my nature, after all, and I must always follow what my temperament inclines me to.' If we need an example of this recruitment to symbolism, one alone will suffice: *The Vision after the Sermon (Jacob Wrestling with the Angel)*, W245, the painting made in Brittany in 1888. The combination of picture planes, the sacred and profane, the rustic and the superstitious, is here in this spiritual vision that complements the real. It is a mental apparition in the copse and the fields; symbolism one hundred per cent. Is this a reverie deployed on several levels, with human beings, demi-gods and animals mingling on a scarlet ground? This is what Gauguin has to say: 'We have fallen into the abominable error of naturalism ... The truth is a purely cerebral art, it is primitive art ...' Writing in the *Mercure de France*, the touchstone of the day, a journal where Gauguin had allies, Albert Aurier hammered in the point: 'You have among you a decorative artist of genius: walls! walls! Give him walls!'

Gauguin wanted to go to the other side of the world in order to find this vital energy. Mallarmé could not but assist him, even though he was later to write about his worrying sense of 'exotic lies and the disappointment of global voyages ...' He launched Octave Mirbeau into the fray and Mirbeau published his article over three columns in *L'Echo de Paris*. 'Monsieur Gauguin is a very outstanding and very disturbing artist ... His art is so complicated and so primitive, so clear and so obscure, so barbarous and so refined ... His work is strangely cerebral, exciting, still uneven, but poignant and superb even in its unevenness ...' In the article he explained that the artist intended to flee from 'civilisation, voluntarily seeking out oblivion and silence ...'

Next came a second piece by Mirbeau in *Le Figaro*, and his enthusiasm was so great that he bought a picture for five hundred francs. This was like a trigger, for the writer's name carried a lot of weight. In the course of February 1891, one article led to another in a snowball effect, with pieces appearing in *Le Voltaire*, *La Justice*, *Le Gaulois*, *Le Rappel*. Delighted, and thoroughly caught up in his own momentum, the Inca told Mette: 'There is a great deal of talk and in the art world there is an enormous stir, which has even reached England, where a newspaper is describing it as an event ... Old Pissarro made a rather jealous remark: "He set out to achieve widespread recognition as a man of genius, and he managed it very skilfully. There was nothing else to be done but allow him this elevation".'

Gauguin became the man of the moment. When he was interviewed by the press on the very morning of the sale, the Inca talked about himself as he struck poses beside his paintings. Mesmerised by his 'mysterious colours', the journalist Jules Huret went so far as to write: 'Take a look at these pictures! Mark my words, in twenty years' time they will be worth twenty thousand francs.' This is the kind of thing that art buyers found gripping; it was the stuff of mythmaking.

The Drouot saleroom was packed solid that afternoon. As the ivory hammer went down, the outcome quickly became apparent: thirty paintings sold at very respectable prices, among them the *Vision*, which was snapped up at nine hundred francs. The buyers included gallery owners with a nose for a bargain, wildly impressed private collectors, like the comte de la Rochefoucauld, and just for good measure, out of solidarity, friends and painters such as Degas and Monfreid. On the evening of 23 February, to his great joy, Gauguin collected nine thousand, three hundred and fifty francs, with an average price of three hundred and twenty francs per painting. This was twice what he had reckoned on bringing in to set himself up in Madagascar. Even though this achievement was to be only a flash in the pan, something he could not have suspected, the boost it gave to his morale was enormous.

A month later, a farewell banquet was organised for him at the café Voltaire, with Mallarmé presiding. There were forty-five guests and the dinner cost five francs a head. Among those present, surrounding the painter at the height of his fame, were Saint-Pol Roux, Moréas, Morice, the writer Rachilde and her husband Alfred Valette, editor of the *Mercure de France*. In the midst of all the toasts, the bursts of applause and the witticisms, there was admiration for this determined man who was deserting the Odéon and the Jardin des Plantes to cast himself towards remote and unknown worlds and the thrill of the exotic. 'I deem my art, which you like, to be no more than a seedling, and I hope to cultivate it out there for my own sake in its primitive and savage state,' he reminded Odilon Redon.

Simultaneously, Gauguin had succeeded in getting a thirty per cent reduction on his fare with the shipping company, as well as an official if somewhat vague cultural mission that required him to go to Tahiti 'with the purpose of studying local customs and landscapes from an artistic perspective and in terms of potential works to be made.' The State undertook to purchase a painting from him for three thousand francs, which would mean his return in triumph, whatever might happen.

But in spite of this success, Gauguin felt depressed at the thought of leaving everything, and even considered giving up the idea. His imminent departure was pathetically far from a reality and his calculations were too pat. In his *Journal*, the writer Jules Renard wrote: 'Daudet was in brilliant form, telling us about Gauguin's plans to take ship for Tahiti; he doesn't know a soul there and keeps putting off his departure. By now even his best friends are telling him: "It's time you left, my dear chap, it's time you left." ' What a cruel irony. The painter broke down in the arms of Morice, confessing that he couldn't bear the sacrifice involved. Not only did he have to leave behind his wife and children, whom he went to see in Copenhagen for a last fond farewell, but also Juliette Huet, his young mistress, who was pregnant by him. On 24 March, out of the blue he announced in a letter to Mette that on his return he would like to resume family life, if she still wanted him. 'So I am sending you a betrothal kiss today.' The difficulties he had to surmount made him think of her with greater tenderness.

Degas had understood the situation very well: the hit-and-run sale had been the winning stroke of a cornered man. Admittedly, Gauguin had pulled it off; but once the agony in the garden was over, there was no turning back. He was only running away to find some clear air in a suffocating world. Now he was condemned to paint, to become himself, to go on seeking, always on the move, driving his incapacity to live in it ever further.

Three hours before Paul's departure, the journalist Eugène Tardieu described him. 'He has a Herculean build, his hair curly and greying, his face clear-eyed and energetic, with a smile all his own: very gentle, modest and faintly mocking.' Paul added this account of his motivations for the newspapers: 'I am leaving to be rid of the influence of civilisation ... I need to immerse myself again in unspoiled nature, to see only savages, to live the life they live with no other pre-occupation but to render, as a child would do, the conceptions of my brain with the help of just those means that primitive arts employ, these being the only good ones, the only true ones...'

It is the end of March 1891, and at the Gare de Lyon he is gripped by a mixture of joy and relief, remorse and intoxication. 'I shall go and take refuge in the woods of an island in Oceania, and live with rapture, tranquillity and art...' Then come the outskirts, the working-class suburbs, the neat countryside. 'A superb awareness which exiles him in the full brightness of his talent, so that he can again be immersed in what is remote and what is himself'; with these ardent words Mallarmé had raised his champagne glass to Gauguin. The locomotive ploughed on towards Marseille behind a plume of smoke which seemed to be writing something in the sky; Marseille where a month later an exhausted Arthur Rimbaud would suddenly arrive back from Ethiopia, to die in France at the age of thirty-seven.

Standing at the gangway of the steamer L'Océanien as it gradually casts off its moorings, the painter no longer knows whether to laugh or weep. There, between the ventilation hoods, Gauguin already sees the purple portholes bristle with masts and coconut palms, past Suez, Aden, and then the island of Mahé, as he sails towards his promised land.

In my mailbox this morning I found a large envelope containing a catalogue of 'Modern Prints' sent to me through the post in error; it was meant for my older brother, who is an art dealer. On pages 28 and 29, there are six Gauguins up for auction next month. These consist of an etching and some woodcuts, among them a portrait of Mallarmé, in profile with a black raven perched on his head, and a print of *Manao Tupapau* presented as a 'proof printed in chocolate brown on canary yellow vellum'. The catalogue lists this woodcut, No 62 priced at 50,000 francs, as having 'traces of oxidisation, dust marks and one corner missing. Undeciphered notations in black lead in a Scandinavian language.'

These notations intrigue me. Whose are they? The owner's? Some friend of Mette's in Denmark? Mette's own? Why did this person jot down these appreciative words, intelligent though they may be, on the print itself, and written backwards? Are they important? These five pencilled words (three on one line, two on the next, with the last word underlined and between brackets, the whole thing unreadable, done quickly as if in code) seem very peculiar. They add mystery to this proof which is signed in the painter's hand, on the bottom right, and printed on the back of another proof, *Washerwomen*.

The reproduction is on page 29 of the catalogue. A woodcut measuring 205 by 290 centimetres, from 1893–4. It shows a sleeping Tahitian woman lying in a foetal position with her back to us, part-foetus, part-Peruvian mummy. She is lying in a white basin, a kind of symbolic egg, which she fills completely. Her braid of hair, which hangs towards the left of the image, is reminiscent of an umbilical cord. Her fist is pressed against her ear: she wants neither to see nor to hear. She is both frightened and sleeping, awake and deep in a dream, sealed off from the outside world and open to it through the perviousness of her skin. On the right, just where her foot happens to be pointing, a small human figure emerges from the inky shadow, as if sardonically; an eerie tawny-faced imp about the height of a child. Is this ghostly gnome-like apparition of a Maori *tupapau* real or imagined? Whatever the case, it is a haunting spirit, a dead dwarf-creature as cold-blooded as a snake, a dead creature reborn from the darkness and returning to torture the warm flesh of the living.

The woodcut is part of the *Noa-Noa* volume, which was meant to record the painter's first stay on Tahiti. It resumes in detail the theme of a famous painting with which Gauguin wished to shock (*Manao Tupapau*, 1892, W457). This time the spectre is on the left, leaning against the post of a couch on which a long-bodied and very young *vahine* lies naked on her stomach, huddled and trembling with fright, exposing her thighs and buttocks in her terror-stricken pose. 'She is lying on a bed covered with a blue sarong and a light chrome-yellow sheet. The ground is violet and purple and scattered with flowers that resemble electric sparks; a rather strange figure is standing beside the bed ... The title *Manao Tupapau* has two meanings: either she is thinking about the revenant or the revenant is thinking about her,' Gauguin explained laboriously.

In a recent edition of *Noa Noa*, in which the woodcut takes pride of place, a piece of writing by Somerset Maugham (from his volume *Purely for My Pleasure*) serves as introduction to the collection. Maugham relates an anecdote about being in Papeete in 1916. He was on holiday in Polynesia at the time and during one of his walks he was told about a *fare*, a traditional Tahitian house, where Gauguin had lived. Without further ado, he made his way to Mataiea by car, turned along a path crowded with playing children and stopped at an ordinary hut set among enormous heliconias, finally to find genuine paintings by Gauguin on the doors of the hut. 'There were three doors; the lower part of each was of wooden panels and the upper of panes of glass held together by strips of wood. The man told me that Gauguin had painted three pictures on the glass panes.'

Although the first two works had been scraped away and almost obliterated (one being fragments of a head, the other the torso of a woman), the third work in this triptych had survived intact; it was an Eve in a sarong holding the *uru*, the fruit of the breadfruit tree. Behind her are stylised white sailing boats and an oily blue sea. Beside her is a rabbit, and a frangipani tree climbing like some broad-leafed creeper. The style was simplified, medieval, synthetist; the date was around 1892. It was a pagan stained-glass window!

'I asked the man if he would sell it. "I should have to buy a new door," he said. "How much would that cost?" I asked him. "Two hundred francs," he answered. I said I would give him that and he took it with pleasure.'

Maugham had the door unscrewed from its hinges and took it away on the roof of his car. Finally, ensuring the utmost care, he had the panel sawn off to remove the glass, then brought it back with him to Europe to have it installed in his villa at Cap-Ferrat. Years later, when he was going through a difficult patch financially, he sold his find for seventeen thousand dollars. This story has no moral.

Of course, I have not had this kind of luck at Pont-Aven or Le Pouldu, areas that have been well cleaned out; and besides, would I have had the practical sense to have the door of some *pen-ty* taken off its hinges after first having stunned my Breton with a wad of notes? A discovery like that would have paralysed me. I might have coped with sketches, but not a stained-glass window or a great painting. Even if someone tells me they've fished some worm-eaten frames out of the depths of the Laïta at Le Pouldu, or that behind a partition in the Buvette they once found some frescoes when they were installing a coffee machine, it isn't quite the same. Admittedly, some drawings and paintings do come to light again. In France, a preparatory drawing in charcoal of a Tahitian woman with half-closed eyes on one side of the paper, and cats on the other, was authenticated and fetched a price of one million, two hundred thousand francs in Bayeux in November 1999. Just a few months ago, an exceptional discovery was unearthed: two Breton watercolours in a portfolio – a goose, a duck, a bowl and a still life with fruit. At auction they went for nearly ten million francs. But what of it? Gauguin's story still has gaps in it, and it is up to us to fill them, those embers of a fire that we can ignite again far away, with others and for others. And that frightened child-woman in the darkness of the woodcut, *Manao Tupapau*, is my daughter as much as she is my sister or primordial wife. And we shall go on together, keeping step with one another, rebellious and open, under the icy eyes of our fears, in the muffled light of our enigmas. She is the mirror in which I am engulfed, when my turn comes; like her, impermanent, a sleepwalker, between dream and reality.

Admittedly, I have a tendency to see *tupapaus* everywhere in Gauguin. It isn't that I invent them, but the more I see of his pictures, the more I recognise them and find them lurking in the pattern of the image; I flush out more of them than expected, see their presence more than ever, in the shadow of the *fares* and the hibiscus shrubs. They come like dark archangels, like devils, sneering, full of power. In distress and turmoil. And they strike poses, assume looks and masks and smiles that verge on grimaces, their eyes so unblinking that they seem eyeless.

This is an obsessive theme, a hole in the work, a nebula that sucks things in. Take for example *Ia orana Maria* (*Hail Mary*, 1891, W428), with that Tahitian mother by a violet path, a virgin of the tropics in her blood-red sarong. The child on her shoulder is a dead Christ, his Mongol face pickled, already green and cold, his limbs stiffened. And he holds only his head, resting heavy on hers, so that their two halos mingle. That's one of them. Likewise in *Parau na te Varua ino* (*Words of the Devil*, 1892, W458), that double presence of a bashful nude and a malignant spirit, its features circled with black, its gaze stony, its teeth bared, tightly encased in a garment of blue. And how can we avoid coming across them in the background of *Te rerioa* (*The Dream*, 1897, W557), where green bodies entwine in a decorative frieze? Or else turned into a raven, 'the Devil's bird keeping watch', as Gauguin put it, its eyes and its beak thrust towards the soft flesh of another *vahine*, in *Nevermore, 'O Tahiti'* (1897, W558)? Even those two horsemen (*Riders on the Beach*, 1902, W620), who are half-human, half-faun, with their deathly faces and hollow eyelids, riding their grey mounts, mingling with the living and galloping off with them, as if there were nothing untoward, just out riding. Riding where? And even Atiti, the little prince hanging in the Dutch museum, isn't he the very image of a *tupapau*?

If I sometimes think of Aristide, the reason is that he takes me back to my childhood in Polynesia, to those three or four sunny years there, almost perfectly insouciant years which held me back from my all too predictable fate. Nothing exists for me further back than that original Polynesia; I have no memory of before then, of my years in France, as if I had been born under the leaves of the mango trees and the tamarinds, swimming among the parrotfish and turtles, sometimes a devilfish whose shadow would zigzag among the mounds of coral. Nor had I any conscious existence before I came to know those spaces purified by light, the wide bands of flat colour in which each element had a sound, a smell, a temperature, had rhythms and capricious movement. My life began there; and this place given to me, appearing and disappearing by magic, takes me back to that older brother who should have lived before me, beside me, a stillborn child whose life, had it been strong and tenacious, would then have cancelled out mine by two years, a life perhaps unmerited or stolen. An unknowable brother left behind in the soil of France, not going with us to those happy shores, that other full and fabulous life, where in some way we were already waiting for Atiti the waxen-faced, the Chinese, Aristide with the hollow eyes, a second self of mine, living and dead, his double and my own double.

Atiti then. A fleshly Tiki with flat hair, a pouting mouth, monkey's ears. A totem. And what of Gauguin's presence by his side, his compassion for this child, his need to draw the corpse; why was he so interested? At one point I suspected that Helena Suhas, the wife of the male nurse, whose photograph I have, and the Anglo-Tahitian woman Titi, who appeared during Gauguin's early months in Polynesia, were one and the same. And that the little boy might be the natural son of the painter and this young woman. I imagined that she might be the one, hidden behind the pseudonym 'Titi' (which means 'breast' in Tahitian), who paraded with him in a ramshackle trap along a coral pathway. But the dates don't match up. Everything suggests that there were two women of mixed race: one of them married to Jean-Jacques Suhas, and the mother of Atiti; the other picked up on the main square of Papeete, the 'meat market', this being Titi, who gave herself only in exchange for presents and money. 'Soon the first vahine will make her appearance; this is Titi, a mixed-race woman whose father was an Englishman. He received frequent visits from her, though he did not live with her,' notes Pierre Leprohon, one of

Gauguin's most ardent biographers. 'She was almost English, but she did speak some French,' Gauguin himself noted in *Noa Noa*. For all that Titi was entertaining, her affair with the painter didn't last long. She had to make way for Tehamana, whom he had seduced on the Taravao road, and whom he later painted as a Maori queen in *Merahi Metua No Tehamana (Ancestors of Tehamana*, 1893, W497), holding in her left hand a fan of woven palms, a symbolic royal sceptre, and with two ripe mangoes beside her. Her hair is adorned with flowers, and despite her black-and-white-striped missionary dress, she is beautiful and mysterious, female grace personified. And hanging in a frame of gilded wood, there in her Chicago museum a century later, she was still the splendid Tehamana, her splendour plundered from the tropical valleys, to be married in exchange for printed cloth and bars of soap, to look him in the face, to look us in the face, sublimely, mockingly flowering.

In the shadow of the basalt peaks of Hiva Oa, Gauguin was bone-weary when he wrote: 'We have exhausted what words can say and we remain in silence. I look at the flowers which like us are still. I listen to the great birds suspended in the air, and I understand the great truth . . .' It is this truth that I discover in the gaze of his models, these shy, elusive girlfriends of the South Sea Islands; this staggering dizziness watching you, watching itself, before its disappearance. This is the power of life, the permanence of corpses whose hands we hold, whose gaze we withstand in the midst of life's incomprehensible uproar.

CHAPTER 14

'The Chinese didn't forgive him for what he wrote about them in *Les Guêpes*, which was a satirical publication that came out in Papeete at the end of the last century. As for the Tahitians, they mistrusted him; he was an outsider, deliberately on the margin. Gauguin drank and womanised. In a very small, conservative social universe influenced by religion and cut off from the world, he was viewed as a deviant. He wasn't a respectable "white". At any rate, he was different from everyone else. He was nothing to do with the colonials and their land, their business projects and their trade. He lived like a native, in a hut, wearing a sarong.'

'And nowadays?'

'Usually, they couldn't care less. Gauguin is quite remote from the Polynesians' concerns, even though he does form part of their heritage and he did defend them against the excesses of the Administration. Our lack of resources, the distance and the modest scope of our collections, act against him. I hope that the centenary commemorations in May 2003 will shift that, change people's way of seeing him.'

I'm in the Madison Hotel, in Paris's sixth arrondissement, on a wet February afternoon. In the lounge overlooking the Boulevard Saint-Germain, I am talking to Gilles Artur, the former curator of the Gauguin Museum in Papeari. This eminent specialist, a Breton, lives in Papeete and is on a visit to France. It was unthinkable for me to write a book about the Inca without consulting him. He is an indefatigable champion of Gauguin and for close on forty years he has been making strenuous efforts to ensure that more is known about the painter. Along with Victor Merlhès, he has worked on Gauguin's correspondence, set up an archive and a library in Polynesia, and runs a bookshop and a publishing house that has republished Gauguin's writings in collectors' editions. Now he is ill and in France for medical care, but his efforts continue.

He is a man of around seventy, with a handsome bald head. Settled comfortably in a Louis Quinze armchair, he considers me with interest. There is something Asiatic about him, a benevolent reserve. Ever since 1965, he has met every future biographer of Gauguin and opened up his collections to them in his museum, which is set in a botanical garden on the edge of the lagoon. His support and assistance are indispensable to me.

'Did you establish the Papeari museum?'

'I had been involved in making some ethnographic films on Vanuatu, at Mallicolo. I spoke English, and that was unusual on Tahiti. The Singer-Polignac foundation gave me my appointment to the museum and I stayed out there. That's all,' he explained modestly. 'I retired this year to devote myself to my publishing house. But let's talk about you instead. Why are you doing this book? What is it that interests you?'

'I like the fact that he cut across the world, his condition as a permanent fugitive. He left everything, he moved through everything like some brilliant and mysterious force. He is like a stubborn gambler who will only bet on the same number, and always on the one colour; that's him, his painting, his work. Of course he was selfish, monstrously selfish. Yet at the same time, if we look closely, we see that he was driven to this: the Stock Exchange made him unemployed, his wife kicked him out, his friends turned away, the dealers abandoned him. But the Drouot sale in 1891 was like a bolt from the blue which made him go towards himself just when he was prepared to give it all up. Economically, he never existed. Socially, he was something of a pariah. People see him as deciding his own fate, when in fact he was primarily its victim, but a stubborn victim who went right to the very end, divesting himself of everything like a snake shedding so many skins. I can also see him being driven to that, there being a conspiracy to make him be himself, to make him become Paul Gauguin. At the end, in 1901, on Hiva Oa, a kind of Golgotha island that was not so much paradisaical as frightening, he was like an ascetic, an enlightened and liberated ascetic. He had lost everything and gained everything; he was painting. I admire that strength of will, his transcendence.'

'And do you know Polynesia?'

'His landscapes are the same as mine. Brittany, where I come from, like you. Tahiti, where I was a child . . . and I spent my adolescence on Madagascar, where he thought about settling. As for Tonkin, which he had seriously in mind, my grandfather was posted there as an infantry officer! The magic of the terraced paddy fields, the Palaeozoic forests, the tigers growling among the bamboos. Or the Montagnard tribes armed with their bows and arrows. I can imagine what Gauguin would have painted in the Red River delta, the imperial city of Huê, or on the high plains of Tananarive, along the Mozambique Canal, in the port of Mahajanga, full of Arab dhows. What's surprising is seeing how much this libertarian liked colonial soldiers of the army and the navy, who were the only true adventurers of the day, along with the scientists. In Arles there was the Zouave, Milliet, on Tahiti Captain Swaton and Sergeant Jénot. And that's without mentioning Loti or Segalen, who had a lot of importance for him, indirectly . . .'

'And what about Gauguin as a personality?'

'I'm not sure whether his contemporaries liked him. At least he has the merit of not covering things up. He was a banker among painters, a painter among the labourers in Panama, an underling as far as the Danes were concerned, a deposed king in the dunes of Brittany, and so on. He wasn't up to climbing coconut trees or catching fish, but he kept his *hauteur* and he remained "the man who paints men"; a stranger in a strange land. He took on everything, even if he complained about it, fumed about it.'

Our conversation lasted for two hours. My background knowledge seems to satisfy him or, at least, is compensated by the passion I bring to it. In my way, I am still a child of Tahiti.

'I went back twice; I've published a few articles and I got involved in a new edition of Marc Chadourne's novel, *Vasco*, on the course at the University of Papeete. I've also got one or two connections there.'

Artur asks me for some names, and of course they are names he knows. In the archipelago, they all know one another. Among the 210,000 inhabitants spread across the whole of Polynesia, which consists of roughly one hundred islands, and with Tahiti's population of 130,000, everyone is more or less related: maybe half-siblings, second cousins, and if there is no better claim they can make they might have been on a drinking binge with someone's son or daughter.

In the end, Artur promises to help me and gives me various telephone numbers. Through his intervention, Victor Merlhès later had me sent the correspondence with Van Gogh (the *Lettres retrouvées*) which was missing from what I had. And since I would soon be out there, he offered to be my guide.

'You'll drop into the bookshop when you arrive, will that be all right?'

I couldn't have hoped for more. A number 86 bus was waiting for me by the statue of Diderot, the author of the famous *Supplément au voyage de Bougainville*. In less than ten weeks I too will be in Papeete. In the footsteps of Uncle Paul.

CHAPTER 15

When Paul disembarked at Tahiti, he was 43 years old and he had in his luggage, like Tintin leaving Oliveira da Figueira's, a Winchester and some cartridge belts, as well as a guitar, a hunting horn, two mandolins, tubes of paint, canvases and brushes, chisels and gouges. In his pocket he had around five thousand francs, the takings from his sale at the Drouot having been cut into by the cost of the journey, the repayment of his debts, the purchase of his equipment, and some allowances to his wife and his mistress, Juliette Huet, to whom he had made a present of a sewing machine. He arrived on 9 June 1891, two days after his birthday. To start with the Inca saw this as an exotic phase of transition. He was to stay in Tahiti for two years, until June 1893.

'On the sea we caught sight of strange fires which followed a zigzag course . . . a dark sky, a jagged black cone standing out against it. We were rounding Moorea just before coming in sight of Tahiti.' At five o'clock in the morning it was already broad daylight. On the quaysides of Papeete he makes people smile as he goes by with his long hair under his Stetson. There are boisterous children, fat Tahitians, thin Chinese, busy missionaries and slovenly looking soldiers. Everywhere there are coconut palms. A green mountain set beside transparent water. Roofs, a red, pointed bell-tower; coral paths between banks of flowers; boats, pirogues that sway about; warehouses baking in the sun; the scent of the ocean and ripe fruit.

Where was he to go after this first bewilderment, this flood of lights and sounds? Having formed a friendship with Captain Swaton after the stopover at Noumea, and becoming acquainted with Sergeant Jénot on his arrival, Gauguin took their advice and lodged in the cathedral district, in a wooden house with the benefit of a veranda. He developed a liking for a couple living next door, Jean-Jacques and Helena Suhas, the parents of little Atiti. Later on, he was introduced to the Governor, Lacascade, who was from Martinique and had a lacklustre reputation. But Gauguin, the 'artistic envoy' with the peculiar appearance, provoked suspicion. Whom had he been sent to spy on? He was obviously someone with political motives, on a mission from France. He was to be mistrusted.

Without venturing beyond Papeete, Gauguin set about tasting local pleasures. He was a visitor to the Military Circle, danced in the park, picked up a number of girls, filled his canvas sketchpad with watercolours, sketches, pencil drawings of animals, landscapes and human types. He also attempted to learn the language with someone called Cadousteau as his teacher. Finally, he shaved his head, and in a fit of respectability bought a white cotton suit. He wrote: 'I have seen so many new things that I am quite unsettled by it. I shall still need some time before I can make a good painting.'

A month after his arrival, he gave Mette his impressions: 'The silence at night in Tahiti is even stranger than everything else. Nowhere but here can you find this; not a single birdcall to disturb your sleep. Somewhere or other, a large dried leaf might fall, but it seems to make no sound. Instead it's like a rustling in the mind ... I can feel all of this about to impinge on me and I am now wonderfully at rest.'

Among his first experiments was a self-portrait with an idol; he is in three-quarter profile, with a yellow square in the background, and a green figurine tucked in the right corner (W415); a portrait of Swaton, who had abandoned his colonial uniform for a slouch hat and a red sarong (W419); and a Tahitian man with a flower behind his left ear (W422). The Inca also had it in mind to make some lucrative bread-and-butter portraits of the bourgeoisie or of traders. He tried for clients and found none. He had no more of a clientele here than in Europe. And no likelihood of a gallery. Had he made a mistake?

By August, our painter-traveller had already lost his drive. His painting was of no interest to these yokels on the far side of the world. He was not tolerated by this small-scale colonial society which had no need to earn a living from this country, because they had company salaries or were civil servants. And, paradoxically, through his drinking bouts and bad company, he had made himself an outsider. The governor did not like him. Why give him any commissions? Well and good, he decided, as he kept up his womanising, his drinking with the soldiers, his sprees with the sailors whose ships were in port. Wasn't he a rebel first and foremost, an artist? He was determinedly outside this sour-tempered little world which aped the manners of a sub-prefecture to the point of caricature. In no time he recorded how he was 'disgusted with this European vulgarity' which saw the whites shouting rowdily on the day of King Pomare's funeral, at the same time as the shy, self-contained Tahitians came in from the outlying districts in silent procession and then sang the chants of mourning. 'Alas, it was civilisation that won the day – the civilisation of soldiers, shopkeepers and bureaucrats . . .'

It was the end of a world, of a people that was now burying its monarch in the midst of military fanfares, merry-go-rounds and snack stands. The King's death 'resembled a financial crash'. Gauguin saw what was happening: civilisation was bound to crush traditional ways of life. Insidiously, it corroded ancient rituals, the gods, the native imagination; the cycle of experience was disappearing in its maw.

'It is the old Tahiti that I loved,' Gauguin noted. Nonetheless he kept on working, turning out numerous roughs and sketches, stocking up the larder. 'On my return I believe I shall have enough pieces of paper in my pocket to paint for a very long time,' was how he put it. But along these streets open to the trade winds, he had found no trace of that primitive, savage Maori art.

In Europe he had dreamt of there being something left; what had become of those flights of romanticism played out in verdant theatres? Perhaps he needed to push further into the island's interior. Yet would anything there have resisted civilisation, resisted the diktats of the missionaries and the arrogance of the colonists? 'I want to make only simple, very simple art; for that I need to immerse myself in unspoiled nature,' was a point he made repeatedly to anyone who would hear it before he left France. So where must he go if he was to find the tikis among the damp ferns or lurking between two narrow valleys, and their *mana*, their artless, raw strength, which would have been like mother's milk to him? The Inca recalled woodcuts in which warriors tattooed from the back of the neck down to their knees sprang up from time immemorial, brandishing clubs or feathered fans. Would he ever see the rock carvings, the tapa clothes woven from mulberry bark, would he encounter telepathic sorcerers or hear the chanted genealogy of clans? That these things have been crushed by modernity, shattered by progress, broken up by missionary evangelism, is something Gauguin sees ahead of Victor Segalen, who was to develop this theme in his novel *Les Immémoriaux* (1907).

The Inca did have to open his eyes; sadly altered, Papeete was nothing but a small town well off the beaten track, with three or four thousand inhabitants, riven by parties and struggles for supremacy between Catholics and Protestants. Every group vied with the others: the Tahitians and those of mixed race made indolent by tasting the pleasures of the 'city'; the Chinese, once coolies on the cotton plantations, now in semi-skilled trades; Anglo-Saxons connected through business interests; French colonists with no restraint, lording it like medieval barons; obtuse bureaucrats and administrators, shoring themselves up with their directives. Alcoholism and prostitution, general neglectfulness and severe epidemics, including typhoid in 1890 and dysentery in 1892, all took their toll on the population. 'This was Europe, the Europe which I had thought I was escaping, still in its worst manifestations of colonial snobbery, grotesque imitation to the point of caricature, of our customs, fashions, vices and civilised absurdities.'

Was he to run even further away? To take ship for the Marquesas, a distance of close on a thousand miles? Money had been frittered away in wild binges, and funds failed to arrive. Hardly any letters came and there was nothing in the newspapers. What were his friends up to? He got word to those meant to follow him: 'Let my friends know: if anyone is inclined to come out here he should take the direct route via New York and San Francisco.' Emile Bernard was utterly furious with him and Schuff had now taken Mette's side, and they paid no heed; only Monfreid was still faithful, but for all that in no hurry to set sail. Monfreid, known as 'the captain', became his confidant, his epistolary companion, his European other half, and a devoted presence in his life until the very end, always looking after his interests in France. Monfreid saw Gauguin, twelve years his elder, as 'a splendid fellow' who was endowed with 'a magnificent gift'. The Inca called him 'his friend', a man with 'the finest, most loyal and open nature that I know.' Between 1891 and 1903, wherever he happened to be, Gauguin confided his doubts and his hopes to Monfreid through the ship's mails. Later, Monfreid's oldest son, Henry, would set off around the world, and become known for his tales of adventure on the white-hot shores of the Red Sea.

Gauguin went back and forth between his furnished lodgings and the tables at the Military Circle, managing to spend his nest egg like water running through a sieve. 'Sometimes it seems fine to me and at the same time I see the ghastly side of it. So far I have done nothing outstanding.' He views Papeete as 'a mistake of the first order'. European-style life, based on merchandise which is imported and then taxed, is too expensive for his pocket; most whites don't eat what the Maoris eat. Jénot describes how this 'began not only to wear down his financial resources but to wear him down too. One morning he came to us and he had been spitting blood, very badly, needing medical care. He experienced problems because he received money from France only irregularly and the same amount went for materials that he couldn't get hold of here; he often complained to me about these difficulties.'

After that he would have to head for the bush, living as the natives did, among them, reducing everything to the very minimum. To get by for a few more months, so as not to come back to Europe empty-handed, Gauguin would have to melt into the landscape, bury himself among the trees, far from any Europeans. His food would have to be raw fish and fruit picked along the roads that overlooked the mirror-smooth lagoon.

'I am strong because I am never swayed from my course by others and I do what is in myself.' One morning in September 1891, his mind made up, Gauguin left in a ramshackle trap, his roll of canvas, his brushes and sculptor's chisel wrapped up in a sarong. His eyes were filled 'with green landscapes and wings', as he made his way towards the coast, in search of bread as well as light.

CHAPTER 16

In the notebook I carry with me there are telephone numbers, sketches, dates, quotations and a lot of notes. It's a small notebook with a black moleskin cover and an elastic band attached at the side. I've bought and got through about twenty of these, taking a new one with me on each trip; I keep it at all times until I run out of pages. As they fill up, they become a foreshadowing of the article or the book to come, its prefiguration: a manuscript in miniature, its skeleton and nervous system. If I lost my notebook it would be like losing myself.

On board the AOM DC-10 for Tahiti, via Los Angeles, leafing through the one I had with me as I sat above the plump Atlantic clouds, I found my notes on the writer and journalist Jean-Paul Kauffmann who had fame thrust upon him because of having been a hostage in Lebanon. I had the pleasure of meeting him when his book on Napoleon, *La Chambre noire de Longwood* (*The Black Room at Longwood*), came out, and I scrupulously made a note of some of the things he said in his interview when he was talking about the Emperor's time on St Helena: like the idea of 'floculation', for example. As if the upheaval, the tragedy of exile and the grip of death upon the Emperor had had an effect on the air of the rooms at Longwood, his prison residence, filling them with an invisible substance which had hung there over the centuries, spreading through these rooms like some malignant gas. In Napoleon's case, the smell of exile, of tedium, of deliquescence. Electrical energies which could not be extinguished, stagnating there and still sputtering on, never at rest, like some kind of amniotic fluid adrift in the corridors whose wood had rotted from so much drizzling rain. A house of ghosts, of revenants. A grave the size of an Atlantic island, a funereal rock, a coffin the size of an English villa, with him inside it, alive, a recluse. 'How dreadful this place is!' Napoleon had observed.

During this interview at his house, Kauffmann had been nice enough to show me a phial containing eau de Cologne. Napoleon's eau de Cologne.

'The only real memento of the Emperor,' said my host.

It had been specially made up, reinvented at St Helena, in accordance with the formula of a 'nose' at the house of Patou, and worn copiously by the victor of Marengo and Jena. His valet, Constant, talks about it in his memoirs: 'I rubbed him with eau de Cologne, which he used in great quantities this way, for every day he would be brushed and groomed. He formed this habit as a matter of hygiene in the East, and it was to his liking; indeed it is excellent ...' There remained a very small number of phials of this 'favourite remedy', and Kauffmann owned one of them.

'Have a sniff ... Napoleon drenched himself in it! Anyone who went near him when he was alive could smell this perfume.'

I took the phial and, piously, I sniffed at it. Lavender, maybe jonquil. For a thousandth of a second ... the Emperor in our school textbooks was there, the high-spirited officer at the Arcola bridge and the Eylau battle charges, the general pinching the cheeks of the men in the imperial guard, prancing on his horse Emir all the way along the front line thick with cannons, was there, in front of me. He still endured; impassive, untouched, and for a second I was carried away by my childhood memories and believed that I saw him as he came out of his bivouac tent, the back of his neck shaved clean under his beaver cocked hat, wearing cashmere trousers, his frock coat stitched with a purple trim; he was flanked by his Mamelukes, Roustan and Ibrahim, the Circassian, who had damascene pistols in their belts. And he was there, his boots prodding the furrows of the sodden earth before he unleashed his regiments of dragoons. Our dear and so terrifying Little Corporal.

I didn't know what to say. I could have quoted Gauguin: 'My pictures from Brittany have become rosewater because of Tahiti; Tahiti will become eau de Cologne because of the Marquesas ...' But I put the stopper back on the phial and Kauffmann returned it to its cotton-wool wrapping. The care he took made me realise that he knew what magic spells it contained: the small miracle of leaps through time.

That is what I was on the trail of with Gauguin: particles, sudden flashes, the exhalations of a presence. At best, an atmosphere. That would be something for a dilettante like me!

CHAPTER 17

Papeete in mid-May, and it is twenty-eight degrees. 'How I pity you for not being in my place, sitting undisturbed in the hut. I have the sea in front of me, and Moorea, whose appearance keeps changing every quarter of an hour. A sarong and nothing more. No suffering from heat or cold. Ah! Europe ...' I have brought my luggage and my thirteen pounds of books to a hotel on the coast, and it is indeed opposite the island of Moorea. An island that right now is green and black, though I can't see it because the views from my room are of 'the mountain' and a car park where two tikis keep an eye on things.

There is no one in the swimming pool; in the restaurant there are five Japanese couples. It is the tourist season's low tide. The sky is amazing, a strong matt blue, like a high wall. It will take at least four days to recover from the twelve-hour time difference and the twenty-one hours of flying. I have changed hemispheres, travelled to the other side of the world, from north to south, from day to night. If it weren't for feeling tired, I would rather enjoy this state of semi-weightlessness. It makes no difference resetting the hands of my wristwatch; it's a matter of getting used to the idea that it is two o'clock in the afternoon, not two o'clock in the morning, and that it might even be a different day of the week, and none of these things matter. When it is out of its matrix the world comes to find a different resonance, a second truth. Like a new stage set conjuring away the one before, just as true, just as false, in the magic of doubling, the succession of masks and fictions.

The coconut palms rustle sixty feet up. Tropic birds flutter about in the tropical garden with its rainbow-hued cassias. A column of ants is transporting leaf fragments ten times larger than themselves. As I chew my 'Tahitian style' fish, I feel a mixture of boredom and complete happiness. Away from any routine, sandwiched between two hemispheres, I am my own person, convalescent and surprised, sleeping badly, taking dips in the lagoon at four o'clock in the morning as a milky dawn is mirrored there, starting my nights at five in the afternoon. Yet, I already feel lighter and more detached. As soon as I arrived I plunged into real life, my own life revealed to me. And I am not here to find some picturesque land, but coming back to what is mine, to the kernel of myself. And if I was straining actively to be there, it was because I wanted to catch hold of the kid that I was – turning into an alleyway, in a mango grove, on a truck heading for Pirae or Arue – as well as the Edenic dream of a far-travelled painter.

Less than three weeks before, there was a performance here of *L'Ile du rêve*, a three-act opera by Reynaldo Hahn (1875–1947), a composer born in Caracas, who was a pupil of Massenet and a friend of Proust. I am sorry to have missed it by so few days, since it was in fact a work inspired by Loti's novel. Yes, really, the same novel that had made Gauguin decide to up sticks and come here. *L'Ile du rêve* had its first performance in 1898 at the Opéra-Comique, was revived at Cannes in 1942, and had not been performed since then, and never at all in the South Seas. The performance by the forty-strong *Orchestre Provence-Alpes-Côte d'Azur*, with Philippe Bender as their conductor, had been quite an event. Robert Fortune was the director of this 'Polynesian idyll' which featured choirs from Papeete and the Temaeva ballet, and was staged in a natural setting of beach and palm trees. It gave the work back to the Tahitians themselves, making them the actors in this rediscovery, and no longer just the extras. Underlying its success was real emotion. All the more so because when Loti wrote it for Reynaldo Hahn, re-transcribing words and rhythms from his book, old songs, now forgotten, had been incorporated into the opera, so the Maoris were rediscovering memories that had been trampled on.

Naval cadet Julien Viaud, the future Pierre Loti, disembarked from the *Flore* in 1872. Carrying his box of watercolours, the young man from Rochefort went out 'on drawing duty', and set to work to bring back 'often up to five versions of the same image, in appalling hot weather. There was to be one for the Minister, one for the Admiral, one for the commander . . . Everyone wanted them.' However, once ashore, he had only one desire: to find the mixed-race children of his brother Gustave, who had died in 1865 on an earlier trip to these islands, where he pursued an interest in photography. Viaud asked questions, met families, rushed around in old traps and hunted around the *fares* along the seashore. On incorrect information he took a hopeful trip to Moorea in a pirogue and was disappointed, almost drowning among the razor-sharp reefs. He had been lied to, and the two naked children brought to him under the shade of a banyan tree were not his nephews; no matter what people said, their birth dates did not match up with his elder brother's time there. No, there was nothing left of him and his love affair with Tarahu, the Tahitian woman with the copper-skinned face of an Apache; nothing left of his dead double, the older brother whom he had sought to embrace through the children he might have left. As the fragile cadet went back to board the *Flore* he hid his tears. Later, he told a correspondent who was going back there: 'Tell the things of that land from me, tell the mountains and the trees that I still love them, but I do not wish to see them again, for fear of my suffering thereupon returning . . .'

Out of this rapturous melancholy, this deathly, sunny mulch of earth, naval cadet Viaud, rechristened 'Loti' from the name for the oleander, was to distil his pseudo-novel, *Le Mariage de Loti*. In the guise of an English officer, Harry Grant, he integrated the story of his brother and himself, the two becoming one in the arms of the sweet native girl 'with the perfection of ancient times' who gave herself to them, her brow tattooed with a diadem of vegetable ink.

Loti was twenty-two, Segalen twenty-five, when they reached the shores of the New Kythera. So astonishingly young. For my part, I turned forty this year. Thirty-four years later, I have returned to the haunts of my childhood in a state of fitful distraction which I maintain as a state of grace. These will be my engine, my energy for the pursuit. Every morning, I turn a new page in my notebook and I write on my blank life, squared with blue, and bound front and back with grainy black boards.

CHAPTER 18

Despite appearances, the side of Gauguin that was a leader preferred a well-ordered life, a regular framework within which he could give himself up to the free-flowing nature of creativity. Nothing must ever stand in his way. He was neither capricious nor extravagant, but determined. He had no compunction about shoving aside anything that might slow him down. 'I am a strong man who knows how to bend luck to his inclinations.' As for what he called 'coït', sexual congress, this too was something that the old mariner made sure to keep in its place. Either with servants as in Brittany or, frequently, with prostitutes, as in Arles, Paris and Papeete, it was a matter of organisation and of channelling vital energies. After that, it was out of the way. Even if...

Emotionally, Gauguin remained ambivalent. As his persistent correspondence shows, he was attached to his wife, Mette, and to his family. In 1888 he had already calculated that 'I can see the possibility of resuming our life together only in seven or eight years time.' Was he trying to convince himself or just being a cad? And at the time of his glorious departure, after having kissed his wife goodbye on his flying visit to Copenhagen, he had spoken without restraint: 'Perhaps you will understand some day what kind of man you gave your children as a father ... Farewell, dear Mette, dear children, and love me well.'

When he was in Brittany and in Oceania, Paul regarded himself as a husband, not separated but 'apart' from his wife through circumstance, financial necessity and context. In his life there is a 'Madame Gauguin' with whom he corresponds in long expository letters full of directives, requests, complaints and expressed wishes: he advises against the piano for their daughter, Aline, but recommends the guitar so that she can accompany him on the mandolin. Letters in which, of course, he lies a great deal, by omission: 'Lots of kisses for the dear children, and the best ones of all for you from your faithful husband and lover' (June 1891). When it came to money, he was quite clear after Copenhagen: the reason he wasn't going to help her any more was his inability to do so. There was no way round this. 'The reason I won't do it is because it is utterly impossible, and is nothing to do with revenge . . .' This is a half-truth.

One of the goals of this 'faithful husband' was to resume their life together as soon as he could earn enough money. He persuaded himself of this: 'When I come back I hope to find all the children as healthy and as well-behaved as when I left them. Next summer, cash permitting, would you like us to spend two months together in the country in Denmark, with the children around me?' (May 1892). However, the painter was writing these ardent lines to a wife who no longer wanted him that much; the irresponsible and stubborn Frenchman had become a burden to her. 'Less calculation and more heart,' Gauguin implored. Mette had made her own life in Denmark, socially at any rate, and was protected by her connections, the Estrup and the Brandes families. She was Zola's Danish translator, she gave French lessons to diplomats, artists and intellectuals, and her apartment with its avant-garde paintings was open to this circle. She had become more confident, had had her hair cut in a masculine style, smoked cigars, felt close to the feminist movement and frequented the cafe Bernina, a well-known haunt of the intelligentsia. Mette had matured; she was intelligent and had achieved independence of mind. She was no longer the wife who had been made pregnant and sat waiting for her fickle husband to come home, but a woman who could be relied upon, surrounded by her clan, in whose midst she demonstrated a capacity for enjoyment, along with a sense of responsibility and strength of character.

Mette had been living alone and bringing up her children single-handed since 1885. Rigour and discipline were called for. She enrolled the children in the best private schools and they had done well; the eldest, Emil, would go to the Military Academy. On the face of things, she had no love life and made a virtuous show of managing without it. Which was not to say ... Gauguin was no fool and, reading between the lines, he sometimes assumed a bourgeois tone: 'I hope that you only sinned in thought with the Danish captain. I may be jealous but I have no right to speak since I have been far away from you for a long time now, and I understand that a woman who spends years of her youth far away from her husband must have times when she feels desire in her flesh and in her heart ...' (March 1892).

With each letter, Mette never failed to ask for money or for paintings which she tried to place. She still had not altered her opinion about the work of her harum-scarum husband, but she had made up her mind to have her share from it. From her point of view things were clear: she had responsibility for the family, five mouths to feed and a house to keep up; she needed cash and her husband never sent any. Therefore she sold what she had to hand: paintings, to whomever would buy them; Gauguin's own pictures as well as those in his very fine private collection. Accordingly she placed a large number of these in the hands of her brother-in-law, Edvard Brandes, a notable liberal, as surety for a sum of money which over the years amounted to ten thousand francs. Brandes subsequently refused to return this collection. Similarly in the case of Doctor Caröe, from whom she obtained cash against some Sisley landscapes, leaving it up to her husband in Tahiti to pay back the money if he wanted to reclaim them.

In the summer of 1892, urged on by artists such as Johan Rhode and Theodor Philipsen and the writer Otto Rung, she even made a round trip to Paris to reclaim certain works from the studios of friends, through Schuff, who was on her side, and Charles Morice, whom she found charming ('you talk about Morice so very enthusiastically that you sound quite plainly like a woman in love ...'). These paintings were in addition to others already secured for her by Schuff. Gauguin's hurried letter shows he saw two sides to these moves. 'I have had news from Paris that you reckoned on selling some pictures in Denmark. If you manage this, do be good enough to send me a small share of the proceeds,' he pleads. 'The more you sell the more it will bring in and guarantee a better outlook for the future. Because one buyer leads to another ... This is the way you have to work, in other words building up a regular clientele,' he insisted from his South Sea exile, sending her eight paintings by sea in December 1892, then another ten in March 1893, in the care of understanding shipboard passengers.

From Mette's point of view, this was investment capital – she hadn't been a banker's wife for nothing. Did this represent an opportunist revision of opinion or had awareness of her husband's genius dawned? She never said, but she brought a formidable amount of energy to the realisation of her interests and therefore, as an indirect consequence, of the painter's. Thus, she saw to it that some fifty Breton and Tahitian works were exhibited at the *Frie Udstilling*, in Copenhagen in 1893. At the same time, for the March exhibition on the Nabis and the Symbolists, she gave the Kleis Gallery seven paintings and six ceramic pieces. In the newspapers, success was instant if controversial: 'We find ourselves faced with a kind of hieroglyphic painting which has thrown overboard an entire capital that has been preciously accumulated,' the *Berlingske* protests. 'Tomorrow, Gauguin's name will be on everyone's lips,' the *Kobenhavn* pronounces in a headline, for its part erasing the stinging failure of 1885. 'One discerns the influence of Van Gogh and of Japanese art . . . He has no apparent precursor, but many imitators.' Madame Gauguin's collection stirred up argument, it was thought-provoking and persuasive. At Philipsen's prompting, Mette sold a number of Breton works for the right price. 'I'm beginning to be collected!' exclaimed the Inca, flabbergasted, on the other side of the world, where, however, not a penny came his way. By an ironic twist of Fate, now Mette would be the one allowing him seven hundred francs so that he could come back.

Later on she would acknowledge how things were: backed up by artists and dealers, she had just achieved her runaway husband's first retrospective. 'I didn't realise that he had become an artist, but I understand now that he had the right to act as he did . . .' This was a subtle combination of affection, calculation and sadness. She felt as sorry for him as she did for herself. But since she needed money and was convinced she had been abandoned, she kept what she made from the sales. In 1907, after lunching with Mette at Monfreid's, Segalen observed: 'Madame Gauguin is, in short, a strong northern-Protestant personality who is thoroughly rotten with virtue and thoroughly corrupted with stern Christianity . . . She recognises that he is very great but very perverted. She had married a man of noble and decent feeling, and says she found him to be a depraved and lying savage . . .'

In short, the Inca was in Tahiti and, even though he professed good behaviour and kept talking about a shared future with a wife who had metamorphosed into a businesswoman, she paid no heed. 'Tahiti is not without its charm and while the women may lack what one might call beauty, they have a certain something that is intuitive and profoundly mysterious,' he told her with sly treachery. This was a 'mystery' that Gauguin deflowered whenever he had the opportunity on the 'delicious island'. On Tahiti as he had done elsewhere. For all his pious talk about fidelity, this was the fellow who had also left behind his mistress, Juliette Huet, in Paris; the little dressmaker whom he had made pregnant. It was Annette Belfils, Monfreid's mistress, who had introduced her twenty-year-old colleague to him.

After having taken her as his model for the painting known as *The Loss of Virginity* (1891, W412), the Inca set her up in a little room near Monfreid's studio, and entrusted him with keeping an eye on her. Then he had made his getaway to Tahiti. A destiny is not something to be wrecked. Thanks to the Drouot sale, Juliette acquired some things and some cash for the bare necessities. The farewells were cursory. For Paul this had been no more than a stop-gap love affair. His illegitimate child was born on 13 August 1891, a little girl who was called Germaine.

'That poor Juliette with the child, and I am unable to help her at the moment. I am not surprised that the little one is not well. Still, she came into the world despite everything; and God knows what state I was in when I made her. So . . .' he wrote to Monfreid in November 1891. A few months later, he issued instructions to Monfreid, making no bones about it: 'The hundred and thirty francs from the piece of photographic apparatus . . . Send me the money (one hundred francs) if you haven't promised it yet to Juliette as my last letter said you should. You will therefore give her thirty francs. I have received a letter from her and the poor girl is not happy. But there is nothing I can do for her.'

While continuing his correspondence with the two women, Mette and Juliette, Gauguin had set up house with Titi, the mixed-race woman from Papeete, with whom he did not get on. What is more, he was nosing around for prospects at dances and on drinking sprees, wearing down his energy to the point of lassitude and disgust. As for the lovely, somewhat empty-headed Titi, Gauguin was no fool. She thought that he had money and that she could live by sponging off him. But though he decided to take her with him on his flight from Papeete, it was because he was apprehensive about solitude, and because she spoke Maori and he didn't.

He headed along the coastal trail towards the districts less touched by 'civilisation'. 'Always on the right, the sea, the coral reefs and the flat sheets of water which sometimes rose up vaporously whenever a wave came crashing against the rocks ...' For Titi, it was like going on a big picnic. 'That day, she had put on her finest dress, and put a flower behind her ear; and the hat she had woven herself out of sugar-cane reeds was decorated with orange-coloured shells over the ribbon trim of straw flowers. With her black hair loose on her shoulders she was really pretty. She was proud of being elegant, proud of being the vahine of a man whom she believed to be important and highly paid.'

Gauguin stopped first at Paea, a coastal hamlet some thirteen miles from Papeete, and visited some acquaintances. Then, after a return journey to Papeete, he settled down in Mataiea, which was twenty-eight miles from the capital and beside a stream called the Vaitura, an out-of-the-way place. 'I went around the district and in the end I found a rather nice hut whose owner rented it to me.' Titi left, then came back when he asked her to, then, weary of this monastic life, she disappeared. Her lover dismissed her with these words: 'That half-white woman who had practically forgotten her race and the way she was different through contact with all those Europeans, could teach me nothing of what I wanted to know, could give me nothing of the special happiness I desired.'

Gauguin had made up his mind to paint and only to paint. To experience that tropical orgy of chrome yellows and reds, mornings that never last, burning afternoons and syncopated nights. To bear the weight of the hemisphere in his brush, in his gouge, in a freedom that was total and disturbing. Here he is at work, at last, in autumn 1891, with his tubes of colours on a sandy embankment of lemon-yellow grasses, his easel set under the pandanus trees, looking out on the blue-black Pacific that washes into the smooth lagoon, burning under spangled glimmers of quicksilver. At the heart of his own legend. Eternity refound, Rimbaud wrote, is 'the sea gone off with the sun'.

CHAPTER 19

At the start of this century, our own, there is nothing idyllic about Papeete. It is a great big village squeezed between the seashore and steeply rising mountains. Traffic jams are permanent, which is just infuriating. There are no old buildings to speak of, since most of the porticoed houses have been razed to the ground, and there are 1970s' constructions, restaurant and banks, shopping centres and car parks in a grid of narrow streets polluted by trading signs. On the Boulevard Pomare, which is clogged with traffic and traffic lights, the seafront buildings and their gaily coloured awnings remind one of Nice. There are very few trees, no clear space, and the road is full of potholes. There is often bad taste, and a sense of junk shop *déjà-vu*, except perhaps for the garish trucks packed with frizzy-haired mothers, the girls in red dresses who sometimes weave in and out of the traffic on their Vespas, gendarmes who are astonishing in shorts and kepis, and, under the canopy of sky, a circular harbour where sailing boats, schooners and tuna-fishing boats gently rise and fall at their moorings under motionless clouds, alongside one or two American steamers.

The capital was founded at the start of the nineteenth century, taking its name from a river for which ships' crews were extremely grateful. A winding puddle covered with waterlilies, it murmurs still in the Bougainville park, the only public green space in the town, under a concrete bridge. *Pape* means water, *ete* means basket or pannier. The inventor of Tahiti, a past master at fantasies and a faker of make-believe, Louis Antoine de Bougainville ('soldier, navigator, writer and man of science', 1729–1811), or rather a bust of him in bronze hemmed in by two German navy-surplus cannons, looks as if he couldn't care less. Although he made Tahiti a myth, he only spent nine days there. Despite being decked out with mango trees and almond trees, his so-called park has the dimensions of a garden square. No one lingers in these cramped surroundings. Opposite, the Grand-Place Tarahoi, once the Place des Fêtes, retains nothing of its past splendours as a parade ground, palace courtyard and focus of power. This wide-open space chosen by Queen Pomare in 1827 has become a car park. Gauguin was fond of drinking rum and lemonade under the branches of its banyan tree – the only remnant – at the open-air bar of the Military Circle.

I went back up rue du Général-de-Gaulle and turned right after the Vaima shopping centre, into the continuation of the rue Jeanne-d'Arc, where I came to the Cathedral of Our Lady of the Immaculate Conception. This is a simple but elegant building, with a red bell-tower, a stone porch and flagstones made of Mangareva coral. Gauguin knew it in its original version and it is possible that he went there on Sundays, so as to be seen by the white community. Inside, the stations of the cross are by Yves Saint-Front, and in them the Jews are Tahitians wearing loincloths, while the female sinners are girls with flowers in their hair. Of course, the vegetation has to be tropical, for how else to evoke the desert and the sands of Mount Sinai to these South Sea parishioners? Similarly, in the Garden of Gethsemane, Christ is beatifically clutching a banana palm, and on his back, when he climbs Golgotha, the cross he shoulders happens to be a racing pirogue. None of this makes any difference to those hard at prayer in the pews this morning: two barefoot children with sweet smiles; a toothless grandmother in a mission dress; and a surfer who has left his surfboard and his Fanta at the door while he implores the God of the Waves.

As for the Rue Paul Gauguin, it has nothing to commend it. Every five yards there is a Chinese bazaar hawking Hawaiian shirts made in Venezuela, mosquito coils, dresses made of greenish lace in cardboard boxes for diminutive little girls, sarongs by the mile, rolls of electric cable and useless tray cloths. Sometimes there's a gap for a café on a raised section of pavement: three tables covered in flies, a dozen chairs and stools, some syrupy music. As if climbing up on stilts to escape the tide of scooters and the hooting cars trying to park bumper to bumper, people take refuge there.

It is seven thirty in the morning in Rue Cardella. I read the

Nouvelles de Tahiti as I nibble at a banana doughnut. On page ten I learn that Air Niugini, the Papuan carrier, is going to make two hundred employees redundant, and that war has been declared on fruit flies in the Marquesas. Elsewhere, the 5th regiment of the Foreign Legion will be pulling out after being disbanded, following thirty-seven years of loyal service; France is taking its counters off the board after making so many clever moves in the South Pacific.

Hunger satisfied, I resume my walk, heading north across the town along Rue Nansouty and Avenue Monseigneur Tepano Jaussen. Finally, I just have to take in the Mission quarter, right behind it, at the foot of the mountain. It still retains something of the Tahiti of earlier times, in the moist shadow of its ancient trees, with its powerful, omnipresent fragrance of the sweet earth. There are Protestant and Catholic schools with metallic saints in the courtyards, their heavy buildings deserted that day; a stone bridge; a memorial to those dogged missionaries, with stuccoed smiles fixed at the top of a pillar. There are paths thickly lined with hibiscus, pistachio trees whose trampled fruits spatter the bitumen. Inside the gardens, garlands of lobed philodendron leaves are hung up to dry, 'long serpentine leaves of a metallic yellow (which) seemed to me like the written characters of some remote Oriental language.'

Distant, attenuated sounds; rusting portals. A dog barks. The mountain is so close that one could reach out and touch it. Once you leave the three avenues that run parallel to the ocean, the silence that comes at night persists in the daytime and impregnates everything; siestas are like the sleep of the dead.

After a disappointing trip to Loti's pool, alas, I still, fortunately, had the Vaiamai hospital, the former colonial hospital. This building goes back to 1848 and is the oldest in Papeete. With its yellow masonry and its blackened, ochre roof tiles stained with damp, it has an Indo-Chinese air about it. Anyone could just walk in, which is what I did, as if on my way to see a doctor, which would be unsurprising. Two coconut palms spread high above the flattened garden, indifferent to the building's transformation into a psychiatric unit. Sitting on one of the steps, among bare-chested fellows muttering away to themselves confusedly, I took notes and made a sketch of the trees. Birds pecked among the shorn grass. Around half past eight a tongue of mist came down and settled calmly over everything. A few nurses in white overalls smoked cigarettes under the verandas. It was like being in a Zen garden.

On several occasions, Gauguin had himself admitted as a patient, poverty-stricken, suffering from heart trouble and riddled with syphilis. Early in 1892 he wrote: 'Just imagine how much blood I'm spitting up, as much as half a pint a day, and there's no way of making it stop; mustard poultices on my legs, cupping glasses on my chest and none of it did any good. The hospital doctor was quite worried and thought I was done for.' He left before his discharge and without proper treatment, so as to avoid paying the fourteen francs for it. In 1896, here again, he wrote, wretchedly: 'I'm in the hospital, worn out with pain. I hope to have recovered a month from now, but how will I pay the hospital?' An amazed Pierre Loti had passed through, searching in the registers filed away in boxes for traces of his brother Gustave, who had been a navy surgeon practising here between 1859 and 1862. As a doctor, Segalen had his time here seeing patients, in 1903. Despite his disappointment and the brevity of his stay, Loti announced loud and clear, Josephine Baker-style: 'I now have two homes, Tahiti and Saintonge,' finding in this archipelago a strain of something powerful and 'elusive'. Probably he caught a fragrant whiff of its blend of life and death, fuel for his nostalgia. Among its torrid mangrove swamps, a stew of pleasures and fears, and the Bay of Tahiti, 'a basket of water', would have been the chalice, the Grail, of nature. A grand stage set, the land that no one ever really reaches.

Rue de la Canonnière-Zélée, Avenue Bruat, rue des Poilus-Tahitiens – this is a lacklustre quarter of barracks and warehouses which have been converted into offices, and the peeling facades of imperial stables. There was nothing left of the painter here among the traffic lights and flower-decked roundabouts, nothing but these meagre vestiges and unlikely trails left by renovated and redeveloped hulks. And yet, in this light keen as a knife blade, the Inca was there all the time, still pulling me along into his work every time I turned and found an intersection where I glimpsed the great mass of the Pacific, or the tilt of palm trees where yellow and blue intermingle, closer, a braid of straight black hair down a girl's back, there, *fe'i* or mangoes in the shape of breasts on display in the market. 'Why did I hold back from letting all of this gold and all of this joy of the sun flow upon my canvas?'

I was hot and sweating like him on the seafront. In the distance three pirogues moved like dipterans across the surface of a lagoon so translucent that it seemed invisible. As the writer Alain Hervé observed about Gauguin, his way of looking remained, the way of looking he taught us. Tahiti is no longer the same since he left it. He contaminated us; he included us in his world. We are invited to be there with him in the unchanged island, within his dream; this suspended time is his eternity.

CHAPTER 20

I went to pick up Gilles Artur at the Vaima bookshop. Besides
newspapers and a stock of classics, he has a selection of paper-
backs and bestsellers, works on Polynesia, old books with yellowing
paper – the climate doesn't help – and a gallery space for signings
and exhibitions. This was where disembarking travellers filled up on
books, just like ships taking on barrels of fresh water.

We left the harbour in my Ford Fiesta for the coast road, heading
towards Papeari. On the programme was Punaauia (PK 15), Paea
(PK 22), Mataiea (PK 46), Papeari (PK 53), and lunch somewhere
around Port-Phaéton. Artur had brought reproductions of some
paintings, including *Te fare* (*The Hut*, 1892, W474), whose location
we were aiming to find.

Although Artur went into retirement at the beginning of the year,
he still retains his authority on the management board of the museum.
The transition was a stormy one. Local politics came into it. When
he left, pictures held in trust by the museum were withdrawn. Because
of the wrangling, there are still no pictures on exhibit to this day;
nothing to be seen. The three oil paintings lent by individuals – the
portrait of *Clovis and Aline* (1883, W82), *The Watering Place* (1885,
W159) and *Still Life with Tahiti Oranges* (1892, W495) – have gone
back to their owners, one of whom is a Chinese Tahitian insurance
magnate and car dealer. The same applies to the portrait of Mallarmé
with the raven (etching on copper, 1891) which belongs to Artur,
and the vase with the Breton women and the geese (terracotta, 1886).
In the white rooms with their poor window light, all you find are
three carved spoons, a few engravings, a pot, and a half coconut shell
with some chisel work. It doesn't justify the two hours it takes to get

there and back. The number of visitors has fallen from sixty thousand to thirty-five thousand a year. The new administrator, Brenda Chin Foo, is counting on stemming this haemorrhage by bringing back the works in question, as well as borrowing another from the Marquesas period from an American museum. These things are in hand, as is the preliminary matter of improving the security system.

By virtue of his job, Artur has seen every would-be painter and crackpot in the Pacific pass through his office. Not long before, one of these, a *Popaa*, a white, had called up bubbling over with a staggering piece of news.

'A painting by Gauguin! I've found one!' he had blurted out on the telephone.

At the back of a damp hut on the north coast, among a dusty jumble of odds and ends, was a worm-eaten picture frame. And, under a crust of grime and mildew, there were indeed two vahines sitting on the sand. The one on the right is face on, has an ill-tempered look, a pinkish-white missionary dress, her hands crossed in her lap; the other, on the left, in profile, wears a cerise-coloured sarong round her hips and a ribbon in her hair. The white guy had left the Tahitian a cheque for 5 million Pacific francs (250,000 French francs) as surety and had dashed to Papeari picturing this stake multiplied a thousandfold, ten thousandfold, even a hundred thousandfold. Think of it, a Gauguin!

Cautiously, using a magnifying glass, Artur had examined this blackened thing pocked with holes.

'Well then?' the owner quizzed anxiously, unable to contain his emotion.

'What is it?'

'What can you tell me?'

'It is certainly one of his,' Artur explained, with amusement in his voice. 'But it's an ordinary reproduction mounted on canvas. The original, *Women of Tahiti*, is in the Musée d'Orsay in quite a different format. I urge you to see it on your next trip to France.'

'I don't believe it! Does that mean it's worth nothing?'

'No more . . . than the cardboard from a box of chocolates.'

The fellow was off like a shot to get his Pacific francs back.

This doesn't mean to say that there aren't ever any finds. Letters, for example. A woman passenger on the *Paul Gauguin*, a floating palace that cruises around the Pacific, with Artur giving lectures on board, told him about one that he had no knowledge of.

'Haven't you ever made a local discovery yourself?' I asked him.

'It's all been raked over, or destroyed. Even on the Marquesas. At one point, however, there was the business of the portrait of a captain. Let's say I got "close", several times. But the trail went cold.'

Could this perhaps have been the painting of that 'adorable vahine with the glowing eyes', who was the companion of the captain on the schooner *Arnaud*, known as 'the White Wolf', commissioned in 1892? Did Gauguin do a sketch of him? And if we are to go by the letter of August 1892, what became of the 'little bits of carved wood' which he gave away for 300 francs to a 'Papeete art lover'? Where have they got to? Maybe swallowed up by the weeds and the compost in that little garden? Or hidden away by a circumspect owner? And those 'two panels carved by Gauguin' which the Hervé family, white settlers from Tuamotu, made a gift of in 1910 to the doctor who had operated on their daughter? They have since disappeared. In his memoir, Aiu Bouillaire notes 'The doctor was not very interested in art and didn't seem to appreciate it; we will never know what became of those two priceless works ...' Mysteries, mysteries.

As I drove on carefully between the mountain and the lagoon, with the air-conditioning running in the background, Artur told me a little about his life. His passion for Gauguin went back a long way; it had been in the family. His father, one of the founders of the Breton daily *L'Ouest-Eclair*, was in the same circle as the poet Théophile Briant, who was a friend of Saint-Pol Roux, the magus of the Crozon Peninsula, 'my' peninsula.

'We lived in Brittany, in Rennes, and I can remember that tall old man who would come and have long conversations with my father, and who dedicated his collections of poetry to him. He was an unusual sort of person; he talked to the seagulls and played Wagner in that manor house of his with the Roman pediment; and on the cliffs at the end of a promontory, he had set up his "dreamery". You have to remember that this was a poet stuck in exile in Brittany and then put back in the saddle by the Surrealists, the foremost being André Breton, who used to visit the chateau. In 1937, Briant gave us the chance of buying a Breton landscape by Gauguin, from the Pont-Aven period. It was the equivalent of a year's salary or more – already quite a sum at the time, but nothing in comparison with what would come later. My father was uncertain and he ended up buying a Maurice Denis, a view of Quimperlé and the Laïta.'

'Do you sometimes regret that he didn't?'

'Of course! However, I was able to buy from Segalen's son, Yvon, one of the Mallarmé etchings from the plate that Gauguin had kept, even up until the Marquesas.'

It was at Punaauia, in 1895, during his second stay on Tahiti, that Gauguin had his hut built, his *fare*, the first Studio of the Tropics. 'Picture a large sparrow-cage made of bamboo sticks, with a coconut-palm thatched roof, divided into two parts by the curtains from my old studio. One of these makes a bedroom, with very little light, so as to keep it cool. The other has a large window high up, to make it a studio. On the floor there are some rush mats and my old Persian rug; the whole thing is decorated with fabrics, drawings and odds and ends,' he wrote.

In a photograph taken by Jules Agostini in 1897, we can see it slightly from an angle: a vast, solid construction set among flowering shrubs and with a statue in front of it, a nude, with its left arm raised skywards. Thanks to a loan of one thousand francs from the Caisse Agricole, on the basis of a declaration that he was going to be a copra producer, Gauguin bought two plots of land for seven hundred francs. He was to stay there until 1901, with ups and downs: a renewed appetite for painting followed by artistic impotence, a terrifying block that only his flight to the Marquesas was able to put an end to.

Nowadays, Punaauia is a residential area. At the end of a twisting road, the villas set in their well-tended gardens spill back into the mountainsides. High up, their owners can enjoy a view of Moorea, along with the evening breeze that cools down the district. These are the same mountains perfumed by the high valley between Mount Diadem and Mount Mahutaa where, in January 1898, Gauguin attempted suicide with arsenic. His decline and the death of his daughter Aline in 1897, his poverty, abysmal loneliness, never-ending failures and even starvation must all have played a part.

Very near his plot of land at Punaauia, the '2 + 2 = 4' private school is still there, now modernised. Gauguin knew it and one of his local acquaintances was Jean Souvy, who was retired and a passionate theosophist. Together, in the cool of twilight, as the butterflies fluttered around the oil lamp, they would talk about Sâr Péladan, leader of the latter-day Rosicrucians, Eliphas Lévi, and Madame Blavatsky, the author of *The Secret Doctrine*, who saw every artist as a prophet and visionary. They talked too about Edouard Schuré and Thomas Carlyle, who asked, in *Sartor Resartus*: 'What am I? A voice, a movement, an appearance – some idea incarnate, visualised at the heart of the eternal Spirit.' Distorted versions of these theories combined and overflowed into the painter's work and writings. 'If I have the strength for it, I shall copy out and send you a piece of work I've done lately on Art, the Catholic Church and the modern mind. From the philosophical point of view it is perhaps the best thing I've put into words,' he told Morice in 1897.

Between the enclosed fragments of a breeze-block wall, a path leads to the beach. Out on the reef, waves hit against the coral platform. What a contrast between the hard blue of the open sea and this amniotic marble calm of the lagoon.

'He lived there; that was his spot. We can picture him staying here on the sand, facing the sea, for hours on end. He lived like a native, wearing a sarong, a straw hat or a beret on his head.'

On this coastal fringe, everything reverberates in a game of mirrors between the water and the sky. A white-headed sea swallow weaves its way across the landscape.

'When people claim that his colours are exaggerated they should come here,' Artur continued. 'They are absolutely faithful! Red earth? You find it near Papeete; it's laterite. Pink lagoons? See for yourself. The play of the clouds and their shadows, the reflections of the water ... the atmosphere changes, depending on the time of day. For instance, around five o'clock there is a kind of renewal: the earth exhales the light that it has stored up and it becomes magical; the trees are phosphorescent. This lasts for a few minutes. Or else after the rain, when the air is so purified that distance seems to be abolished. Gauguin did no more than copy, capturing the precise shades of colour. He was able to see.'

Roots, leaves twisted out of shape, jagged rocks, startled crabs with their claws raised, poised to scuttle into a sand hole, a saffron-coloured dog, vaguely related to the jackal, that comes to sniff us out, then skedaddles. Less than ten yards from us, the water eddies into curls of sea spray. Over there, a man is peering at the horizon, his hand forming a visor – it could be him. When is the next mail due from Rue Laffitte? Will there be any letters from Mette, any news from Monfreid, a hundred-franc note folded in two?

We got back into the Ford and went on to Paea, where we made a halt. On his escape from Papeete in 1891, Gauguin jumped off the rickety, bone-shaking trap and set down his kit on this part of the coast for two or three weeks. He had a few acquaintances in this hamlet and, finding hospitality, he got down to work, hung out with the Tahitians and made some new friendships. This spot on the shore of the lagoon was calm, extremely serene. He wrote: 'That evening, I went to smoke a cigarette on the sand of the seashore. The sun, which had sunk quickly onto the horizon, was half hidden by Moorea on my right. The contrasts in the light were very clear and strongly emphasised, black on the blazing sky, and the mountains with their serrated ridges silhouetted like old crenellated castles.'

In *Noa Noa*, Gauguin hardly mentions this stopover at Paea; he prefers to dwell on Mataiea, further south, where he rented a hut. However, the district of Paea had abundant advantages. Besides its proximity to Papeete, with its banks and shops, the village retained vestiges of the marae of Arahurahu with its pyramid platform; around it unfolded a stately and unblemished landscape in a setting of steep ravine-slashed mountains. Gilles Artur takes the view that this first stay outside the capital was given little importance by the painter for reasons that were either strategic or theatrical. There, in among the coconut groves, sleeping under different roofs, Gauguin embarked on his 'studies' and completed at least two pictures. But he was already mulling over the idea of moving even further on.

After Papara, on the PK 35, we turned into a dirt road on our right and parked under a pistachio tree. It must have been 35 degrees in the shade and it was just before ten in the morning.

'The 1892 painting!' Artur exclaimed excitedly. 'In front of you!'

The grass-covered hillock of black stones with roots as fat as a human arm poking out of it must have been the famous marae erected by Queen Purea. It was a place of worship codified by taboos. The monumental structure was made up of successive platforms of basalt and coral decorated with sculptures and ecstatic tikis. It was an open-air temple for sacred dances, rites and sacrifices, both animal and human. An unpleasant atmosphere lay over this higgledy-piggledy site choked with plants and aggrandised by the banyans. The silence was unbroken and there was an all-enveloping heat that had to be pushed through with effort. Even the fringe of beach at its edge was cluttered with lumps of coral, driftwood and rotten coconuts. So deep that it pulled your feet right in, the sand seemed to be ground glass. The whole place oozed hostility. Built on an extended reef, the marae was a crude piece of wreckage. The ocean surged around the point, sending up a rain of sea spray with ghostly droplets clinging to the crest of the waves. Sometimes birds fought against the wind only to give up and climb higher into the empty sky, like kites with broken strings.

'Cook saw it and had its dimensions taken. It was some forty feet high, with eleven steps, on a base some seventy-two feet long. Gauguin came to paint it, but he turned it into an imaginary thing, making it rather Japanese, reconstructing it as he would have liked to see it.'

'As if he had superimposed his fantasies of a primitive world onto a reality from which they were missing.'

'For all that, local people are certainly afraid of places like this. These sites were taboo; at night you won't see so much as a cat come near it!'

'Yes, it did occur to me that your tikis at the Gauguin Museum were enough of a presence . . .'

'They come from a marae at Raivavae, one of the Austral Islands. Those statues arrived in Papeete in 1933 and there have been countless strange stories about them. The biggest of the three is over eight feet tall and weighs more than two tons. Quite an effective protection system, that's superstition for you!'

The marae painting was done in 1892. *Parahi te marae (There Lies the Temple)*, W483. In the foreground is a bank of flowers; behind it a decorative fence with what is clearly a bark-cloth motif; a mound that is coloured yellow with grass, a tiki in profile and mountains in the distance. *Parahi te marae: There Lies the Temple*. This painting is part of a lot sent to Copenhagen for the exhibition there. In his letter to his wife, Gauguin noted: '*Parahi te marae*: the marae – the temple – remains a place reserved for the cult of the gods and human sacrifice. Not less than seven hundred francs.' In the end it was acquired by Schuff at the Paris sale of 1895 for three hundred and sixty francs.

This painting is of a piece with what Gauguin was looking for in the islands and was hard put to find. A supernatural world relegated to the past. An archaic way of living, in which humanity is new and roles are strictly designated beside the surging of the ocean and the hypnosis of a world without seasons. In the Museum of the Islands, at Punaauia, I had been able to take a look at what was left of this dream. A society that was complicated and extremely simple, where bodies were tattooed from head to foot, crowned with dolphin teeth and red feathers. Phallic weapons, a club made of whale bone, nasal flutes, conch horns, harpoons, javelins, daggers, adzes, reef sandals. But also stilts, spinning tops, quoits, ornamental plumes made of beard bristles, fly-swatters decorated with death's heads, jewels made from mother of pearl or sperm-whale ivory, leaf-shaped paddles, pirogue-coffins ... all of this in among the tikis, their heads sunk into their shoulders, massive, powerful, grimacing stones that sneer, toad-ancestors with outsize mouths and staring eyes. Like some legend of Sun and Water in which men speak to the gods with familiarity because they are brothers with the same fate, like old myths of the Golden Age.

On the road, near the PK 42, Artur again told me to stop. Just before this bridge and the church built of coral we found ourselves in the exact spot where Gauguin painted another of his works, *Te fare*, W474. He got out of the car and unrolled the reproduction. I cut the engine and ran after him. This painting was also made in 1892, and its title means 'the house'.

'There's no tree in the foreground any more,' Artur explained jubilantly. It was a purao, a little purao, a *Hibiscus tiliaceus*.

We were both by the roadside, holding the reproduction out at arm's length, beneath a leaden sun; like magicians, we shifted a few yards to the right, then to the left, to find the perfect angle of view, the perfect energy point. The mountain was our guide, its mass and outline on the sky.

'Let's wait until the clouds disperse, we'll see better. Look, that's it. Just right!'

And he gripped me by the arm. It was like a children's game, finding the subject of a picture painted more than a century ago, by following the sombre contours of the mountain as it makes a big V-shape, then a big U, and another V. The *fare* of those days had been replaced by a new house. And the field, on the right, bushy, even rather blurred, with a brown horse and a cabin under yellow-leaved coconut palms, was now filled with other houses. No matter! We were tempted to have a picnic on the very spot so that we could stay and drool. Happiness lies in the details.

'What a pity we don't have any absinthe to celebrate with,' I said.

We were delighted with one another when we got to Mataiea. In October 1891, Gauguin was already there. Of course, in a letter to Monfreid he admitted that he had made no progress. 'So far, I have done nothing of consequence; I make do with rummaging through myself rather than nature, learning a little drawing, drawing is all there is, and I'm also piling up a record.'

He accumulated sketches, but as yet nothing definitive or fully constructed. 'I am beginning to work: notes and roughs of all kinds. But the landscape's bold, burning colours dazzled me, blinded me ... Yet it was a simple thing to paint what I saw.' He sought and sought himself, accumulating, in his canvas sketchbook, sketches and compositions which he would later use.

It was in the hamlet of Mataiea that everything began, beginning again. The coastal strip was broad there; you could step back further away from the mountains. There were seven hundred inhabitants, with the *fares* and their gardens scattered over an area of around four and a half miles. In charge of the district was chief Tetuanui, who spoke French. 'On one side is the sea, and on the other the mountain – the gaping mountain, with an amazing crack in it stopped up by a huge clump of mango trees right against the rock ...' Far from Papeete, somehow this really is being in the provinces. A fondness for the old Tahiti which Gauguin had called up by wishing for it. And with the area already occupied by missionaries and colonists – there is a rum distillery nearby – he can be sure of finding a good proportion of Francophones.

Gauguin moved into a hut near what today is the football pitch, referred to as the 'stadium', opposite a motu studded with coconut palms, the lagoon, the coral reef and the indigo-coloured ocean. It was a *fare* with bamboo walls, a pandanus roof, and partitions made of *niau*, those woven palm leaves. The floor consisted of dried grasses. A room made out of foliage. The painter is reckoned to have stayed in Mataiea for more than eighteen months, making it the crucible of 'his' first Tahiti. He saw it as life reduced to the essentials, a simple life for a man without needs.

He took possession of his surroundings. In front of him, 'the blue line of the sea was frequently broken by the green of the wave crests falling back against the coral shoals.' And everywhere the 'marvellous colours of this fiery yet softened air, silent . . .' The days were short, molten and biblical. 'This is life in the open air, yet it is intimate, with the bushes for cover.' He lived like a native, barefoot and shirtless. 'We shall end up being able to live for nothing. Free,' he had predicted to Emile Bernard, in 1890. A year later, it was a *fait accompli*, or near enough.

His Tahitian neighbours were benignly indifferent. The whites displayed a certain mistrust, first and foremost the local gendarme. Gauguin avoided them. When it came to provisions, he had to give up the idea of climbing coconut palms or roaming through the mountains gathering fruits or shooting wild pigs with his Winchester rifle. Too high, too far, too arduous. On Tahiti the mountains were still hostile; life was possible only on the coastal strip, in the shade of the valleys, at the foot of ravines with waterfalls in their folds, amid the sweltering crackle of the bamboo plantations. The Tahitians understood this, leaving those areas to the spirits, the revenants, and to the gods themselves. So, despite the prohibitive prices, there was the shop run by the Chinaman, Aoni, who sold everything: tinned food, dried pulses, bottles of spirits. Gauguin saw himself setting about fishing, to save money. Without a pirogue, he had little success. He ate courtesy of the Chinaman's shop, on credit.

At last the painter sent away the lovely Titi, who got on his nerves. His work became better organised in the solitude that was broken only by trips to Papeete, to visit the Suhas or the Drollets. 'I am fairly happy with the last paintings I have done and I feel that I am beginning to acquire the Oceanian temperament, and I can be confident that what I am doing here has never been done before and is not known in France,' he wrote to his wife. A few portraits, village scenes, fields and huts, seashores with occasional female bathers, surprised women, curious children, dogs loitering in the underwood, foliage. And in the evening, lying on his couch in the blue dark, the Inca could feel 'the free space above my head, the celestial vault, the stars. I was very far away from those prisons that are European houses. A Maori hut is no exile, it does not cut you off from life, from space, from the infinite.'

Still on our right, a path runs past the football ground and comes out on the seashore.

'His hut must have been there, near where the football ground is, on the left.' Gilles Artur's hand sketched out a picture in the empty air. 'Between the mountains and the sea rose my hut of bourao wood . . .'

Up by the goalposts, two youths are kicking a ball which seems to bounce with extreme slowness. The mountains are violet behind us. Opposite are a Catholic church, Saint-Jean–Baptiste, and a Protestant one, both with a rather Hindu look about them. In the distance, there's a ringing sound that dies away. A motorcycle goes by, accelerates, then disappears round the bend that is smothered with rubber plants. Rollers roar the moment they smash against the reef. Islets with dishevelled coconut palms, ringed with mist, tremble in the saturated air like apparitions. The grass shivers. A sweet odour of copper rises from the *fares*. The mountains change colour under a cloud; they are darker, almost black. 'On the sea, by the shore, I see a pirogue, and in the pirogue, a woman . . .' Time passes, each second goes by, precious water that pearls into a drop.

Barefoot, I am walking on the sand, fearful of tearing something, of activating some secret mechanism. The ocean swells between the coral excrescences. On the marble-smooth sea there is a strange calligraphy, of stains and honeycombs and bubbles. Everything is there, untouched in that glitter.

CHAPTER 21

Established through the work of the Marist brother Patrick O'Reilly and the Singer-Polignac Foundation, which made a gift of it to the Territory in 1983, the Gauguin Museum awaits us in the middle of a coconut grove on Motu Ovini. Designed by the architect Claude Bach, who won the Grand Prix de Rome, and set in a botanical garden facing the lagoon, it consists of five buildings connected by walkways, their roofs reminiscent of the traditional *fare*. Open, airy and fluid, Papeari stands on lawns surrounded by banks of hibiscus. Being unable to compete with the collections in European and American museums, it has opted wisely for the solution of existing as a memorial: its aim is to present the life story and the painting of Gauguin through reproductions or instructive tableaux. It is therefore a centre for art and history, a place of memory and meetings. For all that, in the forty years of its activities, climate and local rancours have taken their toll.

I went to introduce myself to Brenda Chin Foo, the museum's new director, with whom I had made an appointment on the phone the day before, and meanwhile Gilles Artur spent the time taking care of some business of his own. We met again later for lunch.

Brenda is a tall Chinese woman in a red dress, with a hibiscus flower behind her left ear. She smells of citronella. She rolls her 'r's' charmingly in the Tahitian manner. It is rumoured in Papeete that her appointment is a political one, because the job is strategic. Certainly, Brenda acknowledges that she knows very little about Gauguin. She remains an administrator, but is enthusiastic and eager to learn. She is looking for an assistant to see to the artistic side of things. I stop myself from saying that I would be very tempted to apply.

'We're having renovations done at the moment,' she explained. 'The museum has to be overhauled from top to bottom. We're revising all the textual material and giving it an English version. We need to shake out the dust and breathe some fresh energy back into things.'

Everything is showing its age badly, since none of it has been replaced since 1965. The panels tracing Gauguin's work and biography have turned yellow or are stained with damp patches; sometimes parts of them have fallen off. The scale model of the 'Maison du Jouir' is ruined, and the three copies by Saint-Front are of mediocre quality. Even the Concarneau standing stone, a piece of granite weighing nearly two tons, an Atlantic tiki, brought here to mark the Pont-Aven period, is looking shabby. As for the exhibition 'Loti and the Pacific' in the Bing room, the only one with air-conditioning, it consists of nothing but letters, photographic reprints and ... photocopies! There's a lack of finance, and also a lack of artistic conception.

'We have a number of deadlines,' Brenda explains, inviting me to take a seat in her office. 'We have to be ready for 2003, Gauguin's centenary, without being overtaken by parallel projects like the one on Hiva Oa, in the Marquesas, where the "Maison du Jouir" is being rebuilt on its original plot of land. Then, here, we have to modernise the Bing room to conform with standard security levels. That will allow us to borrow works from French and foreign museums and to get back ... the ones that have left us, for as you probably know, we had three of the paintings on our own walls. I would so much love to see one of the Marquesas pictures here for the centenary! I have made contacts with this in mind. The budget has been approved: sixty million Pacific francs. I'm confident, so long as the board plays its part. We have three years left. Did you see that we've already redecorated?'

What Brenda doesn't say is that she is at daggers drawn with her board, on which Artur has the say, and that he doesn't get on with her. Moreover, even with me there, the two of them avoid one another. In this narrow world, every blow hits hard, and the wounds fester.

'I had found an adviser to be my deputy, a *Popaa*, a woman qualified in art history and a specialist in Gauguin. She was ready to take up the job! They told me that she knew the Breton period better than the rest . . . So they turned down her application!'

Not wishing to get involved in the arguments, I quickly summed up the aim of my visit, telling Brenda about the book I was working on and my two years pursuing the idea of following in Gauguin's footsteps, faint though they sometimes are. She tells me she is willing to help and, knowing it has Artur's backing, puts the library and an office at my disposal.

The shelves are sagging under the weight of the collections. There is a bound series of the review *Le Tour du monde*; there are catalogues of Gauguin exhibitions from all over the world. In front of me I have some half a dozen books about my Peruvian, in different languages and in a variety of formats. This is an Ali Baba's cave painstakingly filled up with treasure over the years by an untiring Gilles Artur.

The room is air-conditioned, the bay windows open onto the garden. There is a sea breeze, the muffled whirr of a lawnmower. The three basalt tikis are warming up in the sun, their eyes empty, their smiles scornful and triumphant. The museum is hushed with that voicelessness of the archipelagoes which seems active, so heavy is it with matter. In the museum shop, the two attendants drowse in a heat that blurs the horizons and makes the bloodstained caladium lilies quiver. I amuse myself by leafing through the museum's 'golden book', whose pages have been signed by General de Gaulle, Ursula Andress, Alfred Hitchcock and Jean-Paul Belmondo.

There are no visitors this morning. Papeete is distant. The lawn shimmers, as if covered in a canopy of light. A crab goes by at a faultless diagonal. All the leaves are hands.

'A coachload of Germans are coming in this afternoon, but they'll be with their guide,' someone murmurs, the relief audible.

In between my circumspect perusal of two different works, I talk a bit more to Brenda. She tells me that she is of the Buddhist faith and has built a temple behind her house. She has in mind to invite the Dalai Lama to make a visit to Tahiti.

'Seriously?'

'Don't forget that the Asian community is very substantial. The first ones landed in 1864, for the cotton harvest; they were Hakkas who found employment on the plantations. Those are my two challenges: the holy man and a picture from the Marquesas!'

In the room at the back, which is also being renovated, I can see the old studio-apartment that Artur used to live in.

'I was happy as a prince. I looked out onto the beach, and to get from my house to the museum all I had to do was push a door open.'

Now, at the edge of the museum complex, a bungalow is being completed for painters in residence. Invitations have started going out. A New Yorker, expensive, insolent and talented, has already said yes. He will stay there, show an exhibition of his works and leave one of them to the museum, which in this way will begin building up a collection.

'We want to rediscover the spirit of the Studio of the Tropics and create a living museum!'

In the library, I come across the facsimile of Gauguin's notebook, the artist's sketchpad that accompanied him throughout his first stay. There are 130 pages, in an 11.5 × 17.2 cm format, with a grey-green cloth cover. At the beginning, in his hand, there is a list of common words and phrases in Tahitian (What is your name? the sea, friend, come in, woman, an orange), accounts (bed 20F, mattress 4F, chairs 8F, large canvas 4F, crate 7F . . .), exchange rates (Chilean pesos, francs, dollars), the notes of a song (la, re, so, ti, mi) and, lastly, the first coloured sketches of his Tahitian adventure: profiles, faces, details, a woman from the back, later to be used for the painting *Vahine no te miti*, which I saw in Buenos Aires. His work is there, in this fermenting of the everyday, this companionship of the pages, this exasperated concern with what the days cost. Sometimes, there is already that sense of wonder which is like an exploding grenade.

'The original was taken apart and sold leaf by leaf, drawing by drawing,' Artur told me. This facsimile came out in 1954 and you can still find some copies of it. The Quatre Chemins bookshop printed five hundred of them. I saw one going for four thousand francs on the Internet – I jumped at the chance.

'You ought to re-publish it in the same format, and with the same binding. Your visitors would be taking Gauguin's notebook away with them!'

'You can be sure we're looking into it.'

Of course, I asked to be allowed into the strongroom to see the reserve collection. I was granted permission as an exception, on the grounds that, as Brenda acknowledged, laughing, 'You're a child of Tahiti. Otherwise, it's out of bounds,' she added.

The strongroom was a big Fichet-Bauche at the far end of an air-conditioned room. There was a wheel on the door, behind which was the collection. Brenda opened the room for me, unlocked the combination then let me inside, through to the other side of the bars. It contained nothing much out of the ordinary, but it did hold documents of great value that were very moving, starting with some photographs of Gauguin's friend, Henry Lemasson, who was head of the postal services in Papeete and an amateur photographer. In the filing cabinets, in numbered transparent envelopes, I found the Tahiti that they knew, in monochrome: some negatives of timorous young girls sitting in rattan armchairs; a melancholy portrait of Queen Marau, the widow of Pomare V; Governor Lacascade and the members of the Military Circle in frock coats and sidewhiskers, in the manner of the Third Republic; Goupil's balustraded house, New Orleans style, with bushy trees in a well-raked parkland; views of Papeete with houses standing by the beginning of a road which went nowhere; landscapes, mountains, beaches, steamships with passengers embarking onto bridges shaded by canvas, gentlemen wearing beards and hats, ladies in white dresses carrying parasols.

And then, also filed and numbered in transparent envelopes, was the correspondence: the originals of letters from Schuffenecker to Gauguin (addressed to 'Artist and Painter, 12, rue Durand-Claye, near Ouest-ceinture, Plaisance, Paris'), amazing letters from Schuff to Mette, and several from Mette to Schuff, seventeen of them to be exact, between 1884 and 1902, their violet ink now rusted to a shade of verdigris. I pluck out these words: 'I write to him so rarely and I think of him even more rarely; but it seems to me that when I learn that he has money, it is my duty to remind him that he has five children and that I cannot manage on my own.' And these: 'I am not travelling round the world like a woman out of her senses! Perhaps, dear friend, you will find me cold, severe and venal, as Paul used to say, but in all honesty this is so exhausting . . .' Another letter says: 'So if you can get some paintings send them on to me and I shall try to

sell them, and I shall certainly not send the money to Paul.' Later:
'He is talking about leaving Tahiti for another island – the devil has
taken hold of him . . .' 'Paul is so criminally selfish . . .' And this, also
by way of Schuff, and never to be received by Gauguin, in which his
Danish wife gives him the news of the death of their son Clovis, in
1900; it is a harsh, malicious letter, lengthy and with pale blue blossoms
scattered across the first three lines, as if she had wept while writing
it and these tears had mingled with the ink: 'I have borne heavy
burdens, I have endured every grief and worry, all alone.'

Finally there are the words of Gauguin himself ('Paul Gauguin,
artist and painter, Punaauia, Tahiti'). The envelopes have turned
yellow; they bear a Papeete postmark and stamps stuck on with saliva.
They are small rectangular envelopes bundled together with an elastic
band. I tremble as I undo it. Gauguin is there, in my hands, in front
of my eyes, and it feels as if I am the one he was writing to. I open
the envelopes, extract the folded paper and read what he wrote to me
across the centuries. I read about those long-gone torments, with
distance now abolished, fractured, nonexistent.

On both sides of the page, the writing is uniformly spidery, a close,
careful hand. A graphologist's report attached to the file explains that
it shows a personality 'that stands out, is independent, enthusiastic,
vibrant . . .' Supremely! But most of the letters are tragic. The one
addressed to Morice refers to the origins of *Where Do We Come from?*,
W561: 'It stands head and shoulders above everything I have done
and that I shall do. Does this mean that I have reached maturity, or is
it great sorrow that made me create it?' The other is for Mette and,
in a PS, her husband adds the numbers of the banknotes attached to
his missive ('R24–307, V92–430'). Then there is this final message
from Hiva Oa, from Gauguin to Pastor Vernier – somewhat medical,
scribbled feverishly on his sick bed with death already pointing its
snout at him: 'I am really afraid that these four days that have passed
without any result might be due to the insufficient dosage I have; so
please send me the dose that you deem appropriate for the cure or at
the very least for calming things down.' He is talking about laudanum,
the morphine that he injects using a glass syringe. Also to be found
in this collection is a copy of his death certificate, an extract from
the registries of the district of Atuona. 'On 8 May 1903, Emile

Frébault, shopkeeper, friend of the deceased, and Tioka Timote, cultivator, aged 55, neighbour of the deceased, came forward.' And referring to the dead man, Frébault noted in his own hand: 'We know that he is married and has children, but we do not know the name of his wife.'

This is quite enough. I come back up from the strongroom, feeling upset. Brenda has left, leaving word that the library and the collections are at my disposal. I tell the attendant that I'll be there the next morning when the museum opens.

Artur is waiting for me under the trees, talking to the workmen who are doing up the bungalow.

'The shop isn't doing well at all,' he grumbles. 'Besides, it's too expensive. Even the awful T-shirts; did you see them! What an embarrassment! Shall we go and eat?' he asks, suddenly weary.

Where should we eat – at the Restaurant Gauguin, whose fish-tanks are renowned? Or what if we were to push further on as far as Port-Phaéton to sample some raw fish and a vanilla *poé* (a Polynesian dessert made with tropical fruits)?

'I need to cheer myself up. All those letters...'

'Whatever you prefer.'

I take the wheel and turn right, heading for Port-Phaéton. But what is a *phaéton*? 'A little white bird with a long pink or white feather on its tail,' wrote Loti, and the fate of this feather was to adorn the heads of chiefs. It was, by extension, the name of a warship which, in 1844, fired on the rebels hostile to the protectorate. A nice paradox, and excellent cuisine served by a Chinese woman in flip-flops. The restaurant was mounted on stilts and the view over the mangroves was splendid. Clamped to one of the stilts by suction, an agama lizard is wondering whether to climb up. The lagoon is a sheet of glass streaked and rippled by slow flashes of light. A truck brings surfers back, their hair slick with salt. A car turning the bends sounds its horn. A mass of mango trees is pierced by the rays of the sun.

'This is what he saw every morning, from his *fare*.'

'It would be good enough for me.'

Tranquil hours at Port-Phaéton. 'God knows what day of the year, as ever the weather was fine ...' Where shall we go tomorrow? Never further than these shores of the bitter and delicious isle.

CHAPTER 22

'I am escaping from the factitious, I am entering nature.' Gauguin attained what he was seeking, at last caressing his dream's reality. 'It seems to me that all this upset of life in Europe no longer exists and that tomorrow will be just the same, and so on until the end ...' Certainly, he had lost weight. Either he ate on credit or he didn't eat at all. To reduce his expenses, he cut out tobacco, alcohol, coffee and meat. He sold his Winchester and sacrificed his hunting horn. His health was not good. He would have to go into hospital because he was vomiting blood. He had heart trouble, and maybe syphilis. Although he was already thinking about his return to France by the beginning of 1892, in the February he thought nothing of putting in for a substitution post in the Administration. Or of taking ship for the Marquesas, which were 'less spoiled by civilisation' and less costly. 'An ox costs three francs or the trouble of hunting it ...' What a lot of flaws in the diamond! 'I am still here working and struggling on.' Tahiti was his powerful dark sun.

However, in spite of material difficulties and his solitude, the first canvases emerged from his brush. Remaining faithful to his principles, he continued working as he did in Martinique and in Brittany: recording in his notebook a subject which he would reinterpret in the subdued light of his *fare*. And, far from any impressionism or a synthetism which he had moved beyond, he buttressed himself upon his very first idea: art is imagination, subjectivity, a language which is able to combine the visible and the invisible, raw animal strength with intelligible sensation. In the chill of Copenhagen, seven years earlier, he had already put it like this: 'The entire visible universe is only a forest of images and signs ... a kind of nourishment which the imagination must digest and transform.'

Gauguin does not seek to represent, but to speak. As if traversed and irradiated by the sensation of being, the artist is metamorphosed into a receiver, a relay post, a tiki. An original manner of painting, with new sources, which engages head-on with exoticism, whose full sunlight gives the colourist scope to excel. In the view of the historian Françoise Cachin, there are two principal axes: firstly, landscapes with large flat blocks of freely applied colour; dark blues, dull reds, electric yellows and strong shades of orange ('all of these marvellous colours of this fiery air'); Golden-Age nudes, sumptuous and indifferent, their faces closed on some mystery; rural scenes imprinted with Edenic calm and laid out under low skies, sharply defined mountain peaks, magnetic waterfalls. And then, with a decorative inflection, there is a refashioned mythology, whose symbols are taken both from the ancients and from reminiscences: here, on beaches of volcanic sand, under the sarcastic gaze of the Maori gods, are Egypt, Japan, the Greeks, Christianity and the Buddhism of Borabudur, all telescoped and enmeshed. These are already masterpieces and, employing a careful stylisation and a contrived primitiveness, they drown or exalt the painter's own existential anxieties. Among the finest of these are *Vahine no te tiare*, W420, which Gauguin regarded as very 'new' and which he sent to Paris, and *Ia Orana Maria*, W428, a paradise of tangled trees and ferns, peopled with lavender angels and nubile young women. Then *Under the Pandanus*, W431, *Women of Tahiti*, W434, *Woman with a Mango*, W449, *Vahine no te miti*, W465, *Manao Tupapau*, W457, and lastly the imperious *Arearea* (*The Red Dog*, W468), and the strange *Ta Matete* (*We Shall Not Go to Market Today*, W476). What a sublime harvest.

'Bit by bit, civilisation is leaving me ... I have all the pleasures of a free life, both animal and human.' By the start of March 1892, he had thirty paintings ('I have worked hard of late and at this moment I have forty yards of canvas covered with Lefranc & Co paint'), sixty-six by the time he left, as well as some 'ultra-savage' sculptures.

In *Noa Noa*, Gauguin gives an account of these two years 'far away from filthy Europe', in which he subdues the district and the people, re-acclimatises his art and melts into the suffocating heat. With his broken Maori, he made a few friends in Mataiea; sometimes, he would go with the vahines who were fishing for giant green prawns or gathering giant clams with a knife on the barrier of the reef, waist deep in water. 'My neighbours have well-nigh become my friends. I dress and I eat like them, and when I am not working I share their way of living, indolent and joyful, with abrupt changes of mood to gravity.' As a man living alone, he had a reputation for bedding girls easily; while on occasion he did allow himself this pleasure, the reality had less rough and tumble.

Lost in his own thoughts, the Inca never stopped fretting about his children left back in Europe, and his allies who had forgotten him. Primarily Charles Morice, who had kept the money from paintings that were sold, and his wife, who was 'taking over' the artistic commerce in which he no longer played a part. Admittedly, Albert Aurier celebrated him in the *Mercure de France* as 'the indisputable initiator of symbolism', in April 1892. There were also a few pieces sparingly exhibited, for example at the Paris gallery Le Barc de Bouteville. But was that enough when it was a matter of survival on the other side of the world?

His stay continued to be a challenge and his revenge for a life of privations and failures: to reverse all of that with spectacular paintings that will draw attention to him again, sweep away his 'followers' and let him take his place among the moderns; to attain a level of sales that will be enough to live off, and to keep that clientele. As he puts it: 'The conditions in which I am working are unfavourable and anyone who does what I am doing has to be a colossus' (March 1892).

The struggle is relentless. When his letters arrive, by way of America, the first thing he does is look to see if there is a banknote. And any confidence he displays in the future is 'because he wills it to be so'. Five months later: 'Nonetheless I have merchandise crated, and it is good; but on Tahiti it has no currency. No one has any money and besides they are all twopenny traders and petty clerks.' Paradoxically, at a distance of thousands of miles, only Europe can let him live from his art, and allow him to stay there, so far from it.

He is obsessed by his loneliness. 'I had been gloomy for some time. It was affecting my work ...' His escapades with those girls 'taken in the Maori way, roughly, without a word', their bodies covered in monoï oil, give him no satisfaction. What he would like is a companion. To get the better of his sadness and take his mind off things, every time the boat arrives from Europe, he pays the fare of eighteen francs and travels to Papeete on the diligence pulled by three horses. On the quaysides and in the harbour cafés, he offers to do portraits or carved figurines. In March, he takes this opportunity to visit the Suhas. He gets on well with the father, Jean-Jacques, a nurse in bacteriology at the colonial hospital. He has lent Gauguin money and on more than one occasion has offered him a place to stay. But this is 5 March 1892, the day when the couple's son Aristide has just died; Atiti, the little boy that Gauguin was so fond of, and who reminded him of his own children. The family is in a hurry to have the child buried at the end of the day, once the heat has abated. The child is lying on his bed, absurd in his lace alb and horribly swollen. A few friends come by to pray. We know the rest: Gauguin's good intentions, the dreadful painting dashed off in the yellow light, Helena's anger and the embarrassment all-round when they see the goitrous body with the livid eyelids. A *tupapau*, a frightening mummified creature.

This scene shows the confusion of a man discarded by a society which he has wanted to escape from and which has marginalised him. The recluse of Mataiea is a castaway, his proud ship has become a drifting raft. His 'private planet' has a sorry ring to it. The point has come when Gauguin realises that he cannot go on like this. This dead child in the streets of Papeete, painted by a man who is destitute, sick, at the end of his tether, will be a watershed, a light illuminating the dark spiral into which he was unwittingly drawn.

Early in the summer of 1892, Gauguin made a decision: he had to put an end to these fetid days of solitude and selfishness. He had to begin all over again. Since he could not find his Eve in Papeete, where the women were corrupt, nor in Mataiea, where they were married, he would go in search of her further on, on the other side of the island beyond the Bay of Taravao. What he describes in *Noa Noa* resembles a Nordic saga: a man on his white horse, moved by noble intentions, rides to the other side of a butterfly-shaped island to find a soulmate. And this ideal, this flower-love, has always been waiting for him: Tehamana, 'she who gives strength', also known as

Tehura. The story is charming and mawkish, like Loti's. Despite that, these scenes as described by the majority of biographers so much correspond to the reality of the time that they can only have a basis in the truth. And both Tehamana's existence and her relationship with Gauguin are moreover confirmed. The Inca took the diligence as far as Taravao, then a gendarme lent him his mount. He went back round the isthmus in the direction of Hitia and, worn out by crossing rivers and sodden undergrowth, stopped at Faaone.

There, Gauguin was invited to eat in one of the huts. He sat on the ground, chatting and smoking. He was asked about where he was going. He answered that he was looking for a female companion. Without further ado, a woman spoke up: 'If you like, I'll give you one. She's my daughter,' and she brought her to him. She was a tall young girl in a pink muslin dress, already carrying her parcelled-up linen. She had a charming face and the raw beauty of youth, her hair falling down her back, 'unruly like the undergrowth, and slightly frizzy.' Gauguin was embarrassed. He felt old, intimidated and ashamed, ashamed of his desire, and now also afraid: of this beauty, of this new youth and vitality and its mocking indifference, of Tehamana.

'Through her dress, the golden skin of her arms and shoulders could be seen. Two little buds pushed out firmly from her chest,' he noted nonetheless. She was no more than thirteen or fourteen years old, already tall and with ravishing skin. This is how their conversation began, in Tahitian, from what Gauguin describes:

'Aren't you afraid of me?'

'*Aita* (no).'

'Would you like to live always in my hut?'

'*E* (yes).'

'Have you ever been sick?'

'*Aita.*'

That was all.

After giving small presents to her family from the local Chinese shop, which marked the official status of the cohabitation, he took her away and headed back to the other side of Tahiti. At Mataiea, the young woman showed herself to have a loving nature. She was simple and straightforward, often full of gaiety. Her presence by his side disturbed and galvanised him. And after the first few days, and the nights of love, Tehamana was happy to stay with the *Popaa*, agreeing to live with him and give him the freshness of her fourteen years. 'I loved her and I told her so, which made her smile . . . She seemed in return to love me and did not tell me so. But sometimes, at night, the gold of Tehura's skin was alive with light.'

What a new flowering there was! This was the key of carnal knowledge, the threshold of the secret, the joy of the senses in his arms, the pleasure of living; this was peace of mind and energy itself. 'She is a balm to me!' the old Inca pronounced of this child who went fishing, brought him fruits and crayfish, sang, laughed at everything, found entertainment in small things, liked to take siestas and make love, lazy as a cat. He returned to his brushes and his canvas and painted like a fortunate man with a new muse by his side, a little savage princess. 'I had gone back to work and happiness lived in my house.' And on this longed-for land, where he is made dizzy by the perfume of gardenias, in the light's fullness she is the gift that is at last given and accepted. Nothing is depleted, everything is enhanced, among the bamboos and the vanilla plants, the waterfalls where they bathe and then hold one another close among the blue ferns. 'Life exists and everything moves . . .'

Beneath the rustling of the agamas, before that pale line of the horizon, Gauguin rediscovered the childhood of the world, that margin between nothing and infinity. 'On the veranda, a sweet siesta and everything is at rest. My eyes see the space before me without any understanding, and I have a sense of the endlessness whose beginning I am.'

Madeleine Bernard, 1888. Musée des Beaux-Arts, Grenoble.

ABOVE: Haymaking in Brittany,
1888. Musée d'Orsay, Paris.

RIGHT: Yellow Christ, 1889.
Albright Knox Art Gallery, Buffalo,
New York.

OPPOSITE
ABOVE: The Loss of Virginity,
1890-1. Chrysler Museum, Norfolk,
Virginia.

BELOW: The Vision after the
Sermon, (Jacob Wrestling with the
Angel), 1888. National Gallery of
Scotland, Edinburgh.

LEFT: The Brooding Woman, 1891. Worcester Art Museum, Massachusetts.

BELOW: Aha oe Feii? (Are You Jealous?), 1892. Pushkin Museum, Moscow.

OPPOSITE
Vahine No Te Tiare (Woman with a Flower), 1891. Ny Carlsberg Glyptotek, Copenhagen.

RIGHT: Annah the Javanese, 1893–4. Private Collection.

BELOW: Where Do We Come From? Who Are We? Where Are We Going?, 1897. © Museum of Fine Arts, Boston, Massachusetts.

OPPOSITE
Nevermore, 1897.
Courtauld Gallery, London.

OVERLEAF: Photograph of Paul Gauguin with The Brooding Woman. Private Collection.

Transparencies courtesy The Bridgeman Art Library, London.

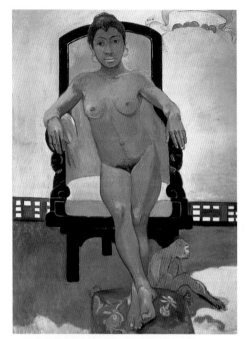

CHAPTER 23

'Bit by bit, civilisation is leaving me.' The bloom of purple foliage streaked with yellow, the tousled tops of coconut palms, the murmur of the ocean, a distant drum. Faint whiffs of burning fires. What day is it beneath the almond trees whose horizontal branches make a parasol? It hardly matters. 'I share their way of living, indolent and joyful, with abrupt changes of mood to gravity.' In the evening, the women chant the potent *himene*, and the old people recite the clan histories which are so many legends of Oceania. Although Gauguin hasn't completely mastered Maori, he speaks it better now. He fishes on the reef in the mist, with sandals made of vegetable fibres and a trident. In Mataiea, with the house and a companion, he feels at home. A dog sleeps under the hut.

In September 1892, when the artist had used up his rolls of canvas, he took some copra sacks and cut out squares and rectangles from them, to go on painting. Everything was good for exhausting this fever he was in. He was carving too. Idols either of his own invention or transplanted from the Maori pantheon; he calls them his 'ultra-savage ornaments'. These are stylised figures of divinities in *toa* or *aito* (casuarina or she-oak) wood; heads of Tahitian women in *pua* wood, mini-totems in *tamanu*, a convoluted tree with hooked branches, as well as plates made of *popoï*, bowls and spoons which he decorates with polychrome motifs. Often these are fantastic objects which he manages to put on the Papeete market, displayed to visiting sailors or the first tourist arrivals as local 'souvenirs', which didn't bother him.

In search of raw materials, Gauguin decided to head for the mountains, a decision not to be taken lightly. Beyond the coastal strip and the valleys densely wooded with trees and plants, the interior of Tahiti was harsh and wild. It was studded with high peaks, some of them rising to more than six thousand five hundred feet, in a steep and indomitable terrain full of sheer slopes, where needles, spurs of lava, and knife-edge ridges cut into the sky and tore at the clouds. According to the terminology, Tahiti is a 'high' island, in the sense that it is a volcanic mountain that has erupted from the sea and is encircled with a coral reef. Because of the relative absence of viable paths, and out of superstition, very few people ventured into this hinterland. 'The *tupapau* will torment you ... You must be mad or foolhardy to go and disturb the spirits,' they told him. The interior was empty, little-known, engulfed in an otherworldly silence, scattered with petroglyphs and sacrificial marae. It was the kingdom of the dead.

Accompanied by one of his neighbours from Mataiea, Jotefa (Joseph), Gauguin went off in search of rosewood for carving his 'strange gods'. This is a hard wood that will stand up better to the damp climate. As Gauguin describes him in *Noa Noa*, Jotefa is 'a very simple and very handsome young man'. He had struck up a friendship with Gauguin and the latter painted him a number of times. 'When I am painting, not a single day goes by without him coming to watch me.' We find his portrait in *Man with an Axe*, W430, as a well-muscled ephebe from a Greek frieze – a painting that bowled over Alfred Jarry – and also in profile or as a contrapuntal figure in the paintings of the same period (*The Rendezvous* or *Landscape with a Man and a Horse*, W443, or *Matamoe*, W484).

'If you like, I'll take you, and we'll cut down the tree you want and bring it back together.' Bare-chested, 'clad only in loincloths', they struck out through two cracks in the basalt rock. 'The semblance of a path among some trees, sprawling in confusion ... Nothing but wild vegetation, getting more overgrown all the time, and the higher we went the more impenetrable it became...'

In *Noa Noa*, the account of this escapade becomes the shift from one state to another, the supreme shedding of old skin. Their ascent is long, taking several hours; they cross streams of water, discover forgotten paths, throw themselves into the high forest that Jotefa hacks at with his axe and instinctively finds familiar. The Inca follows, carrying his tools, short of breath and finding the going rough. He is twenty years older than his athletically built guide and suffers from 'the fatal heredity of a society which is morally and physically diseased'. The younger man, enjoying it all, scampers ahead, sure-footed as a kid. He is sniffing out the way, thinks Gauguin, the essences of the trees guiding him, drawing him on from the deep parts of the island. The mountain is riven with torrents, scree, sharp-edged rocks; it is an arduous climb. 'The silence was total, despite the plaintive sound of the water among the rocks, a monotone, a sound to accompany the silence . . .'

In the distance, the austere outline of Mount Tetufera, some 5,400 feet, blocks the horizon. The higher the two men climb into the foothills, the more the light is obscured, darkening by degrees. 'It was broad daylight and we could almost see the stars,' notes Gauguin. Time after time they wade waist-deep in water to reach the far bank of a stream, axes held above it. On dry land there are yet more mounds of stones, colonies of ferns exploding in their thousands among the scree, thickets of wild flowers, tree trunks that sprout to sixty feet.

They slip between two pools of sunlight. They have to make good time to spare themselves the heat and get back down again before nightfall and its procession of *tupapau*. Both of them are copiously bathed in sweat. They climb on for three hours, four hours, into the very centre of the island and its dark beating heart.

During this ascent, Gauguin experienced a hallucination. 'Was this a man walking there in front of me?' he wondered, his exhaustion making him prey to anxiety. 'It seemed to me that I saw in him the breathing embodiment of all this vegetable splendour which hemmed us in. And in him and through him it released and sent out a fragrance of beauty that intoxicated my soul . . .'

In this enchanted forest, this other world far from the shore and the populated hamlets, Jotefa became once more a being apart, superior because of his innocence, in close harmony with nature: the very emanation of life, momentarily human. An androgyne to whom Gauguin wants to submit, like someone bowing down, surrendering to a superior being. Gauguin accepts and acknowledges this searing attraction, its sacredness and sensuality; it would be his own struggle with the angel, one that begins with an embrace. He reaches out towards him, open to whatever might ensue, even caresses. Confused, the Inca moves closer to the shining back in front of him, magnetised by its power, 'my temples racing'. Jotefa turns round; Gauguin backs away and lowers his eyes. The apparition has gone. The Tahitian stares at him through 'his innocent eyes', unsuspecting of the Frenchman's intent, that 'desire for the unknown' that smothered him. Out of vexation, on the mountainside where their breath makes echoes, the painter plunged into the icy water of a stream. To punish himself as much as for the sake of purification.

'*To'eto'e* (it's cold),' Jotefa said.

' "Oh no!" I answered.'

Back on the move, Gauguin thrust himself into the thickets, 'as if I wanted to dissolve into this maternal immensity of nature.' They reached a flat clearing, where 'the steep wails of the mountain drew apart', and finally found what they were looking for behind a tangled curtain of scrub: a dozen or so rosewood trees with an exceptional spread of branches. A piece of paradise.

Of course, Gauguin indicates the finest, the biggest, the most extensive of these. The two men take turns, hewing at the magnificent trunk until their hands bleed. The wound begins to gape, and finally the rosewood tree collapses under the gouging axe blows that ring out. Once it is on the ground, they lop off the branches and cut it into long logs, a victim and an offering to the gods, in the light that blazes over the southern coast. 'Cut the foot off the whole of the forest, cut your self-love out of yourself,' whispers his axe. Gauguin is the dead tree, reborn, and essentially from himself, like an initiate, a mystic, a visionary. Red with the blood on his hands, sticky with the rose-pink sap, wood shavings in his hair, his arms and legs scratched by the thorny vegetation, in Gauguin's words: 'I was a different man, a savage now.'

They went back down to the village, the fragrant wood across their shoulders; weighed down by this forbidden fruit, they were the conquerors of the magic mountain. By twilight, they were home, beside the sea's quivering surge over the coral, their skin drenched with sweat, sap and blood. Shattered with fatigue, fulfilled with their joy, they were new made as if on the very first day.

Tehamana brings them water in a gourd, and mouthfuls of coconut. Jotefa leaves them. He will return. They have set the rosewood to dry against the *niau* partition. Three red blocks almost phosphorescent with sap, which tomorrow will be three totems, three tikis, so many carved figures.

'Are you glad?'

'Yes.'

'And deep in my heart, I said so again, to myself: Yes.'

At this moment, Gauguin was a Maori. Every blow hammered by the chisel into this precious wood will quicken his breath, will make him stronger. Only this matters, life itself through it and its fragrance. *Noa Noa!*

CHAPTER 24

What did he read in his South Seas hut? To start with, what he took with him, which is very little, given the cost of freight. For someone with his funds, books were expensive and hard to find in Papeete. But though his country library contained scarcely forty volumes, it was supplemented by a boxful of documents (photographs of people from the Marquesas and tattoos, diverse illustrations, plates of monuments, of Borabudur and the Parthenon; statues, of Dionysus and ecstatic Buddhas; reproductions of paintings by Puvis de Chavannes, Delacroix, Manet, Degas, but also Holbein, Cranach and Italian primitives) which served as stimuli and constituted his 'visual larder'. 'I am taking photographs and drawings, a whole little world of companions who will speak to me every day,' he told Odilon Redon before he left France.

Among the literary works he had were Poe, Loti and Balzac, naturally; Mallarmé whom he revered, and probably Baudelaire and the novels of Octave Mirbeau. Also the poems of Saint-Pol Roux, who stressed that poetry 'is God made manifest in the human, all the formless chaos of the world made clear by the mediator who is the poet.' Also there, lent to him by his Punaauia neighbour, were mystics and theoretical maguses such as Sâr Péladan or Eliphas Lévi.

And in particular there was Ernest Renan, whose books changed his life. In his young days, when he was a seaman, Gauguin had caught a glimpse of the sulphurous intellectual on board the *Jérôme Napoleon*, during the 1870 scientific expedition which was scuppered at the Pole because of the Franco-Prussian War. His book *La Vie de Jésus* (*The Life of Jesus*, 1863), the first volume in his *Histoire des origines du christianisme* (*History of the Origins of Christianity*, 1863–81), raised doubts about Christ's divine nature, emphasising his human and subjective side. It caused a great uproar that Jesus Christ should be seen as a man of flesh and blood, fear and desire, 'someone real and pure' but 'so great that I should not like to contradict those who are so impressed by the outstanding qualities of his work that they call him God', announced Renan, who was then suspended from the Collège de France. The outcry turned into an upheaval.

Gauguin took as his own this theory of a man-god, the very symbol of the human condition, and the mediator of another world. Stuck in his village by the sea, he endlessly brooded over its elements without mastering them. But with his skills as a sculptor, he bent them to his needs like wrought iron. Jesus of Nazareth remains the man 'who has made his species take the greatest step towards the divine', Renan insisted. Christ is the cornerstone and behind him hides Joshua, the son of an artisan and a Jew of Galilee. He is the supreme yardstick, the highest example and the most humble model; his drama lies at the very heart of things. His story is revolutionary: he wanted to change life, to refashion it, to give it different words; he 'ushered a new spirit into the world'. Gauguin took up many of Renan's ideas as his own, deliberately painting himself as Christ (the series of the yellow Christ, the green Christ, Christ in the garden of olives, etc), persuaded that he too in his way, as an artist, was a 'diviner', the holder and captor of that truth, and thereafter placed his art in the realm of the visionary. Painting was communion with the world, the joy of every moment and every thing, freed from constraints, loosened from contingencies, coming together with the great flow.

In Papeete Auguste Goupil, a colonial whose interest in Gauguin – an unusual enough occurrence – led him to commission a painting (a portrait of his daughter, Vaite, W535, 1896), also lent him Jacques-Antoine Moerenhout's *Voyages aux îles du Grand Ocean*. This two-volume work, written by a former diplomat, was published in 1837, and its 600 pages contain a history of each group of islands through its customs, mythology and ethnography. This assiduous survey, which has its share of inaccuracies and improbabilities, attempted to take stock of the earlier Polynesian world by way of personal accounts collected by the author. Included in it are descriptions of the handsome Ariois, hedonistic initiates in sacrificial rites to Venus, who practise dances and sexual exhibitions. Captivated during his brief sojourn, after several months at sea, Louis Antoine de Bougainville had earlier observed: 'Venus is the goddess whom people turn to here ... There is no mystery in her cult of worship, and every act of sexual pleasure is a national festival ... Several of our men have had reason to be very happy with the customs of this place.' Indeed, this religious sect had made its appearance on the sacred island of Raiatea, and then spread through the archipelagoes from the fifteenth century on. Apostles of Oro, the god of Fertility and War, its initiates advocated hedonism, free love, infanticide and, from what Gauguin understood of it, a life without constraints and entirely directed towards pleasure and adoration. According to Bob Putigny, the author of a study on supernatural powers in Polynesia, 'the people venerated (them) like superior beings in close contact with the gods who inspired them, and directly approved their actions and words.' Men and women were chosen for their physical beauty, their vitality, their natural *mana*. This honour transcended the caste structure of a pyramidal society (royal chiefs, high priests, landowners, and at the bottom farmers and fishermen, slaves and prisoners destined for sacrifice), giving them rights and precedence and effectively placing them in a separate, different sphere from that of mortals. Once initiated into the secret, each member of the elect would become a dancer and a poet; and when the neophytes took part in orgiastic celebrations that were halfway between a Mass and a carnival, they became the link between two worlds, and, incidentally, a force of subversion in any struggle between fiefdoms.

Gauguin copied out a number of passages into a notebook with a cloth cover. He titled it *The Ancient Maori Cult*, and he gives his version of this cult in at least two of his paintings: *Vairaumati tei oa* (*Her Name is Vairaumati*), W450, and *Te aa no Areois*, W451. He used Tehamana as the model for his full-length portrait of two naked young women sitting on sarongs, waiting for the goodwill of avid gods. This very summary reading was the basis of his Maori knowledge and gave him the material for his manuscript *Noa Noa*. From this we can say that he invented his own ideal Polynesia, which he transmuted like poor-quality lead into solid gold, making it a fiction, a material for dreams, a material to be worked on, the yeast for his painting. As he had done with each one of his masters and his fellow painters – Pissarro, Cézanne, Degas, as well as Emile Bernard and Van Gogh – the Inca took what he himself lacked, made it completely his own and transformed it. He was more instinctive than intellectual; a self-taught wild man, he leapt ferally on his prey and made it his. On Tahiti, for want of interlocutors and methodically collected facts, Gauguin had just found what he needed to make his exile fulfilling: the remains of an imaginary world, the figures in a pantheon, a mythology alongside an erotico-esoteric atmosphere. Much of this albeit superficial know-ledge which Gauguin staged in an arbitrary manner, without any anthropological concern, he put in Tehamana's mouth: 'At night, in bed, we had great conversations, which were long and often very serious. In her child's soul I tried to see the traces of a distant past.' These were esoteric allegories, parables and metaphorical legends, which in any case were not to be got out of a fourteen-year-old girl with little worldly wisdom. This didn't matter. Gauguin was the deviser of his own fictional exile: he smoothed down its phases, and worked on every contour. He became the actor in his own vision. Tahiti *was* his painting; what he burned up here was primarily his desire for it, the theme to which he responded with brushes and gouges. It is his own immoderation that took shape, his lack that was filled. The immensity of his dream and the breadth of his quest was him and him alone.

'What a religion the old Oceanian religion is! What a wonder! My brain is buzzing with it, and all it prompts in me will certainly scare people,' he pronounced theatrically in a letter to Sérusier, left behind in Brittany. And, through the lessons of that Golden Age, Gauguin knew how to reframe this bloodless Polynesia which had been denatured by European civilisation. In this fabric of rituals and legends, celebrations and combat, abductions and seductions, can-nibalism and infanticide, sex is omnipresent, or rather, love is free and without complexes, between fornicating gods, vahines offered to them, warriors tattooed with star-shaped jellyfish, and priests with superhuman powers bowing down before magic tikis.

'All the joyful pleasures of a free life, animal and human!' This was Mystery, on the threshold of a mystery, the start of the spiritual adventure which Gauguin transferred to his painting. 'Putting a red or a blue on my canvas, without thinking too much about it!' In his destitution, the artist, dizzied by philosophy, had an intimation of it: he was no longer there to line up paintings for sale, to supply a market or give an impetus to a modernist movement, but to get close to Truth by transposing reality through the filter of his vision. In his way, he was a white Arioi, the last initiate of the sect that had been dispatched by missionaries' psalms, a monster outside any norms, detached from society and its theatre. 'Painting must be made very simply, with a subject that is savage, like a child.' Stripped down, listening to the dictates of the world, the Inca in metamorphosis glimpsed that all this 'can only invade me'. He did not know how true his words were. Now he was a shaman.

CHAPTER 25

There were to be three versions of *Noa Noa*. The original text, in Gauguin's hand, is a series of relatively happy memories of his stay on Tahiti. He eventually returned to Paris in 1893, and he viewed these notes, along with another text he had outlined, *The Ancient Maori Cult*, as the basis for a promotional work which would give the background to his experience, clarifying his two years in the tropics and treading somewhat on Loti's heels. 'I am preparing a book about Tahiti which will be very useful as a way of understanding my painting. What a lot of work!' he told Mette in 1893, writing from France.

Subsequent interventions, primarily that of Charles Morice, who was called upon to help out, led to some parts of the text being developed or cut down, to names being changed or the actions of certain protagonists being altered. Gauguin's intention was to compare 'savages' to 'civilised people', the former category's raw material to the classical regulation of the latter. A second manuscript saw the light of day. It was the product of Morice's rewriting, the painter's lies or second thoughts, and divers fresh transcriptions, like the co-author's extravagant insertion of poems, whereby he could flatter himself as having joint status in the enterprise.

After much procrastination, in 1897 Morice published extracts in *La Revue blanche*, then, hard pressed, in 1901, 'a very simple little volume', with no illustrations, at his own expense. The title, *Noa Noa*, is a reference to the Polynesian Eden, *Rohutu noanoa*: fragrant paradise. Monfreid lucidly summed up the poems as 'trivial'. In an emphatic, incantatory vein, they are nothing short of derisory: 'Smiling at the dream sun, as it rises/This continent of flowers in these seas of golden fire/Eden, Eldorado, Florida, Labrador/Is this a land before my eyes, or just my dream?' While he did not disown it, Gauguin was likewise severely critical of this publication. Meanwhile, in the tradition of Poe and Manet's deluxe edition of *The Raven*, he had branched out into a series of ten woodcuts, nocturnal and oneiric pieces which were intended to accompany his book, though without any connection to the narrative.

When he went back to Polynesia for good in 1895, Gauguin took a copy of this second version with him. Over the years he kept on going over it, interspersing watercolours, engravings and photographs, pushing this collection towards a kind of manifesto, an essay which was an extension of an anticlerical pamphlet, *L'Esprit moderne et le catholicisme* (*Catholicism and the Modern Mind*). By the time he died, in 1903, this version had become a third manuscript, an illuminated book-cum-art object running to two hundred pages, diverging from its earlier versions. It is now preserved in the Department of Drawings at the Louvre.

In short, in *Noa Noa*, the veracity of events and their chronology should be viewed with circumspection. From Morice's version onwards, it became a mixture of true lies and false truth, based on Gauguin's fictionalisation. Thus, the episode at the Maraa grotto does not exist in the first version. However, Gauguin could have dictated it to his collaborator for the second version, or touched it up with details for Morice to develop. Whatever the case, it is a passage that I have always liked. And when I drove my car to a stop at Maraa in front of the curtain of banyans, my heart was pounding. 'Almost entirely hidden by guava trees, the grotto only appeared by the roadside as if the rock had detached itself by pure accident ...' I had to experience *in situ* what had been described in *Noa Noa*. At last.

Let us return to the text. Gauguin lived in Mataiea with his girlfriend Tehamana (Tehura). At the invitation of friends, they set out at around six in the morning, before it got hot, on a walk of nearly six and a half miles. They were to have a lunch of two roast chickens, an octopus, and a pig cooked by the method of braising in a covering of stones. Along the way, he, Tehamana and four neighbours stopped at this grotto by the side of the coast road, the PK 28. It consisted of a wide natural cavity scooped out in the basalt cliff, with its edges and walls lined with ferns. From the roof, which was some thirty feet high, hundreds of stalactites hung in permanent frozen drips, forming a foreground curtain of milky rain that spattered onto the surface. Further back, is a subterranean lake of dull blue water, as deep as Loch Ness. It seems limitless and bottomless, and the only thing that can be distinguished, vaguely, is a reddish elevation, a kind of theatre stage within the blur of paleness. It is a deserted spot, choked with plants and twisted roots; it is cold in this semi-darkness and the silence weighs heavy.

Gauguin tells us: 'Push aside the branches, let yourself slide up some three feet and you will be in a dark hole ... On the walls, either side there are huge snakes, at least that is what they seem, slithering slowly to go and drink from the surface of this interior lake. They are roots that emerge through the fissures of the rock...'

The painter suggested that they bathe there; his companions took fright. He insisted; they were reluctant to take a dip in among that mass of sharp stones, just for the sake of stretching their legs. Tahitians are known to prefer bathing in the fresh water of rivers and waterfalls rather than in the lukewarm lagoon. Under cover of foliage, where the sun is kept out, the water is cooler and more refreshing. But this grotto was so strange.

In the illustrations to *Noa Noa*, the woodcut titled *Auti te Pape* ('the fresh water is in movement') brings back something of this oppressive atmosphere. One might easily be at Maraa. On the right, while a vahine ventures into the water which cuts diagonally across the print, the rocks suggest the forms of grimacing monsters: a giant raven's head with staring eyes points its beak towards the victim, intent on piercing her. A second nymph, also naked, with a garland on her brow, stands by the edge. Her back is turned as she falters, feigning not to understand this surrender, this sacrifice to the forces of darkness, her feet on a bed of flat stones. Will she live a little longer, to taste life in the yellow sun, or will she disappear into the blue-black water?

' "Are you coming with me?" I asked Tehura, pointing to the back of the cave. "Are you mad? It's very deep there. And the eels! People never go there!" '

Proud of 'showing off his swimming skills', Gauguin went into the cave. He wanted to see what was there beyond the dimming light, in the darkness. By his account, he swam for an hour.

It must have been four in the afternoon at Maraa, beneath the foliage with its stink of camphor ointment. I put my things down on a stone, hid my keys and wristwatch in my shoes, and put on my swimming trunks. I took a few steps, careful of where I trod. Above, the ground was muddy, seeping between my toes; below, there was cloudy crystal, the colour of an opal. Finally, immersed up to the waist, I swam straight ahead, my breathing good, calm in this brilliant, slightly viscous water. The water that dripped from the stalactites dotted the lake with white sparks like so many small electric charges. I had to cross this liquid curtain; a few drops ran into my hair. Finally, in front of me, the cave rounded out in a hollow, revealing ochre reliefs, orange-coloured shapes and stripey residues. At intervals, I had noticed a puzzling lapping motion from right to left: these waves came towards me, passed under me, caressingly, to be finally smoothed away. Gauguin surmised: 'For a moment I thought I saw a large tortoise floating in the water; more exactly I thought I saw its head rise above the surface in a challenge to me.' Could this be the movement of eels, made invisible by being the same colour as the water, drawn out of curiosity and swirling around any intruder? I speeded up my breast stroke, feeling rather small. The further in I went, the more the light dwindled. In the end I could make out that natural diving board, a shelf of reddish stone, and then a hole. Where did it lead, and to what?

Gauguin did this before me, a century ago. He wrote: 'By what strange phenomenon did the far end of the grotto recede even further away the more I advanced towards it?' I had the same sensation of making no progress, despite steady movement, as if in a bad dream of being on an endless staircase where each landing is reached only to reveal the same prospect as before. The Inca tried to touch the bottom. 'This terror had to be overcome; I let myself sink to the bottom but could not reach it and came back up. I could not even touch it with my heel thereby to regain my confidence.'

I dared not tempt fate by getting too close to the sharp-beaked raven outlined by the dark wave. Besides, Tehamana was not there to worry about me. The same Tehura-Tehamana who was standing on the far side, behind the stalactites, seen by Gauguin as 'now only a small black dot on a luminous centre'.

'Come back!' she shouts in desperation.

When he turned round, the painter saw her from a very long way away. He expressed his surprise: 'What other phenomenon makes distance keep moving towards infinity?' He swam on in the same direction and after half an hour he reached his goal. Hoisting himself up onto the rim to catch his breath, he sank back against the damp wall; it seemed to bleed. 'A very ordinary little platform and a gaping hole; where does it go? It's a mystery. I have to admit that I'm frightened.' Then he splashed off back in the other direction.

It was late in the afternoon. Here, in this isolated cave, a mere muscle cramp would have done for me. After some fifty yards, I stopped and looked around, kicking my legs all the time to stay in the same spot. My movements caused ripples right back to the far end of the cave, then, hitting it, they washed back towards me. I was at the centre of an ebb and flow that I myself had created. The echo amplified my breathing. Some internal reverberation made everything blur, sending up a white haze. And the red platform still appeared distant, as if it had moved still further, at any rate sliding away and not easily reached. A piece of graffiti on the wall to my left had disconcerted me. Was it a ritualistic inscription, an optical illusion or a declaration of love? What if I were suddenly to find the painter's signature scratched there on the wall? Out of bravado, following the line of the rock, I advanced a further twenty yards. An eddy from the left was a little alarming as it slicked beneath me then went off in the other direction. Eels? I turned tail.

Ten minutes later, I swam back under the stalactite curtain at a steady crawl and reached the edge, frozen stiff. It would seem that the Inca had indeed done that swim, for the details and sensations were exact.

Leaving the cave, proud of his exploits, the painter went off to pick gardenias for his beloved. He set a flower in her bushy hair. The warm air and the caresses of his companion, who clung to him, getting her sarong wet against his skin, perked up this mad dog of a Frenchman. 'How good it is to be alive and, when we are hungry, to gobble up the little pig waiting for us at home,' he pronounced, resuming his walk with a springy step. 'The road was beautiful, the sea superb, with Moorea opposite grandiose and haughty . . .'

Through the windscreen of my Ford, the landscape was radiant, 'blue and green from end to end'. A silly little song was playing on the local radio: 'Among the wild flowers, at the foot of the waterfall, I'll wait for you . . .' I headed for Papeete again. A capricious but insistent May downpour contrived to get in front of me by a good half-mile. First it created turmoil among the thickets and the shrubs, strummed on the soft trunks and broad leaves of the banana trees, rinsing the landscape before rushing from one valley to another, swept along by the wind. Adjusting my speed to the bad weather, I only reached the village when the victorious sun came out in full dazzle. Tahiti glittered like magic. In the gardens dewy with water, the grass had a blinding sparkle. On the left, a dense heat came off the lagoon and through its limpid waters you could see the complicated castles of coral; some of them were so wildly formed, topsy-turvy, that they seemed to spell out a Hebrew script. Rays of sunlight fell straight down, clean like knife blades, between two spangled hedges; the road was a tongue of silver. Ravenous, I stopped at the Chinese shop to buy a packet of manioc cakes and a bottle of water. That day, at Maraa, Gauguin had been there to meet me. I didn't dare tell the mixed-race man who was hunched behind the cash register.

CHAPTER 26

On the harbour front, between the harbour master's office and the East Coast truck terminal, I went to sip a Fanta while waiting to have dinner with Gilles Artur. Beside a score or so of lorries fitted out as trailers, you can snack on fish, kebabs, pizzas, chicken Chinese-style, and even crêpes. Alongside the ferries, and sometimes huge foreign liners, docked there, seamen, workers and tourists flock to this improvised encampment which will be gone in a few hours' time. In the warm night, as insects drone and buzz, with the Pacific close by licking at the quaysides and tossing yachts about, amid this nocturnal music it is good to wander where the air is cool. There is no more traffic. The city-centre car parks have turned back into what they were at the start: sand beside the ocean. Papeete goes to bed as soon as its mountains darken. The pirogues have come back in through the Motu Uta channel. Under the trees, a few beauties idle, panther-like peasant girls, mingling with the lithe *rae rae*, transvestites who have huge laughs, swimmer's thighs, hair brushed down their backs and the fixed joyless smile worn by the *filles de joie*.

On the Boulevard Pomare I noticed a child who looked like me. He wore unbleached linen shorts, a short-sleeved blue shirt patterned with shells, and flip-flops made locally. At six or seven, living in the Pirae district, admiring the schooners circling at twilight, I was just like him. And, all these years later, the father holding him by the hand could have been my father: obviously an officer, a lieutenant or a captain newly promoted. Even out of uniform, I can tell them by their close-shorn hair at the back, their gymnastic gait, full of no-nonsense muscularity.

On my previous trip, in 1996, I had stopped here on my way back

173

from the Tuamotu Archipelago and stayed in the town centre, at the hotel Tiare, the one Somerset Maugham also stayed at. Twice, at Rangiroa and Papeete, I had been mistaken for 'the dentist from Moorea'. I was greeted by two different people, asked how I was and how was my wife. At the arrivals terminal for domestic flights, collecting my luggage from the carousel disgorging surfboards, boxes tied with string and packs of Hinano beer, a little boy even took me for the man 'who had treated his tooth decay'. I told myself that I must have a double in the South Seas. At the time, it was an amusing anecdote; an episode with comic potential. Yet, the more I thought about it, the more I was disturbed by the thought. What if I had an identical twin on Tahiti's twin island? I wondered. Another me, in a white overall, a dab hand with the dentist's drill and filling amalgam. With complete impunity, on the other side of the world, more than eleven thousand miles away from my Paris apartment, my Maori version performed his surgical procedures in the most perfect ano-nymity, unsuspecting of my existence. And which of us two, with the same face, the same build, probably the same demeanour, the same voice, would have been truer than the other? My double! My double on Moorea, I kept repeating, foolishly, on Prince Hinoi Avenue.

Why couldn't I cross the reef? Take the first ferry tomorrow morning, and forget about Gauguin. After all, wasn't Polynesia just this, the never-ending other side where the grass is always greener, the ever-elusive faraway place which allows everything to be possible? But, behind this coincidence, I was less afraid of seeming ridiculous than of the disappointment that I brooded on every day. In the land of my childhood, everything in this archipelago was so different, had moved on so perfidiously under seeming similarities: like a play in the theatre where the set might have stayed the same, but someone had altered the spatial dimensions, tampered with the lighting and changed the cast.

The day before, at Saint Joseph's School, where I had been a pupil, and of which I retained very distinct memories, I had hardly recognised the covered playground and the vast courtyard, and found nothing left at all of the football ground, or the beehives, or the pistachio trees along the path, or the Chinese shop. I might as well have made them up. Yet the building was the same, the site identical, as was the arrangement of the classrooms, and I could still taste in my mouth the slightly acid flavour of the fruits that the hawkers would sell to us through the railings: star fruits and genips. I had become a stranger, or rather life here had gone on without me, reaching a maturity from which I was excluded, through metamorphoses that were not mine. By returning to what I had been in Tahiti, through these differences and maturations I contemplated my own foreignness. Having been an other, it was myself that I could no longer find there. Where, then, could I assume I belonged?

As for our house in Pirae, the first house I can remember living in, at the far end of a housing development I had found a shrunken villa, too close to the road, at the end of the path which had been tarred over in the interval. A *Popaa* was taking an afternoon nap. My ring on the doorbell had woken her up.

'Do you want to rent it?'

'Just to take a look around, I mean, to see it again; I lived here once.'

I couldn't manage to convince the Frenchwoman. And even though she could scarcely have taken me for a thief, she wouldn't let me see my old bedroom, the living room with the rattan chairs and the decorative bamboos, or let me sit down in that kitchen with the cool floor underfoot, which was out of sight through a curtain of gaudily-coloured beads, and where once my father's Hungarian orderly, Sergeant Kraft, would tell me about the family mill in Szeged, or how cold Lake Balaton was, or about the estimable town of Pecs where he had studied.

'You can take a walk round the garden, if that's what you fancy,' she conceded before disappearing inside the house.

I went there, her mangy dog barking at my heels. The garden of cassias and tamarinds was no more, nor was the hibiscus hedge; it had been amputated by construction work next door. Where was the garage for the Zodiac, the sun awning for the Renault 4L? The neighbours had decamped to Los Angeles; their *fare* on stilts had been demolished. Teva's banana plantation had been decapitated, and where was the low wall whose curtain of fencing we would lift to slip away into the bushes and the gardens, and the clammy heat of the plantations? It overlooked a car park. I even found Taoone beach reduced to two-thirds of its size and spattered with refuse. I had learned to swim here, across from the Taunoa Channel, in this deep ocean where Moray eels undulated among the rocks. Had I dreamt this or was it reality that kept eluding me? What was the point of going back over these snares, these will-o'-the-wisps, a string of fictions? I remember having had three cats, Pussy, Jules and Mareta, a harpoon, an overseas subscription to *Spirou* and a chicken-pox rash. My playmates next door were called Teva, Toyo and Moana. Their mum, Marama, wore a sarong and cooked us tinned beans in tomato sauce, and to me nothing seemed more delicious. I swam like a god, climbed the tamarinds and thought myself Robinson Crusoe on every one of the South Coast motus. And Sergeant Kraft would sometimes come and pick me up from school behind the wheel of the Jeep. How proud that made me! To me his Hungary had become a land of Cockayne, filled with sprites and spells, and he too was in his way a knight, a figure of legend. Had he not passed the final test by crossing what he called the Iron Curtain? Secretly, I desired his mistress, a tall, lunar half-Chinese lady, white as porcelain, who went around on a Vespa and smelled of a haunting musky perfume that made me dizzy.

At the end of my walk I turned into a street at right angles. I had an appointment in a French restaurant, and that evening Gilles Artur introduced me to his female companion. From her accent, I thought she was Tahitian, but not at all, the lady was a Lapp, from Lapland, and she spoke Finnish! Every year, she went back to Europe to ski, to have saunas, to roll around in the snow and reconnect with her relatives. Those Lapps, with their brightly coloured little skirts and their pointed woollen caps, who gave up their permafrost for firewater and had the same fate as the American Indians. By coincidence I had Arto Paasilinna's extraordinary novel *Prisoners of Paradise* in my luggage.

'How do you say in Finnish: "the lagoon is the colour of amethysts"?' I asked her curiously.

'We have no word for that. However, everything wintry . . .'

And I was charmed by having dinner in a fake Normandy cottage in Papeete, in the company of a Lapp lady and a Gauguin specialist who had known Saint-Pol Roux. The three of us polished off the succulent bonito and celebrated my first article with a bottle of 1992

Saint-Estèphe. Through Artur's mediation, *La Dépêche de Tahiti* had just done an interview with me, published under the title 'In Search of Paul Gauguin'. For the photograph, I had posed under a tiki.

'Here's the first article to refer to my book before it's even published! It's probably something to do with time differences.'

'How much longer are you staying?'

'Only seven or eight days. I'm leaving tomorrow for Hiva Oa.'

I seemed to have exhausted the delights of Tahiti. The Marquesas were pulling me. In their bitter solitude, these volcanic stumps, isolated in the Pacific and battered by southern swells, struck me as embodying the painter's destiny, his geographical materialisation. These twelve islands, in two groups over nine hundred miles from the Society Archipelago, were stubborn and insolent, like a pair of black knuckle-bones thrown onto the blue carpet of the ocean. Paul Gauguin, yet again. 'Alone, far-flung in distant seas', as one critic wrote. To invent and to invent himself, always in flight, hoping for rebirth.

CHAPTER 27

Would he have lied? Tampered with his memories? What of Tehura-Tehamana? Seduced and abandoned, pregnant by him. 'I am soon going to be a father again in Oceania. Heavens! I have to sow my seed everywhere,' (March 1893). This child was never to see the light of day. And what about that sweet and simple life he had out there? That 'awakening' in the mountains and the caves? Might he not have exaggerated, wanting to return to Europe in triumph, his adventure transformed into an epic?

Let's come back to his correspondence; in it, his exacerbated state of mind is transparent. Money obsesses him. 'I'm in the most utter depression. Down to my last fifty francs and no prospect of anything whatsoever,' (December 1892). There is his fury to win and his certainty of being right, his need to find a dealer of Theo's calibre and a dependable market: 'I have worked hard latterly ... I think I am on a winning streak,' (June 1892). And simultaneously there is his fear of competition: 'I'm told there is a whole pack of young people following on my coat tails and prospering. Since they are younger, have more advantages than I do, and greater skill, I shall perhaps be squeezed out. I'm relying on this Tahiti period to put me ahead; it will take my work beyond the range of what I did in Brittany ...' (March 1893). Sometimes there is also despair to the point of thoughts of giving up: 'When I get back I will have to abandon painting, since it does not earn me a living.'

Because of his delicate health, worsened by his privations and excesses, the Inca sought repatriation at the government's expense, on the basis of his destitution. In a letter to Mette dated April 1893, he describes his daily existence in pitiful terms: 'For two months now,

I have had to cut out all expenditure on food. Every day I have uru, a flavourless fruit which resembles bread, and a glass of water. I cannot even treat myself to a cup of tea because sugar is so expensive ... If you had sent me some money from the last painting, you would have been saving my life ...'

This is the dream reaching its end. No sales on Tahiti, a paucity of money orders from France, declining health, exhausted energy, and a wife who is indifferent. His first Tahitian stay ends 'in a total mess'. In this letter to Monfreid in February 1893, he explains the situation: 'I'll have to wait for at least three months before I can hope to leave, assuming that the Ministry will repatriate me.' In Europe he intends to see his children and his wife as soon as possible. He hopes to patch things up with Mette, or at any rate to establish better terms with her and clarify the business of the Scandinavian sales and exhibitions. 'You are right, I must go back ... I close my letter with a kiss to you and to the children, and I'll see you soon. I may well arrive a month and a half after you get this letter' (April 1893).

He has packed. He has also said his farewells. He is leaving his hut in Mataiea, and has found temporary lodgings at Paofai, with the Jénot family and the Suhas, while he waits for the boat. Tehamana sobs beside the lagoon, like Rarahu in Loti's novel. Gauguin doesn't have a penny to his name. 'I have to live in such a way that I can do my duty right to the end, and I can only do this by bringing my illusions to account.'

Yet, the results are there: sixty-six canvases, woodcarvings, drawings and roughs, plans for engravings, and hundreds of sketches so that, like Delacroix coming back from Morocco with seven sketchbooks, he can 'go on with his Tahitian work' even in Europe. 'It's enough for just one man!' Among his papers there is also his *Cahier pour Aline*, Aline being his favourite child, 'notes scattered disconnectedly, like dreams, like life made up of scraps.' In this harvest, there are some crucial masterpieces, for instance, that *Manao Tupapau*, W457, one of Gauguin's favourite paintings, already sent to Europe. It shows Tehamana lying on her stomach, her buttocks on show like some plump tropical fruit. She lies on a yellow sheet, her pupils dilated with fear, while a black-hooded *tupapau* stands sneering behind her, in the midst of phosphorescent flowers. This is dream and reality unashamed, the intimate fusion of two worlds. It can rival Manet's *Olympia* (1863) in attracting journalistic attention, creating a public stir, and even scandal. But the only thing that matters is that he will be talked about. 'I would gladly have gone to work in the Marquesas, which would have been enormously useful to me, but I am tired and taking care of my affairs in Paris is an urgent necessity.'

Were it even just a matter of those two years, the new direction of his work was proof of his genius and it would be saved. But, having taken ship as 'a destitute repatriate travelling in steerage'. Gauguin did not know this and still had doubts about his future. He left Papeete harbour on 14 June on board the *Duchaffault*, to make a connection in New Caledonia with the liner *l'Armand Béhic*. During the voyage he paid a supplement to avoid being quartered along with the herd and the sheep, in third class down in the hold.

On 3 August 1893, our wandering Ulysses reached Marseille with four francs in his pocket. The town was in a sweltering heat and no one was waiting for him. 'Would you telegraph your concierge so that when I get to Paris on Friday I shall have some kind of landing place,' he asked Monfreid, who was still in the Pyrenees. There, standing on the quayside, was the man from the archipelagoes, the suntanned savage, the shaman back from the islands. What a fine thing.

CHAPTER 28

So where were his friends? From Marseille, stuck in a hotel on credit, he sent telegrams rounding up Sérusier, Schuff and Monfreid. A money order for 250 francs arrived for him and he took the train. He wrote to Mette: 'Come as soon as possible!' On 3 August, he had written from Marseille: 'Write to me at length about how everything is at home; I have been without news from you for five months now. Also tell me where things are with our finances so that I can start doing some calculations.' Was this love or self-interest? Maurice Joyant, Theo Van Gogh's replacement at Boussod & Valadon, had now left, and no one knew what to do with his brightly coloured paintings. Nor what to do with this rowdy mahogany-skinned character who would cadge ten francs and ask to be lodged without charge.

'You're a free man,' they would say tartly.

Free, indeed, but to do what? 'I found the door closed at Boussod.' At the Ministry of Fine Arts, where the old administration had promised to buy one of his works for three thousand francs, they surveyed his Latino seafarer's looks and shoved him into the upholstered corridor with the parting words: 'Your art is too revolutionary.' He took his canvases, his gris-gris, his trunks filled with fetishes, sarongs and seashell necklaces, and cleared out. He ended up in a pied-à-terre in Rue de la Grande Chaumière, where a certain Alphonse Mucha lent him his studio. 'Without the little restaurant that lets me eat on credit I don't really know how I would feed myself.'

However, at the end of this year luck finally smiled on him. At Degas' insistence, Durand Ruel, who had already bought some of the Inca's works, agreed to the idea of an exhibition at Rue Laffitte. This was the gallery that had spearheaded the early Impressionists, and at the time was backing Maufra and Moret, former followers of Gauguin in Brittany. It had been taken over by the dealer's two sons, while Durand Ruel the elder, having established himself in New York, contrived to sell Monet and Renoir to sugar magnates. The Paris gallery therefore planned a show for Gauguin, though it didn't take any chances: the catalogue, the posters and the coloured frames were his responsibility. 'It is a great step forward and I believe that with a few newspaper articles this exhibition will be a success,' he explained to Mette, who had no intention of following her husband's suggestion that she come to France with one of the children. 'Besides, we could have a talk, and we need to, since by letter it's out of the question...'

This would be killing two birds with the one stone, for if she were to come from Denmark she would bring his paintings, the Breton and Tahitian ones and the ones in the old collection from his banking days. This was war plunder that Mette had sold off on the quiet. A crate of paintings reached Paris in October. Some were missing, Gauguin saw with alarm; the best ones. Where were the Manets, the Sisleys, the Cézannes and the Renoirs? There was no explanation. 'From now on I need to keep an account of all this, so when you have the time write to me with a list of the pictures you have and a list of those you have sold since I left for Tahiti, along with the prices...'

A second piece of news came, and no small thing: his uncle in the provinces, Isidore Gauguin, uncle Zizi, the younger brother of his father Clovis, had obligingly died in Orléans. This was a miracle. He had left an inheritance of twenty-five thousand francs, with shares and bonds, to be divided between his maid, Gauguin's sister, Marie Uribe, and Gauguin himself. Gauguin was in good spirits: 'My uncle's death will solve everything.' Now he had a private income! He would receive thirteen thousand francs, a sum which, with some sales in addition, would keep him going for several years. He had left for Tahiti with less than that.

Had the tide changed at last? Feverishly, he paid off his most pressing debts of some two thousand francs. He told Monfreid: 'My notary has put the funds in my chaste hands ... which means that you won't have to be troubled for any cash.' He went on some heavy binges, gave two hundred francs to Juliette Huet, whom he saw something of, bought three hundred-franc shares in the *Mercure de France*, took a trip to Belgium for the pleasure of seeing some works by Memling and Rubens, settled the bill of nine hundred francs for the exhibition, and, after much prevarication, sent only 1500 francs to Denmark. 'If I had sent her six thousand francs ... what would have become of me?' This hastened his final break with Mette. 'We can hope for nothing from him! He will never think of anyone but himself and his own comfort!' she raged, appalled. In a letter of 15 September to Schuff, she gave her disgusted verdict on Gauguin: 'So he's back now! And by what I can tell from his letters, he's the same as when he left, full of his own monstrously unfeeling selfishness, which is something I find extraordinary, incomprehensible...'

The exhibition at the Durand Ruel gallery opened on 4 November 1893. It showed thirty-eight paintings from Tahiti, six from Brittany and two carvings. The works on the walls, now retouched and varnished, were in white, yellow and blue frames: *Manao Tupapau, Ia orana Maria, Vahine no te miti, Vahine no te tiare* ... Among the finest, we can still see *Merahi metua no Teha' amana* (W497); *Vahine no te vi* (W449); *Fatata te miti* (W463), a bathing scene with shadowy greens and deep blues; *Aha oe feii?* (W461), a piece of lagunar paradise where the vahines are naked queens crowned with gardenias, lying and resting on the sand; *Otahi* (W502), in which the model's body is a languorous arabesque; and his *Pastorales Tahitiennes* (W470), a hanging Garden of Eden, flowered with frangipani trees, with a woman playing the flute, an orange-coloured dog, and a vermilion-red lagoon where the banks of coral are like an animal's eyes. 'It is extraordinary that so much mystery can be located in so much dazzling brightness,' Mallarmé would exclaim. The catalogue had a preface by the indefatigable Charles Morice and the prices were audaciously displayed at around two thousand to three thousand francs apiece.

On the evening of the opening, Gauguin wore an astrakhan cap, together with a petrol-blue cape and checked trousers. Champagne glass in hand, the impression he made was by turns affable and aloof, charming and blunt. He was tense because he knew that the stakes were high beneath this electric light that distorted the effect of his work. Was he an artist of the highest order? His protective inner circle, Morice, Jean Dolent and Julien Leclercq, intellectuals of the avant-garde, proclaimed that this was so to anyone prepared to listen.

While the public was taken aback, the press remained puzzled by this work, described as 'barbarous, opulent and taciturn'. Who are these peculiar gods with bronze torsos? These obscene Eves in among the violet bushes? These Christian saints in the guise of sleepwalking little savages, women carrying mongoloid Christ figures on their backs? And why these colours that shade the sky pink, the animals red, and smear the idols with some greenish hue, that squeeze Prussian blue straight out of the tube onto locks of hair and flatten things into so many abstract blocks? Technically, how could anyone justify the absence of the model, the abandonment of perspective and the arbitrary framing?

While Gauguin's great talent was proclaimed by Thadée Natanson in *La Revue blanche*, as well as by Félix Fénéon and Octave Mirbeau ('What he sought in Brittany, he ultimately found in Tahiti: the simplification of line and of colour, and their corresponding harmonies in the scene'), four articles cruelly stress their disagreement. 'At Rue Laffitte, one can see works by Monsieur Gauguin, whose rapturous enthusiasts declare him to be the greatest painter of modern and past times! What misfortune to be unable to share this opinion! It would be so nice to be the contemporary of the greatest painter ever!' said one. 'I know nothing more childish than this affected return to faltering primitives . . .'

Renoir and Monet turned away from this 'joke'. Their colleague was playing at being a primitive, mimicking them. A posture! This art was not his. 'He does not lack talent, but what trouble he has controlling it. He is always poaching on other people's ground; nowadays, he is plagiarising the savages in Oceania,' mocked Camille Pissarro.

Nonetheless, some works were sold, ten or so, at greatly reduced prices. Two pictures went to Degas, one to Ambroise Vollard, who would become the dealer of Matisse and Picasso, and the marvellous *Ia orana Maria* to an enlightened art collector, Maurice Manzi, for two thousand francs. But the public was still taken aback. 'Brightly coloured pictures representing quadrumanous females stretched out on a billiard-table cloth . . .' In a gallery where the curious were no longer sure whether to applaud or to hiss, the Inca made a final gesture. He took down from the wall a walking stick with its knob decorated with tikis, and he gave it, in princely fashion, to the elderly Degas, who was just leaving.

'Monsieur Degas, you've forgotten your stick!'

It was a homage to his friend, to the master. An act of testimony between two great artists.

'My exhibition has not really delivered the result which could have been expected of it,' he confirmed to his wife, who had been alerted by the press coverage. Allowing for his expenses, he can't have earned more than a few hundred francs. But the main thing was that he was talked about, and he stirred up controversy; he had started something. Alas, therefore, at the end of this exhibition there were no profits to send to Copenhagen. All the more so because Mette had not given him the details of what she had sold, and he had no intention of being duped. The two of them were cheating. 'I must therefore have precise information, and be kept informed about whatever paintings you sell. In accordance with all of these accounts, made bi-monthly, I shall do what I ought. I ALONE am the judge of what that duty shall be,' he argued in December 1893. These are sordid calculations. 'Since you have recently told me that I must shift for myself (I am all too well aware of this), and with no goods other than my sellable work (which you have entire possession of), so I shall allow myself to take precautions to avoid any occurrence in the future of what happened when I arrived at Marseille.'

Mette felt she had been swindled. Their correspondence became a succession of figures, additions and subtractions, replacing promises and sapping hopes. Down to squalid details like these: 'Bedding 100 F, dentist and optician 75 F, underwear 100 F, tobacco 50 F, clothes and shoes 125 F.' The idea of renting a fisherman's house on the Norwegian coast in the summer of 1894, as a way of re-cementing the family, was abandoned. Of course, he would have liked to see his children, to sweep away the past that gnawed at him, but he only ever did this in his letters, never going so far as to get on a train. Nor did she. In December, he wrote: 'Thank you for your suggestion of my going to Denmark, but I am taken up here all winter with a very big piece of work.' Then came a change of tone: 'If you can only write to me in future in the same terms as your letters since I arrived, I request you to stop writing,' he wrote, berating her, in February 1894. Finally, he told her: 'My work is not finished and I have to live. Think about that and put an end to your perpetual grievances.'

At the end of 1893, spending his uncle Zizi's inheritance, Gauguin moved to a wooden house at 6, Rue Vercingétorix. It was decorated with carvings, spears and war clubs, bark cloth hangings and glass cabinets full of seashells. The chrome yellow walls were adorned with works by Redon, Van Gogh Monfreid, Cézanne and himself. Maori frescoes 'showing love-making' embellished the window panes. This was the Montparnasse version of the Studio of the Tropics, with carpets and a piano, and our artist in a Breton waistcoat.

Behind these theatrics, with which he sought incessantly to per-suade, he defended his cause, his art, and his new work against his enemies and the loneliness which pressed upon him. He spent time with Maillol, Maufra, Durrio and Jehan Rictus, and continued to see his dear companions, Leclercq, Monfreid and Morice. After the laughter and the drinking and the conversations that went on until dawn, there were, however, spells of dark melancholy. He paced about among his easels, as if he were imprisoned. When Morice found out about these moods he proclaimed hysterically: 'He may leave again, travel far away from our decadence, from these coteries and cabals. If he does, we will have driven him to it.'

Every Thursday, Gauguin held open house, playing music, giving demonstrations of upa-upa dancing, and whispering sweet nothings to the young Judith Molard, a thirteen-year-old who had a romantic air about her, although she was not exactly pretty. Her Swedish mother, Ida Ericson-Molard, an artist and sculptor, and her stepfather William, a composer, lived next door. Without intending to, Gauguin inflamed the young girl's feelings. After a couple of loving looks, a caress and a lingering kiss, she agreed to pose nude. At his request, she gave him a pledge: a tuft of her pubic hair. But Gauguin didn't touch her. He already had Juliette Huet and Annah, who was known as 'the Javanese', a 'half-Indian, half-Malay' model Vollard had found him. She had come from Ceylon, it seemed, was dark-skinned and astonishingly impertinent. She would amaze guests by appearing with a female monkey on her shoulder, then give her arm to her island escort, the Maori Inca in the blue cape. Talk of all this exoticism echoed through the whole arrondissement.

In Brittany, where they went in April for the sake of saving money, Gauguin reassembled his court. As ever, he needed followers. A few new arrivals, replacing Bernard and de Haan, were impressed: Slewinski, Seguin, Jourdan and an Irishman, O'Conor. But the country villages had changed and the phalanstery atmosphere was gone. There were too many people. Pont-Aven had become fashionable; its bridges and alleyways were awash with clusters of 'cloisonnist' daubers and bourgeois on holiday, just off the train, were tucking into cured sausage at the Bois d'Amour. Marie-Jeanne Gloanec had a new hotel, the 'Ajoncs d'or'. Grumbling about these morons in shirt-sleeves, Gauguin settled in like the old lord of the manor.

Little now remained of Le Pouldu, which had been invaded by English bathers and loudmouthed families. Though de Haan had abandoned Marie Henry and her baby, she had given up her inn and married a *rentier*. She had no intention of going back to the old bohemian days; what is more, she knew better than to return the paintings Gauguin had once left with her to pay for his board and lodging, and refused to do so. Gauguin even went to court to get them back, but he lost the case.

On 25 May 1894, at Concarneau harbour, where Gauguin's gang were parading about, the men arm in arm with their girlfriends, there was an incident. Sailors and fishermen made fun of Annah the Javanese and her monkey. The women retorted and things escalated on the quayside when the ensuing fight turned into a pitched battle. The artists, outnumbered, came off worst. To escape from a beating, Seguin jumped into the water. Now alone, Gauguin stood up to the sailors, then collapsed with an agonising pain in his leg. His tibia was broken above the ankle, an open fracture from the men kicking him with their clogs. 'The bone stuck out through the skin ...' Half-conscious, he was carried to hospital on a stretcher, and from there to Pont-Aven in a trap. He would never walk in the same way again.

The weeks that followed were the start of a long convalescence. Confined to his hotel room, he alternated between phials of morphine and coarse red wine. He brooded over his disappointments and slept scarcely three hours a night. His friends had left; it was raining heavily over Brittany; Taoa, the pet monkey, had been poisoned and was now buried, and Annah had gone off, subsequently looting his Paris studio. Problems were piling up: the case against his Concarneau assailants, which he would rightly win; the court battle with Marie Henry, which would work out badly; his wrangling with the Dane Edvard Brandes, who was equally determined not to give back certain paintings. Brandes wrote: 'Over the last two years I have bought pictures from Mette for a total of ten thousand francs ... I have not the slightest desire to give any of them up. I perfectly understand this whim of yours – you are an artist – but you will understand that you are really asking too much.' The paintings were therefore not being seen as a pledge against a loan, but an outright bargain sale of pictures whose value had constantly risen. Gauguin had let himself be fleeced like a lamb.

The sky was overcast, its colour a dark slatey-blue. Windblown Brittany can be dismal. The paths were waterlogged, the undergrowth smelled of death; a man could well hang himself in these depressing strips of field. The struggle against so many petty interests, such indifference, seemed too hard. 'I've had to endure so much that I've lost heart ... and that of course means four wretched months and a lot of expense, with nothing to show for it ...' In another letter to Molard he lets slip the terrifying words: 'Done for ... can't go on ...'

Among the hydrangeas in the hotel's small garden, he could stagger no further than from the chair to the bench. He was to be plagued with pain to the end of his days because of this accident. His damned right leg! Still bedridden, he tackled work on the series of illustrations for his book *Noa Noa*. 'My leg is getting better, but I don't know whether it's because of the morphine or the endless rain, every bone in my body is hurting terribly ...' He confided in Molard: 'For the last two months I have had to take morphine at night and I am now dulled and exhausted; to deal with my insomnia I have to resort to alcohol every day ... Yes, I limp around with a stick and I am in despair at not being able to get far enough to paint a landscape.'

In Paris he learned that six of his paintings from the collection of Julien ('Père') Tanguy had found a buyer at a mere one hundred francs apiece. Yet again his genius was being spat upon. How was it possible to be hailed by Degas and Mallarmé, to be exhibited by Durand Ruel, have so many followers and continue to do battle for the avant-garde, yet be worth so little on the market: commercially next to nothing, at knockdown prices, just something put to one side? Why should he keep on painting, why should he be chained to this continent where nothing smiled on him? He thought about another departure for his New World.

Mette gave no answer. He hadn't seen his children. 'I am beginning to wonder whether I exist for my family . . .' He had neither a dealer nor a gallery any more. With envious eyes on the Durand Ruel stable, Ambroise Vollard had certainly offered him a helping hand, but though he set himself up at Rue Laffitte and subsequently exhibited some of Gauguin's works in March 1895, at this point he was only starting out as a dealer, without any clients and without a penny to his name. Vollard was a Creole from Réunion, a strange character known to be stingy as well as parasitical. Gauguin deeply mistrusted him. He described him as more of a scoundrel than Cartouche, the notorious eighteenth-century brigand. Once he had sniffed out his prey, he would circle closer and closer around him. He would play at being indifferent then be a charmer, and buy what he pretended to disdain for a rock-bottom price. Yet in 1900 this 'Cayman' would be Gauguin's lifebelt.

Where did he want to go now? Would it be Samoa, following in the footsteps of Robert Louis Stevenson? They speak Samoan and English there; would Molard find him a dictionary? Or would it again be Polynesia, enhanced in retrospect? He could take advantage of the hospital in Papeete to have his leg seen to. 'This whole series of misfortunes, the difficulty of earning a regular living despite my reputation, along with my taste for the exotic, have made me take an irrevocable decision. And this is it. In December I shall return and I shall work day in day out to sell everything I own, either all together or broken up piecemeal. Once I have the capital in my pocket, I shall leave again,' he told Molard in September. He elaborated to his friend Monfreid: 'If I am successful, I shall leave at once in February. I could then end my days free and undisturbed, without having to worry about what lies ahead and without perpetual battles with imbeciles . . .'

He still thought of taking one or two friends with him into exile: Seguin and O'Conor. Laval, his companion on the trip to Martinique, and the only one who had had the guts to go with him, had just died. Of course, his intentions could well have frightened people off, given his expressed desire to bury himself in the Pacific islands. Despite his pseudo-intrigues ('I was fighting to raise the stock of my pictures and I was putting about rumours of my departure to give them a certain rarity value', March 1895), he was prostrate with doubt: might it not be time to give up painting? 'Fame; what a futile word, what a futile recompense! As soon as I can, I'll be off to bury my talents among the savages and nothing more shall be heard of me . . .' His son Pola later wrote: 'He wanted to retreat under the palm trees, to try and find some serenity and wait for either life or death to come and seek him out.'

He got back to Paris, then came the hastily organised final selling-off of everything. 'Selling the whole caboodle, no matter what the price. The lot. If I can manage it, I'll leave right away . . .' First there is an exhibition in his studio, ecstatically received but without any sales. After this comes an auction at the Drouot, with forty-seven canvases, as well as engravings and woodcarvings. He asked the Swedish playwright August Strindberg to write a preface for the catalogue. Strindberg was then a wildly fashionable figure and the Molard family knew him socially. In his presence, the limping Gauguin had felt 'the shock between your civilisation and my barbarism'. However, Strindberg didn't know what to think of Gauguin, recognising the power of his work but at a loss for words when confronted with this 'tumult of sun-filled pictures'. His letter of refusal was published as it was in the catalogue, an ambiguous, paradoxical piece of writing that had its own effect. 'What is this? It is Gauguin, the savage who hates a civilisation that stands in his way; there is something of the Titan in him, jealous of his creator, in his spare time producing his own little work of creation . . .' It concludes: 'Goodspeed, master; just be sure to come back and come and see me. By then perhaps I will have learned how to understand your art better.' Gauguin sent this text to the newspapers and some of them published extracts. He saw it all as publicity, imagining that this would put him in the news. But in these few months public interest had been gripped by more serious events: the assassination of Sadi-Carnot, the president of the Republic, by an Italian anarchist in Lyon, in June 1894; and more recently, in December, the sentencing of Captain Dreyfus, in the celebrated affair that would occupy many column inches, as France became passionately divided over it. Social agitation was at its peak. The Republic was seen to be in danger and increasingly the police were picking up people for questioning. Artistic circles were targeted, under suspicion of anarchism. The critic Fénéon was arrested; Pissarro fled to Belgium; Mirbeau panicked. The last thing on people's minds was those forty-seven barbarian paintings.

On 18 February 1895, at three in the afternoon, echoing through an empty auction room, the chief auctioneer's hammer fell for the sale of eight paintings and nine drawings at pathetic prices. Schuff, Seguin, O'Conor, Maufra and Slewinski were there when Gauguin wound up by buying back his own paintings, through intermediaries, because they didn't fetch adequate prices. Degas took away six drawings at between twenty-five and eighty francs, a copy of *Olympia* for 230 francs, and the painting *Vahine no te vi* (*Woman with a Mango*, W449, 1892) for 450 francs. Slewinski, Maufra, the collector Halévy and the dealer Bernheim picked up small lots. Vollard got two engravings for a mere seven francs. After deductions for expenses, the final profit totalled around 2000 francs. This was the sum by the Inca in a letter to his wife, who demanded her share: exactly 464 francs and 80 centimes.

This was the knockout blow that sent him out of the ring. He had no illusions left. As if someone had given him a kick in the seat of his pants; so much for his uncompromising dreams. He summed things up in a letter to Mallarmé: 'For me the sale was pointless.' That night, Gauguin collapsed sobbing into Maufra's arms. They went to Maufra's, on Boulevard de Clichy, to have dinner. The 'painter of the century', as Aurier proclaimed him, remained a pariah. 'At the age of forty-seven, I do not want to descend into poverty and yet I am very close to it; I am on the ground and no one in the world will pick me up ...' What is more, he had contracted syphilis from a prostitute in Montparnasse.

Tirelessly, Morice kept up his efforts. In *Le Soir* of 28 June he wrote: 'Tomorrow a great artist will leave Paris, France and Europe, with no hope of return, and disgusted once and for all with the foul-smelling, rundown air that we breathe in this West of ours ... Yes, Gauguin is right to leave, and we should envy him for having a free homeland out there that can give him consolation for this one.'

On the platform at the Gare de Lyon, Judith gave him an armful of lilies. Dragging his bad leg behind him, the Inca went on with his wandering, in flight like a badly treated animal, a few thousand francs in his pocket. Just like Bernard and de Haan, Seguin and O'Conor failed to join him. 'Was he bluffing?' Morice wondered. 'I think he was. But he called his own bluff without weakening...'

The black-bolted hull was reflected in the dull water of the harbour. After he climbed the ladder, Gauguin was the loneliest person on board. This time, his tin trunk sitting on the bridge looked like a coffin. A sarcophagus. He was never to come back.

CHAPTER 29

The steamship *L'Australien* set sail from Marseilles on 3 July 1895. It called in at Port Said, where Gauguin bought a batch of forty-five pornographic photographs, and Sydney. He had a connection with the *Richmond* for Papeete from New Zealand on 29 August. While he walked around the gallery of Maori art in the ethnology museum in Auckland, filling his notebook with decorative motifs, like a vagabond pocketing alms, his wife imagined he was still at Rue Vercingétorix.

'I made my escape without any warning. My family will have to manage on their own,' he wrote to Monfreid.

This time he was bound on no official mission, no artistic sojourn. This wasn't a pleasure trip for the sake of bracing new horizons, but an exile, a desperate flight. His failure was confirmed. 'I fully intend to live out the rest of my life here, quite peacefully in my hut.' Behind him, he had left his paintings and the remains of his collection stored with a handful of friends, art collectors or brokers who were to deal on his behalf. In addition to his own works, what was left of his collection comprised some forty pieces, the bulk of them drawings, by Van Gogh, Lautrec, Pissarro and Signac. A certain Bauchy bought eight of these for 2500 francs, although this was on credit. He was already owed 800 francs by someone else, and 600 francs by another buyer. At Rue Saint Lazare, his broker Lévy assured him that his stock would rise again. When it came to his canvases, 'It is perhaps a matter of time, since your painting is not easy to swallow, but I'll do what is necessary,' Lévy affirmed. Gauguin trusted these people, particularly Georges Chaudet, a young artist with a great deal of tact and an interest in the Inca. As well he might have.

September 1895, arrival at the Society Archipelago and Papeete, where everything has changed. 'The capital of this Eden is now lit with electricity . . .' There are far more merchant ships in the harbour, and more coaches and traps on the quayside. The roads have been resurfaced, an abattoir has been built, and street lighting, along the roads and the seafront, bestows a greenish halo on the complexion of the *vahines*. Modernisation is under way in the administrative services, the Postal Service in particular, under the guiding hand of Henry Lemasson, the amateur photographer who was a friend of Gauguin. On Tarahoi Square there is even a merry-go-round with wooden horses revolving to the sound of the hurdy-gurdy.

There too, the political atmosphere is in turmoil: to the northwest, the islands of Bora Bora and Huahine were creating difficulties, while Raiatea-Tahaa continued to be unstable. These territories wanted to remain autonomous and were rashly playing into the hands of the British and of private interests. The battleship *Aube* was despatched with a delegation on board, and after numerous speeches, promises, celebrations, dances and banquets, order was restored. 'Four extra-ordinary days and nights of rejoicing, as on Kythera.' This was done by a combination of instilling fear, and giving small presents and assurances. 'Red balloons, little music boxes and other baubles.' The troops caught up with the last recalcitrants, who were armed with spears and war clubs, and deported the leaders. The French tricolour flew among the coconut palms. 'The work of civilisation, so it appears,' noted Gauguin, in part disgusted, as he made the most of the occasion to visit the islands.

Within a week or two, the Inca had returned to his old obsessions and was keen to strike out further: 'Next month I will be on La Dominique, a stunning little island in the Marquesas, where you can live practically for nothing and without any Europeans around. I'll be like a lord there, with my relative riches and my nicely set up studio.' While life in the capital was still beyond his means, he could get by with 500 francs a month in the districts, and with even less on a small far-flung island. And the Marquesas were certainly remote, necessitating a five- or six-day voyage due north by schooner.

For now, Gauguin set his baggage down in Punaauia, on the west coast, and rented a *fare* that looked out to Moorea. 'It is in a superb position, by the roadside, with a staggering view of the mountains behind me.'

'My hut was Space and Freedom!' The remainder of his legacy from Uncle Zizi was used to make improvements and enlargements to his rented home. He had 900 francs left in the kitty. However, thanks to the favourable exchange rate ('I used to get 125 Chilean francs for 100 French francs, and now they give me 200'), his nest egg was worth considerably more. And in Europe, with some paintings sold and money owed to him, he had more than 4000 francs due. With such a sum, alas only potential, he could envisage getting by for at least two and a half years – except that the potential was never realised.

At this time, the beginning of 1896, at Punaauia, on the shores of the opaline lagoon, Gauguin didn't give a hoot for fame and its accoutrements. Theories and groupings, declarations and aesthetic manifestoes could go to the devil; he had turned a fresh page. These last few years had knocked the stuffing out of him. 'The more I go on, the further I go down . . .' Let people give him what he is owed, leave him to his own devices to paint and carve what he sees fit, and then perhaps he'll go back to Europe. He expects nothing more from life except to be paid monies outstanding.

The mildness of the climate helped and he began to settle down: he found some of his old friends, made a number of female conquests, and he celebrated heartily, treating his people to rum and red wine. Tehamana came and left again, frightened by the sores on his legs, but a new *vahine* joined him: the fourteen-year-old Pahura, who gave him a son, Emile, born in 1899, after giving birth, in 1896, to a daughter who did not survive. Pahura was a docile companion, with him more out of self-interest than affection, but of little importance in the eyes of the painter. Finally he found the heart to get back to work, producing four canvases in 1895, and twenty-two the following year, one of these being the sumptuous *Te arii vahine (The King's Wife)*, W 542, where the Maori queen naked upon a green carpet is a more sensual evocation of Cranach's *Venus*. He considered this to be his best painting. 'As far as colour is concerned, I don't think I've ever done anything of greater resonance.' A primitive Venus, simultaneously innocent and perverse, sensual and indifferent, lying among menacing trees and fallen fruit, against a background of the seashore and the barrier reef. He also did a series of six paintings in the same format in warm and muted tones.

Imperceptibly, his art had changed because he himself had changed. Gauguin was on a different level; he responded to a different order. Destitute and inwardly broken, he was no longer the South Seas orientalist of old, the traveller with an eye to picturesque detail and shimmering textures. He had forgotten conventional lessons and immersed himself in the reality of this landscape, listening to its deep human reverie with empathy. Tahiti was part of him, or rather he was this reinvented Tahiti, the yeast that made the dough rise. His itinerary became his trajectory, each test a station in his stations of the cross. He climbed towards his revelation by way of renunciation.

One of the finest paintings in this series of six is *Nave nave Mahana (Delightful Days)*, W548, an archaic frieze in the manner of Puvis de Chavannes. It uses a range of muted reds, greens and yellows in a setting formed by column-like trees and long, decorative flowers, where women stand gazing out at the viewer, while a man and a child sit on the ground. In another, *No Te aha oe riri (Why Are You Angry?)*, W550, a vexed young woman in a blue sarong steps through the Edenic calm of her surroundings, against the pale, almost abstract mass of a *fare*. Returning to the Christian imagery which he was never to shake off, he also painted a powerful self-portrait; in it he is part prophet, part condemned man mounting the scaffold, face on, wearing a white collarless undershirt. He is accompanied by two thieves, these being *tupapau* outlined dimly in the shadows, and he looks like a vanquished warrior, still rebellious, with a bitter smile on his pinched lips – *Ecce Homo!* This painting is titled *Self-portrait Nearing Golgotha*, W534.

In June 1896, in the hospital where he had been admitted for his leg ('I have two open wounds that the doctor can't manage to close; in hot countries this is difficult'), the Inca dreamed up a scheme which would get him out of his financial predicament: fifteen people – friends or collectors – would each send him 160 francs, thus making a total of 2400 francs, in exchange for a painting each, or a consignment of fifteen paintings which would be allocated individually by lottery. To this end he asked Monfreid to contact Sérusier, Rouart,

Dolent, the Comte de la Rochefoucauld and Seguin, and to put this plan into action over a period of five years. He drew up a certificate: 'I take it upon myself to send every year in advance fifteen paintings executed conscientiously with artistic integrity, to be shared out between the signatories of this undertaking, which commits them to sending me annually the total sum of 2400 francs, signed: Paul Gauguin.' He added: 'It is clearly understood that I am lowering my prices, because this entails a commitment of five years.' This heartrending and original idea was never to come to fruition.

A year and a half after his arrival he was bailed out by two money orders from Georges Chaudet; 1200 francs came in December 1896, and the same amount the following month. In Paris, however, this loyal friend was unable to go on, since Gauguin's affairs were becoming burdensome. There were limits to his devotion, now that he was ill and indeed would not live long, and Gauguin did not realise this. He was weary of these letters from overseas that demanded, ordered and asked him to lend this or that canvas to one or other of the dealers, or to take it back and try with Vollard, Lévy or Schuff, who unfortunately took it upon himself to send Mette 'two sun paintings by Van Gogh'. It was Vollard who began to buy up Gauguin's works at knockdown prices, putting them on show in November 1896. The critics hailed this exhibition, but Gauguin only learned about its success later on. Vollard kept the proceeds for himself.

In Tahiti, Gauguin procured a portrait commission from the notary and businessman Goupil, and some work teaching drawing at his opulent villa in Outomaoro. This was paltry consolation when he was classified as a 'pauper' at the hospital. One unit of morphine a day for his leg, his wounds, his chronic eczema, his double conjunctivitis, his ulcerations and his syphilis, which had finally been cured. According to one of his biographers, Maurice Malingue, he spent no less than five stays in the common ward at Vaiamai. His medical record gives these details: weight 71 kilos 500 grams, and a scapulalgia, a disorder of the shoulder joint. He was treated with sulphur baths, zinc oxide salves, mercury ointment and injections of cacodylic sodium. Morphine became necessary.

The rest of the time, he survived as best he could, painting in his hut. 'Nothing comes for me, it is driving me mad.' Europe was like a mirage, an obliterated dream. News arrived with a three-, sometimes four-month delay. When he replied his letters were read a month or two later. His copies of the *Mercure* smelled stale. Moreover, sapped by his feelings of emptiness, he eventually sold off his shares. He had realised that in his *Vision after the Sermon (Jacob Wrestling with the Angel)*, W245, painted at Pont-Aven in 1888, from the point of view of the Bretons and the baffled Tahitians alike, he could be both the golden-winged angel and the Jacob in his homespun robe. Himself against his painting, against the others, himself against the void, himself against himself and against his double. Painting that, nothing but that.

At Punaauia, the *vahines* avoided him, suspecting him of carrying the plague. He now had fewer friends. His girlfriend Pahura bored him; he found her as lazy and foolish as a mare just broken in. Of course, he wasn't an easy man. His melancholic state made him violent and unpredictable, and he wasn't always in the mood for tenderness, with his legs swathed in pus-stained bandages, and with his jug of absinthe, taking sips of it hidden away in the coconut groves. 'All I wish for is silence, silence, and more silence.' He wrote to William Molard: 'Ever since my childhood misfortune has dogged me. I've never had any luck, never any happiness...'

Beneath the fearsome palms, in the roaring of the waves against the reef, like the beating of a giant pulse, a mystical crisis looms. Who can he hold on to, to stop himself from falling, to catch his breath again? Who is there to help him find the next question to ask, the next step to take him forward, the riddle of the Sphinx? 'Human beings need an open ear in order to hear, but God's ear has no hole, nothing. He hears and sees, perceives things without the aid of senses, which only exist to make things tangible to men; everything flows into him, by way of his soul...'

Could it be that this hollow reality was what he sought: God himself, in the crushing void?

CHAPTER 30

At Punaauia, the wooden house was mounted on stilts; it measured sixty feet by twenty-four and *niau* partitions separated the studio from the living area. It faced the lagoon and Moorea. Here at last was the Studio of the South Seas! After being thrown out by his landlord, Gauguin gave up his plot and had another hut built a stone's throw from the previous one, in April 1897. The piece of land cost seven hundred francs, 'too big for me but the only one for sale.' He was able to make this investment because of a ploy: the loan he had secured from the Caisse Agricole on the basis that he would be settling to work the land. As he put it in May 1897: 'I made an effort of will and overcame my pride; I persisted, I pleaded, I plotted and finally I succeeded . . .'

Indeed, as he had claimed to the bank with responsibility for development in the archipelago, he planned to reap a profit from the one hundred coconut palms on his property, 'which can bring me in 500 francs a year.' Vanilla would be an ideal complement, and fruit trees. Monfreid sent him seeds. Would it be mother of pearl or poultry next? 'Who knows! Perhaps one day I will manage to be free and safe from everything!' These ideas were forgotten as soon as he had pocketed the money. Gauguin the landowner painted, sculpted and engraved once again, not caring in the least about turning his patch of land to advantage.

It was then, in April, that he received a 'short, ghastly' letter from Mette, which hit him like a bomb and abruptly shattered his spirit: their daughter Aline had died. She was nineteen. Leaving a ball, she had caught a chill, come down with pneumonia, and died in Copenhagen on 19 January.

The version given by Pola, her brother, is that Aline had lost the will to live because of a disappointment in love, a marriage made impossible by rejection. She had not been 'good enough' for the parents of her fiancé. Sweet Aline who drew like her daddy, played the piano, spoke French better than the others, said she was in love with him, and whose photograph he treasured, one 'of her alone', with her light eyes, like those of a nordic Madonna.

For the Inca, under 'redoubled blows of unhappiness', this was the final nail in the coffin. If there was only this low ebb, how could he give anything? He became obsessed by suicide. His health deteriorated. This is his reply to Mette in June 1897: 'I have just lost my daughter and I no longer love God ... Her grave back there, the flowers, all that is mere semblance. Her grave is here close beside me; my tears are living flowers ...' This letter was to be the last between him and his wife. His closing words were: 'may your conscience sleep to prevent you from awaiting death like a deliverance.' Mette cut off all links; both of them had moved beyond hatred, to indifference.

'Where do we come from? What are we? Where are we going?' asked Gauguin, as his heart trouble worsened in the sun. 'My health is collapsing completely!' However, it was in this gruelling climate that one of his greatest works came into being. 'In terms of its execution this canvas is far from perfect, for it was done in just one month without any preparation or preliminary study. I wanted to die and in this state of despair I painted it without stopping for breath ...' This is W561, the painting whose title is that triple question; it is a huge oil painting, the pivotal fresco to which the eight pictures of the 96 × 130 series are attached. It is both a great spiritual testament and an artistic and philosophical summation; it measures four and a half metres by one metre and seventy centimetres, and has twelve figures scattered in four groups against a blue and green landscape, with the island of Moorea in the background. It brings in earlier studies and fragments of paintings. All of its decorative motifs, its symbols, and its unease as well as its lyricism, are mixed together into this 'musical poem'. In the centre a naked man, Saint Sebastian waiting for his arrows, is picking a red mango; to the left is a large Buddhist idol, whose 'arms raised mysteriously and rhythmically seem to point to the beyond'. There is an old man, a Peruvian mummy watching for death; a newborn baby lying on a blue stone; dogs, two cats, birds, a nanny goat; dreamy, solemn women, trees twisted above green lagoons. This is an Eden traversed by doubt, made hollow by the anguish of being human, mortal in other words, voiceless in the face of the enigma.

This masterwork was accomplished in a fever. 'Into it I put all the energy I could before I die, a passion so grief-stricken in terrible circumstances, and a vision so clear, without corrections, that its haste disappeared and the life in it emerged ...' The symphony was unrefined, complex and coded. 'I shall never make a better one nor another like it.' When he went to Punaauia to photograph it, Henry Lemasson returned with the painter's explanation: 'On the right, there is a child who has just been born; on the left there is an old woman with a symbolic bird, an omen of approaching death. Between these two extremes of life, there is an active and loving humanity. And within this terrestrial framework, is a statue symbolising the divinity inherent in humanity.'

At the beginning of 1898, seeing absolutely nothing arrive in the mail, and convinced that he had been forgotten by the entire human race, Gauguin went up into the mountains to kill himself. 'I had no revolver but I had some arsenic which I had hoarded during my bout of eczema.' He climbed onto a rocky plateau overlooking the lagoon and swallowed the grey powder, then burrowed into the ferns like a gundog, sheltering from the sun and waiting for deliverance. In vain: he must have taken too much arsenic and he had such dreadful spasms that he vomited up the poison. Hollow-eyed, his head buzzing, and distraught with the pounding in his temples and the burning pain in his gut, he staggered back down to the coast after a night of misery. He had lost out again; death had not deigned to take him.

In the dawn, as the cock crowed and spray bubbled up over the lagoon, Gauguin was both an old man and a child. His limping steps echoed on the coral path. Under the humming coconut palms, he was still alive. Hope was a thin seam of diamonds deep inside the mountain. He pushed open the door of his *fare* and collapsed onto his pallet, without having noticed the honey-gold colour of the sky.

'What a mad adventure was my travelling to Tahiti, but a sorry and dismal one...'

Gauguin kept going, 'harassed by creditors'. In July 1898, he entrusted the large W561 and the eight smaller canvases to an officer returning to France. It was exhibited by Vollard in December. Gauguin answered the objections of a number of critics with the retort: 'My dream cannot easily be taken hold of.'

He let go, became a poor white, for a time employed as a draughts-man in the office of Public Works for six francs a day, and with some renewed vitriol, took up journalism and pamphleteering, writing when he had something in particular to say. First he contributed to *Les Guêpes*, then he wrote for *Le Sourire*, producing four pages of satire on his own Edison duplicator. There was rage and bitterness in the articles he wrote for this waspish publication; serving interests other than his own, he launched attacks against the Governor, Gallet, the bureaucrats and Catholic priests, and the Protestant party. He even strayed head first into this stinking little colonial world that he execrated with diatribes against the Chinese, whose growing number disturbed the French. This was a shady compromise that diluted his powers and eroded his vital energies.

Up until 1900, the erratic money orders that came from Chaudet and Monfreid allowed him to keep his head above water and to juggle with loans, repayments and hospital expenses. Here and there a canvas would be sold, a collector would pay up. In Paris, Degas bought some pieces, as did Henri and Ernest Rouart, while Emmanuel Bibesco, a wealthy Romanian, became keenly interested in his work. Three hundred francs arrived in May 1898, six hundred and fifty francs in June, a thousand francs in November. This income was irregular, subject to the vagaries of shipping services and quarantine restrictions, at the mercy of rates of exchange and badly written addresses. Some-times it took six months between a sale and the money being cashed at the Tahitian branch of a bank. Polynesia was so far away. A few masterpieces were still to come, in one final burst: *Rupe Rupe (Fruit Gathering)*, W585; *Two Tahitian Women*, W583, where one of the two women, bare-breasted, holds out a dish of red flowers. There was also *The White Horse*, W571, commissioned by a pharmacist who turned down the finished painting because the animal had a greenish tinge.

But hope gave way to despondency. Sometimes he did sustain hope, and then not at all. It depended on his health and on the money orders. He limped miserably, he had an infection in one eye and the hot humid climate produced regular 'skin eruptions'. He no longer got on with his companion, Pahura. Although his mixed-race son, Emile, born in 1899, had the same name as his Danish elder sibling, Gauguin seems not to have had any interest in him. 'I am condemned to live after losing every moral reason to live.' It is true that he went on writing up until 1901, producing a number of treatises, including an essay on colour and another on religion, made wood engravings, carved sculptures, continued to inundate his correspondents with entreaties, and on three occasions despatched canvases to Europe from what he had left in his *fare*, but he never took up a brush again. Just his thumb running back and forth over the dried brush hairs, which were hard as stone. What did it matter, when Monfreid had his cellar bulging with unsold paintings?

Everyday life took up his attention, and its humiliating drudgery: 'What a lot of time is wasted in the search for our daily bread! The most menial tasks, shoddy studios and a thousand other hindrances. All this leads to despondency, and then to impotence, fury and violence ...' he wrote to André Fontainas in March 1899. 'I don't paint any more, except on Sundays and holidays,' he informed Maurice Denis with some irony. And his 'Papuan art' lacked any *raison d'être* once he heard about the breakthrough of his former Post Impressionist and symbolist colleagues, along with other Nabis. When Emmanuel Bibesco wanted to come to his aid, he told him, while remaining tactful, that 'I am currently organising my life so as gradually to give up my interest in painting, and withdraw, as people say, from the scene. I'll get on with writing, and perhaps do a little work on my bit of land.' Gauguin the gentleman farmer.

For all this posture of disengagement, when he heard about Chaudet's death at the end of 1899, he was choked with panic. The tap had been turned off. Who would represent him in Paris now? 'At all costs I need someone who is willing to replace Chaudet,' he insisted anxiously. Monfreid was in the provinces, Morice had no inclination for business; he thought of Sérusier or Portier, through Degas. De Haan and Mallarmé were dead. There remained Vollard, who looked after the interests of Cézanne and Redon.

Gauguin offered him an arrangement. 'I am placing all my hopes in this now.' After all, hadn't the dealer already exhibited his work? In March 1900, following a great deal of negotiation, a contract was signed for a monthly payment of three hundred francs, along with a supply of paint and canvas, against a yearly consignment of twenty to twenty-five works, which Vollard could sell at whatever price he wanted. Gauguin accepted, though not without reservations: 'It is Vollard's intention to exploit me.' But he was well aware that he had come to the end of the road, after taking up everything that had come his way in Tahiti.

However, although he mistrusted Vollard, with the exception of Theo Van Gogh, no dealer had ever offered him such a worthwhile proposition. In a letter to Monfreid in August 1901, he outlined his strategy: 'As soon as I have enough to live on for a year or two, I shall end things with Vollard, not abruptly but diplomatically . . . I have no intention of letting myself be exploited by a gentleman who has left me to languish in poverty for long enough to get my pictures at shameful prices.' So he agreed on terms with this uncaring, devious and self-interested dealer. He was saved, even if his instalments were already late and he had, paradoxically, stopped painting. 'I don't know how I shall manage to make good what Vollard has advanced to me . . .'

But there was a solution after all: one last shock of regeneration, virgin territory, a new emotional charge: moving on. Gauguin sold his *fare* for four thousand five hundred francs, repaid his debts and the interest he owed, and made ready to weigh anchor for the Marquesas, aiming to find the vital impulse to paint in those small islands. This was a financial as well as an artistic tangent.

This is the last act. One of the Marquesas islands, Hiva Oa or Fatu Hiva, the wildest if possible, 'still almost cannibalistic'. In this isolated part of the world there were very few functionaries, and above all very few whites. There were fruit-laden trees and docile girls who gave themselves for a handful of sweets. Their art was intact, and he had been able to copy decorative motifs from rare privately owned examples, weapons and tools. Moreover, he imagined that there would be immemorial customs still kept alive.

'It was time to head off to a simpler land . . .' Gauguin was fifty-two, with two years left to live. 'I think that with the ease of finding models, and with landscapes still to be discovered, in short with completely new and more savage elements, I am going to do good work on the Marquesas . . .' When he wrote to Morice he also said: 'The complete solitude I'll have there will give me a final blaze of enthusiasm before I die.'

He was ready for his final metamorphosis among the funerary tikis and the valleys smothered in lemon trees. He was called again; stripped by his art, his quest, dry as a climbing stem. All the better to burn.

CHAPTER 3I

Air Tahiti operates a shuttle service to Hiva Oa with a forty-eight-seater ATR 42-500. It gets to the Rangiroa atoll in the Tuamotu group in fifty minutes, and reaches Nuku Hiva in two hours and twenty minutes. After a half hour supply stop, the twin-engined plane heads on to Hiva Oa, 160 miles to the south west. Then it takes off in the other direction, its propellers scooping out holes in the hot air.

It's a daylight flight. Nothing ever seems to blemish this liquid eternity, except sometimes, as the nasal-voiced pilot points out, the white and green jellyfish shapes of the scattered islands, ringed with their diadem of coral. The plane is almost empty. A kid with 'Bulls of Chicago' on his baseball cap drowses among the seats, hiding facial burns behind big sunglasses. He is on his way back from New Caledonia, where he has had a skin graft.

We make our stop at Nuku Hiva. In the Terre-Déserte aerodrome, swept by the ocean wind from end to end as if this forms part of the decor, a noticeboard asks people 'to take care to collect fruit that has fallen to the ground in gardens and destroy it by burning.' In fact, the *Bactrocera tryoni*, the fruit fly, has spread through the valleys of Hatiheu, Aakapa and Tapivai. Tapivai? That's Melville's valley! The one the novelist went to in 1842 when he deserted from the whaler *Acushnet* with a shipmate and they headed for the mountains to elude their captain. Adopted by the 'noble savages', Melville spent eight weeks in what he would later described as a land of Cockayne. 'Over all the landscape there reigned the most hushed repose, which I almost feared to break, lest, like the enchanted gardens in the fairytale, a single syllable might dissolve the spell.' The first encounter with the inhabitants sets the tone. 'They were a boy and girl, slender and graceful, and completely naked, with the exception of a slight girdle of bark, from which depended at opposite points two of the russet leaves of the bread-fruit tree.' These people are tattooed cannibals, fierce-tempered but charming and childlike underneath. He has a romance with a beautiful Typee, Fayaway (Fay as in fairy). They swim in the mountain lakes and make love under the giant ferns. For the whaler, this escape is wonderful, plunging him into an enchanting Eden. Then, uncertain whether he is a guest or a captive, he outwits his vigilant hosts and flees to the coast where he finds another ship in port. *Typee*, the novel that narrates these adventures, was published in 1846, winning him instant fame 'for having lived among cannibals'.

Gauguin was not familiar with this extraordinary story when he exiled himself to the Marquesas. He had probably heard about it but could not have read it, since it hadn't been translated. The same goes for *Moby Dick*, published in 1851, in which the tattooed harpooner Queequeg appears on board, a South Seas 'savage', probably a Marquesas islander, his face and body 'checkered with squares', who is never without his notched spear and his coffin. This coffin gives the hero Ishmael a means of survival as a makeshift boat when the *Pequod* is shipwrecked. After Loti's tale, Melville's would have appealed to Gauguin. Even if the American writer did not stick to the truth, this picture of a newly embraced paradise would have been irresistible. It would have tickled his fancy and would probably have drawn him to stay in the valleys of Nuku Hiva, the trapeze-shaped island formed from two compacted volcanoes.

At Terre-Déserte I wait patiently if uncomfortably. Under the windswept foliage of the trees, scores of large wood wasps hover about threateningly. The kid with the burns that make him look like a *tupapau* has parked himself in the shade. Every fifteen minutes the helicopter takes on a load of five passengers whom it will deposit at Taiohae, population 1600, sparing them three hours on the road. In the time between, there is an extraordinary silence over these sea-girt fragments of lava which remind me of Ireland. A palpable, almost frightening silence that vibrates like a high-tension cable.

A young woman comes up to me, and in the Tahitian style she is instantly familiar, giving me a welcome kiss. Her name is Ida Clark and she works in tourism. She is my contact on Hiva Oa. For family reasons, she had made a return trip to Papeete and had been on the plane, though she hadn't ventured to approach me. It must have been my cannibal looks. Without further ado, I eagerly bring up the subject of Gauguin.

'Here, people said that he wasn't a good man,' she tells me. 'He drank and was a womaniser. He had a bad image, not like a settler sent out from France. You had to watch out for Koké.'

Koké, that was the name his Maori friends gave him. Gauguin, Coquin, Koké. I find it moving to hear it still used.

I ask her if there are many people who still have things of his here, even paltry objects. Ida confirms that there is a sewing machine at Puamau, on the north coast of Hiva Oa, the sewing machine Gauguin gave to his mistress, Marie-Rose Vaeoho, in 1901. She also tells me, naively: 'My older sister also has a painting she bought for five thousand Pacific francs from the nuns at Atuona. It's a Gauguin.'

'A painting of what?'

'A girl with a bare breast. It's red.'

'An original?'

'Yes, I think so. It's hanging in the living room. You should come and see it.'

'Tell her if she wants to redecorate, I can easily find her some nice wallpaper – it's no trouble.'

Gauguin took ship on the steamer *La Croix-du-Sud*, on 10 September 1901. He had trunks, furniture, a harmonium, a harp, three easels, a set of crockery, tools and utensils, a camera, timber and rolls of canvas. And a one-way ticket. It was a six-day crossing; the vessel was dependable and made regular connections. In addition to a cargo of sugar, biscuits and tinned goods, a number of planters, functionaries and missionaries were on board, variously disembarking at the different ports of call.

On September the 15th, the steamer sailed into the Bay of Taiohae at Nuku Hiva; on the 16th it reached Atuona on the island of Hiva Oa, in the southern group. Now weary, Gauguin decided not to go on as far as Fatu Hiva, which would have meant another stage, aboard a cutter. He disembarked on this reefless island, shaped like a seahorse, some 25 miles long and dominated by the 4000-feet-high Mount Temetiu. The Bay of Tahauku – known as the Bay of Traitors, in memory of the sailors lured into ambush there – is formed from a sunken crater, its slopes covered in bushy vegetation, and is quite staggeringly beautiful. A pale blue tongue reaches into the cove of black sand fringed with coconut palms. Tucked at the foot of mounts Temetiu and Feani, sheltered from the movements of the earth, the village of Atuona languishes in the shade. Its setting is imposing and it gives a warm welcome. At the beginning of the twentieth century, Atuona had 500 inhabitants, among them some acquaintances of Gauguin's: police sergeant Charpillet, and Doctor Buisson, who had attended him in Papeete. It also had a bank, two missions, a church, five shops and two bakeries. Why go any further? Gauguin set down bag and baggage in 'this outpost of civilisation'. It was an Asian man called Ky Dong who lent a hand and found him a room.

The landing strip is some eight miles north of the village. It was bulldozed out of the mountainside and seems very short. We manage to land nonetheless. I had made a reservation at the Hanakee Hotel and, behind the aerodrome building, a car is waiting to take me there. A man called Maurice awkwardly bedecks me with a garland of gardenias. Along with three other clients, a couple on holiday and a Customs official, we drive down the winding road to Atuona.

Hiva Oa, formerly known as La Dominique, is one of the three inhabited islands in the southern group of the Marquesas. It is 25 miles long and 10 miles wide, making an area of 150 square miles, and has a population of 1700, scattered over the valleys in clan groupings. A high ridge, the seahorse's backbone, runs from north to south. The island is a tropical hothouse, drooping with humidity, the air heavy with fragrances, the foliage of glossy trees reaching the ground. A land shrouded in kapok and mango trees, ringed by an ocean that seethes against the lava. In the island's interior, it is hard to breathe, while the coast is battered by a hostile wind. Magisterial downpours rinse the earth, soak it and scour it away before capriciously whirling off to another peak that darkens and flashes. With sudden shifts between deluges and sunshine, the climate is so unpredictable that it seems to be playing a game. There might be rain on the right side of the road but not on the left. The roadway dries so quickly it is like a sodden paste that hardens at once; there are permanent metamorphoses in the singing foliage.

Bend follows bend. I had set out at five that morning and feel more dead than alive. The scent of the gardenias makes me dizzy. I need to lift my spirits. When we arrive, the bungalows overlooking the Bay of Traitors and the 360-degree panorama of the mountains and the sea only leave me cold. I'm shattered and queasy and don't cast a glance at the Hanakee rock, a boat of stones and scrub out at sea off the beach at Atuona, where Gauguin painted his riders on the pink sand. I sit with a cocktail of fruits in my hand and scarcely hear a word of what I'm told by Serge Gatinel, the likeable manager of the hotel. His establishment, owned by an adoptive Marquesas islander, Serge Lecordier, is the only one open on Hiva Oa.

This is low season and only three bungalows are occupied, one of them mine; six others are being renovated. There are no bookings until the following Saturday, apart from someone's birthday evening. All the better! This makes me happy. Now that I've got as close to Gauguin as I can, I am drifting along in an obsessive daydream, which I have no wish to be drawn out of by conversations or incidental meetings. What is there to talk about? This project which has carried me across the world on the heels of vanished footsteps?

My bungalow has a sheer drop to the ocean. The hotel has been built on the mountainside, jutting out by means of terraces and overhanging supports; it gives the impression of being set amid two explosions of foliage above the Pacific. A band of cloud hovers over a ridge then tears and drifts off in shreds to be sucked into the trees. A sailing boat enters the Bay of Tahauku and joins the fleet of pleasure craft sheltered there. As far as the horizon you can see the wake of a tuna boat heading for Tahuata, where six hundred islanders work on copra production in enchanting bays that rise in steep verticals. Here there is no difference between sea and sky.

I spend an hour on the telephone, with Guy Rauzy, the mayor of Atuona, Joe Reus, who is in charge of the museum, and Louis Frébault, the great-grandson of Emile Frébault, the trader who was a friend of Gauguin. I shall see them later. Organising my stay to a strict schedule, after lunch I have a Landrover booked so that I can get to the other side of the island, towards Eiaone, Puamau and the Oipona site, where Gauguin made a drawing of the great Takaii, an idol carved from red tufa stone. I also plan to get to the valleys of

Taaoa and Tehueto to take a look at the petroglyphs. And, if possible, to make an appointment with the chief archaeologist, Pierre Ottino-Garanger. Meanwhile, I send a fax to Gilles Artur to confirm our dinner together the following week, and two more to France. Yes, I'm now the one all set to start work in the South Seas.

After a short nap and an iced tea, I pick up my pencil and tackle the master's correspondence again, from 1901. There are letters to Monfreid, Molard, Fontainas and Morice. Next to my bed with its mosquito net, I've pinned up reproductions of the Marquesas paintings: *And the Gold of Their Bodies*, W584; *Girl with a Fan*, W609; *The Enchanter* or *The Sorcerer of Hiva Oa*, W616. I have also arranged my travelling library and gathered my notes together, like a soldier polishing up his kit before battle.

Being here is a test for me; it's the point of impact between my book and reality. In the bay, behind the beach and that curtain of slender coconut palms, are his house, his plot of land, his grave, Oviri, his descendants. Him, still there. Soon night falls, dense and blueish like carbon paper. The stars are brand-new nails. Three agama lizards watch me from the thatched roof.

CHAPTER 32

'Hey, trousers! White trousers! I want your trousers!'

The guy was lounging against a mango tree, and he was mean-looking. A girl was beside him. She too was drunk on Hinano beer, or on something else. Downy creatures glided through the moist Atuona air, their wings beating back. The sun wasn't unbearably hot yet; I could feel it on the back of my neck and my shoulders.

'And what will you give me for them?' I replied.

'Two coconuts!'

'So I'll be left with nothing on?'

'With nothing on and without your shoes because they're too smart by half!'

'I'll make a deal with you. You stay here, don't move, and when I come by again a year and a day from now, they'll be yours because you asked for them first. OK?'

The girl wasn't so drunk as he was, and she was laughing even more now. The guy hadn't caught my drift and was shouting. I turned my back on him before things turned nasty. For a first encounter it was unpleasant.

I have an appointment with Joe Reus, a Frenchman who settled on Hiva Oa in 1984, and an amateur painter. In his villa surrounded by flowering plants in pots, he has a lodger: a Spanish woman who has made the village her temporary home. People have told me that she's a stunning young woman, and a fierce one, getting over an unhappy love affair in these blessed islands. I shall try to catch a glimpse of her.

'She's given the whole of Hiva Oa a hard-on!' Maurice told me at reception.

Reus takes care of the Segalen-Gauguin museum and the Maison du Jouir on a voluntary basis. Or rather, what is left of its reconstruction. Not very much, in fact: a rickety, broken-down wooden *fare*, empty. On the outside steps, a guy in the same mould as the one I met earlier is smoking some ganja and muttering to himself, vacant-eyed. At Joe's arrival, he scoots off towards a line of banana trees.

This first copy of the Maison du Jouir is in a sorry state. You could easily break a leg on that rotting floor, where light pokes in through the wooden planks. There's not a single piece of furniture, just a board on a trestle, with three or four warped photographic prints which have gone mouldy. The portrait of Segalen in his naval officer's uniform is badly fly-blown. There are holes in the roof. It's pitiful. We make our exit.

'The next one will be much better and this time it will face the right way,' my host promises.

Reus is as skinny as a rake, balding and pale-eyed. He wears a red T-shirt, linen trousers and flip-flops. He developed a passion for the wild man of the Marquesas, 'the man who makes men', and collects whatever he can find. He shows the site to enthusiasts and offers them a tour of the adjacent museum. This displays a number of letters, photographs and facsimile documents, as well as some forty-odd copies of works, made by Alin Marthouret, an eccentric who arrived here one day in a sailing boat and got it into his head that he would reproduce Gauguin's work, or at least the work of his Marquesas period. The project was supported by the mayor of Atuona, Guy Rauzy, but Papeete didn't like it. Marthouret's work had served as the basis for a local exhibition in 1996, with forty-one paintings on display, but the people who set this up saw the copies as the potential basis of a second Gauguin museum which would short-circuit the one in Tahiti. In exchange for lodging and a monthly fee, Alin Marthouret had undertaken to deliver two hundred major works, to the increasing annoyance of Gilles Artur, who was making strenuous efforts to secure original pieces in Papeete. The issue was to do with quality, philosophy too. It sometimes happened that Marthouret gave away one or two of the paintings to generous visitors.

'We often find ourselves dealing with hysterics,' Reus told me. 'Gauguin is our Eiffel Tower! You get Americans coming off the

Aranui, the cargo ship that runs between the islands, and wanting to grab everything. They want us to take the works off the wall and wrap them up in newspaper for them, and would you believe, they bring out their American Express cards. It's crazy! Then there have been things like that Asian television channel that asked me to pose in a sarong, naked from the waist up; I was supposed to pretend to be Gauguin. They couldn't have cared less about the chronology! Another time, I had a Japanese woman who felt faint when she was fondling the Master's printing press. It was from Gauguin's day, but of course it didn't actually belong to him. You should have seen her moaning and stroking the handle of the thing, whispering "Gauguin, Gauguin ..." I think she had an orgasm.'

So the copies are there on the walls, in brilliant colours, almost fluorescent, overdone. The original dimensions have been disregarded, and though the drawing has been captured in its outlines, the colours are very approximate. They have neither the subtlety nor, above all, the sheen of the originals. They are fakes, that's obvious. Does it matter?

'I warn my visitors: everything here is artificial. Otherwise, to be honest, what would there be for them to see? Why come to our island? For Gauguin's grave and Jacques Brel's? That's not enough for a twenty-five-hour flight from Europe.'

'What about Marthouret?'

'He went on his way, not very happy about it. He'll be in France now.'

Reus locked the door to the museum and went on talking.

'We get school groups coming. I try to make them see that this is their heritage; and sometimes it's their own great-grandmothers in the paintings. But that's all in the past.'

In fact, for the centenary of Gauguin's death and the Marquesas Festival of Arts in 2003, the municipality has released a budget of fifty million Pacific francs, which is to say a quarter of Hiva Oa's entire annual budget. This means the purchase of the painter's original plot of land, clearing this land and reconstructing the Maison du Jouir according to exact plans and materials. In addition, there is to be a library and the opening of a cultural centre designed around a permanent exhibition, two or three *fares* to be made available for grant-aided artists, and the employment of two copyists to complete Marthouret's project.

A short drive in Joe's car brings us to the building site, opposite the old colonial grocery of Ben Varney, the sole vestige of the time, where Gauguin bought his wine and his tinned goods. A sharp turn to the right and the four-wheel-drive pitches about as we plough on and over a ditch, then we come to a halt. All at once I can see Gauguin's plot of land as it was, as he described it 'covered in stones and scrub'; now it is levelled and bare, scored with wheel marks from the heavy vehicles of the Public Works department. This was his last plot, a rectangle measuring a little over an acre. This was the very spot where he found his 'splendid isolation', between the house of Tioka, to the west, and the school run by the monks, to the east. To the north is the razor-edged mountain, seamed with cataracts. To the south, beyond a line of dazed coconut palms and a few lopsided shacks in yellow, green and blue, is the shore with its concrete landing pier to one side.

When I got out of the car I bent down to gather a small handful of the damp, greasy, blood-red soil. This was what he owned. The Inca's last patch. 'A hammock for taking a nap out of the sun, cooled by the sea breezes that waft through the coconut palms from the sea just three hundred yards away. I am right in the centre of the village and yet it would be hard to tell my house is here because it is so well surrounded with trees,' he wrote, glowingly. This was the final refuge of the man and the artist who was driven by his solitude, his desire for revenge, his need to be reborn. 'You have no idea how peacefully I live here in my solitude, quite alone, greenery all around me . . .' It was indeed a Maison du Jouir, a house of joy and pleasure.

It is hot as I walk. I try to memorise the stale, overpowering taste of this turned-over earth, the violet mass of the peaks, the vegetation that sprouts from them like a beard, the fragrant breath of the wind. It's a theatre. A natural sloping theatre, rolled out and open right to the Pacific's heaving edge, a tamed monster that licks the lava of extinct volcanoes.

In the adjacent field, a horse vacantly grazes on tufts of yellow grass. A motorcycle putters towards Tahauku Bay. It vibrates through the trees and the bushes. Further away, out of sight, someone is listening to the radio. Each sputter and crackle dies out in this superior silence that swallows it up, drinks it in and takes possession of it.

Reus goes on with his expansively detailed technical explanations.

'The Jouir was set on this axis, with the door facing the mountains. It had an upper floor, which was quite unusual for a private dwelling.'

The fact was that, with the help of two carpenters whom he plied with rum, Gauguin had designed his house to meet his needs precisely. The building was some forty feet by eighteen, had a roof thatched with pandanus leaves and was mounted on stilts. The ground floor was divided by bamboo partitions covered in *niau*, into a kitchen, a dining room, a sculpture studio with a workbench, and a shed for the trap. Close by was a well and 'a bathtub made of lime and shingle, raised some twenty inches above the ground and this deep.' To get to the floor above there were stairs with a handrail; here was a bedroom which extended into another studio and a music corner. There were a few bookshelves and trunks that could be locked. As decoration he had 'barbarian paintings, trophies, war clubs and boomerangs'; reproductions of works by Degas, Holbein, Raphael and Manet; Japanese prints, and the pornographic photographs from Port Said. Like Maori huts in New Zealand, the front door and its frame comprised five carved panels, with the famous 'MAISON DU JOUIR' engraved on the lintel. On the left, there was a clear invitation to women: '*Soyez mystérieuses*' (Be mysterious), and on the right: '*Soyez amoureuses et vous serez heureuses*' (Be in love and you will be happy). A rule as much as it was an entreaty.

Although it was exceptional for this part of the world, the house was nonetheless rustic and sparsely furnished. Gauguin was no nest-builder. This was a den and a larder rather than a residence. The liquor salesman Louis Grelet, who visited the place while the artist was alive, left his description: 'A thin partition separated this room (his bedroom) from his studio, which seemed extremely big but extraordinarily untidy – a real pigsty! In the middle of it was a small harmonium, and at the back were some easels, beside a large picture window, where the artist worked.' He added: 'I had been struck by seeing how a man who had known affluence could make do with such lack of comfort!'

In the village, the atmosphere was very friendly. At least to begin with. With the Catholic missionaries he acted the part of a good parishioner, going to mass, the point being to win them over. In addition to Ky Dong, he had quickly made friends among the whites. The shopkeepers marked him down as a customer, and the exiles as a fellow-boozer and something of a daredevil. When it came to women, he wasted no time, and had his eye on the girls' boarding school. 'You can be a little Sardanapalus here without any trouble or cost,' he quipped.

The devil was in Atuona, and he looked like a faun; limping and laughing, sunny and ready for action. The Inca proclaimed loud and clear that he had regained his desire and the source of his power to paint: 'Here, poetry flowers of its own accord and all I have to do to prompt it is let myself dream while I paint. I ask for just two years of good health and not too many money worries so that my art can achieve some maturity.'

Delighted and a bit puzzled, I walk up and down, getting my trousers and my shoes in a mess, reconstructing what I know about his time here in the space of this empty rectangle, his 'final setting'.

'What about the Makemake, the river that ran through his garden?'

'Over there, further up. It flooded in 1903; he talks about it in his letters to Monfreid.'

'Do you think these coconut palms were here then?'

'They're too young. The tallest can't be any more than forty years old.'

Fifteen yards further on, three metal sheets laid out crosswise bring me to a halt. What are they covering up? I go over and lift one of them with the tip of a finger. Reus is watching me. He is deliberately holding back and relishing my curiosity.

'You've found it.'

'Sorry?'

'I'm going to tell you something. We managed to locate his well. And that's how we worked out which way the house faced.'

'The well where he hung his bottles of absinthe at the end of a fishing rod to chill them? The well of the Jouir?'

'Nobody knew where it was, because the river was unstable and it shifted the ground and its boundary lines. For years it was nearly ten feet deep in undergrowth. When he died, in 1903, after the gendarme's sale that meant his possessions were dispersed, the Jouir was dismantled, and the wood and stone shared out. The last of his things, if they were deemed to be without any value or use, were thrown into the well. The plot changed hands several times; it belonged to the Taporo company, then Donald & Co, which was a shop, then it had a Chinese owner, Sin Tung Hing, who sold it to the municipality. By then, of course, people had forgotten the whole story.'

'It became a legend.'

'Less than three months ago we brought some things up out of it.'

'How come?'

'On 10 February, we were clearing the ground for the work ahead; there were four of us: Saucourt, a guy from Resources, Lecordier, who owns the Hanakee, Gaubil, who's a shopkeeper in Atuona, and myself. The earth plough came up against some stones in a semicircle. We started digging and found more stones underneath, in a circle supporting these, and it went deeper and deeper. So here was a stone structure below a crust of earth. And it was the well! We had to clear out rubble, detritus, broken glass, to a depth of nearly five feet, and empty out stagnant water with buckets. Finally, we used an electric pump and we managed to bring up what was there as far as eleven or so feet down.'

'And then?'

'We didn't want to broadcast our find, we wanted to keep it for the museum inauguration. There was an article in the local press. The amazing thing was that the sandy mud in the well had kept the things that had been thrown down there in a state of preservation.'

As he spoke, Reus removed the cross-laid metal sheets one by one. Underneath was a dark, deep hole. The well of the Maison du Jouir. Like an eye put out, a trap door, an uncovered grave.

'What things?' I asked, staring into the abyss, my heartbeat quickening. I knew there had been a walking stick with its knob carved in the shape of a phallus, thrown into the well.

'Various objects.'

'Do you still have them?'

'I just have to get them together. They are divided up between the four of us for the sake of security. We amateur archaeologists! In principle, there's no problem about you seeing them.'

'What exactly are they?'

'I don't want to go into too much detail: let's say that there are shards of plates, medicine phials, a glass syringe, teeth in a container.'

'Did these belong to Gauguin?'

'We can't tell.'

'All the same, his well!'

'Well . . . so it seems.'

Facing me, on the other side of the road, a golden shaft of sunlight poured into the colonial shop, lighting up the glass shelves, the tins and the bottles of Hinano beer. A Chinese man came out of the Varney grocery and mounted his scooter. Then the shaft of light shifted, adjusted by the clouds, combining with another shaft, and this beamed out like a spotlight. Under its veil of foliage and palms, the plot of land became a chequerboard of light and shadow, and the black well, Reus and myself became the chess pieces in an esoteric game. The air vibrated with it. I dared not move another inch. I was at Gauguin's house, and he was still there. My voice and his among the tangle of things growing.

CHAPTER 33

Among his new friends were Tioka, a warmhearted Marquesas islander with whom, in accordance with custom, he exchanged his name; Reiner, a former gendarme; Guilletout, a Basque, a hunter and woodsman, and Emile Frébault, a former non-commissioned officer in the infantry who had become a shopkeeper. There was also Nguyên Van Cam, known as Ky Dong.

'Who is he really, this Ky Dong?' Gauguin wondered maliciously. It was a startling encounter all these thousands of miles from civilisation. Ky Dong was an educated and cultivated young man of twenty-six. He had had a scholarship at the court of Huê and then at the lycée in Algiers, was a bachelor of science, spoke and wrote French, dabbled in painting, composed verses, and had a qualification as a physical education instructor. Ky Dong means the rare child, the wondrous child, and, as it seemed, he had been an extremely gifted boy, so much impressing the French Resident at Nam Dinh that the latter helped him along the way with his studies. Behind his affable countenance, the young man was a politico, a former anti-colonialist leader who had united students and intellectuals around him in far-off Indochina, the Indochina that Gauguin had planned to get to in 1889. When Ky Dong had been sentenced to deportation to Guyana in 1897 for subversive activities, the authorities had left him here, on the way, at the Governor's charitable request. He had married a Marquesan woman and settled down to start a family. His official job was as an orderly. When he met the painter as he got out of the rowing boat, he already knew him, not through his work but because of the stands he had taken in the satirical journal *Les Guêpes*. They were two rebels, two outcasts greeting one another on the black sand of the beach.

In the early weeks, Ky Dong found Gauguin a lodging while he waited for the Maison du Jouir to be completed. He also found him girls, since the painter was looking for them. The first was a twenty-year-old Marquesan, Fetuhonu, who had a club foot. The limping pair made people laugh.

'What wonderful models!' Gauguin proclaimed, back at work, urged on by his contract with Vollard. By contrast with 1900, a year that produced nothing, in 1901 he completed fourteen paintings, and twenty-four in 1902. 'From the beginning my work forms a whole ... Moreover, my living so utterly far away is proof enough of how little I seek some transient glory ...'

During this period, Gauguin was in his element. His standard of living was higher than what he had known. He owned a house, a horse and a trap. As was his habit, he spent his money carelessly, mostly at Varney's, where he got credit in the periods between the ship's arrivals in port. 'My neighbour is an American, a charming fellow, with a well-stocked shop where I can find everything I need.' The accounts records show that he laid on plenty of refreshments for his friends. In December 1901 Gauguin paid a bill for 90 bottles of red wine and 16 bottles of rum. In March 1902, this lover of Bordeaux in preference to Burgundy, tired of inferior quality, tried to have a cask of good wine sent from France, through Monfreid and Fayet. 'I say good, because wine that travels so far and arrives in a hot country must be specially selected. I think that wines from the Midi turn bad easily, becoming vinegary. Of course, in exchange for a painting ...'

To brighten up their parties, where there was singing, dancing and playing of the mandolin and the harmonium, Ky Dong wrote a play, *Les Amours d'un vieux peintre aux îles Marquises* (*The Loves of an Old Painter in the Marquesas*), about the erotic arguments between a driven artist and a hunchbacked woman. There were three acts, written in alexandrines and, amid much raising of glasses, this strong-minded bunch laughed until the tears streamed down their faces.

One of Gauguin's acquaintances, in a different mould, was the pastor Paul Vernier who ran the Protestant mission. A widower, isolated, with the Catholics powerfully ranged against him in great numbers, he too was an intellectual. As a fervent reader of Flaubert, he enjoyed discussing the master of Croisset under the papaya trees with Gauguin. Both of them were thrilled by *Salammbô*, the 1862 novel set in Carthage, somewhere between an antique costume drama and an operetta. Gauguin lent him Mallarmé's poems, *L'Après-midi d'un faune*, and made him a present of a drawing. After Doctor Buisson went back to Papeete, Vernier, who had some medical experience, supplied the painter with morphine from his mission hospital.

For, by fits and starts, even with brief remissions, his state of health was deteriorating. His heart was getting weaker, he suffered from eczema and the after-effects of syphilis, and his badly healed ankle tortured him in the humidity of the climate. Flies plagued him, settling on the sores in his legs. 'I have begun to get back to work quite seriously, even though I am always ill.' In the portrait of him sketched out by Ky Dong before Gauguin himself painted it, *Self-portrait with Spectacles* (W634, 1903), he has sunken cheeks, his short hair is turning white and he wears thick spectacles. Privations and excesses meant that he was living his life on a short fuse. 'A quite premature old age,' he had concluded when he was still in Tahiti. 'For some years now I have endured eczema on both feet, and halfway up my legs, and over the last year in particular I have suffered a great deal.' From 1902, he got about only in the trap, holding the reins of his bay horse and following the tracks at a jog. He used a phallic walking stick to lean on if he needed to stand up.

As for the women in his life, after he tired of Fetuhonu, he seduced Tohotaua, a magnetic Maori redhead from the island of Tahuata. She was a mistress whom he would use as his model for two major canvases: *Girl with a Fan*, W609, painted from a photograph taken by Grelet, and *Contes Barbares*, W625. But, underneath this licentiousness, he still suffered from a profound loneliness, and kept looking towards the boarding school with the aim of finding a serious involvement with a woman. For Atuona was precisely where pupils from the whole archipelago were brought for schooling. The boys went to the Ploërmel Brothers and the girls were entrusted to the care of the Sisters of Saint Joseph of Cluny. The old goat was hoping to come up with a catch from this playful adolescent hothouse. Which is exactly what he did, by enticing the fourteen-year-old beauty Marie-Rose Vaheoho; she had a bronze body, the hair of a goddess and the laugh of a child.

This boarding school still exists today. On Sunday afternoons the young girls go to the beach to bathe, with the nuns encircling them. Around four, when it's time for a snack, they go back to their dormitories. In an orderly procession, they file past Gauguin's plot of land, passing the Varney grocery and, leaving the church behind them on the right, walk through Atuona as the boys ogle them and act tough on their mopeds. This was a sight that I myself did not want to miss, in that sweetish scent of late afternoon, when the whole island released the breath of its sap and the copra exuded its buttery fragrance from the drying sheds. That Sunday, I too found a parapet to perch on, let my legs dangle and, while pretending to be making notes, waited for them beside Maurice, who was seething with impatience. Finally they arrived, with wet hair and towels around their necks, their flip-flops dragging on the bitumen. Two or three of them were singing a silly little song; others clumped together arm in arm, or with arms around waists, their satin-smooth skins reflecting the blue of the sky or the moist shade whenever they stepped under it. Some of them walked alone, a Walkman fastened to their heads. But all of them looked back at those who watched them, certain of their power, their grace, and this provisional freedom. Thirty, forty, fifty naiads, aged from thirteen to sixteen, who chortled as they passed you, holding your gaze with aplomb; a small battalion of prisoners simultaneously calmed and excited by the sea air, and whom the local fellows would probably meet up with in the garden of the boarding school that night, following the 'motoro' tradition.

As he had done for Tehamana in Tahiti, Gauguin went to the shop with the beautiful Marie-Rose and made what was essentially a contract of cohabitation. This was done over the counter at Varney's on 18 November 1901. Since the purchase was recorded in the register it had the value of a notarised deed; for 244.50 F: six yards of cotton fabric, eight yards of chintz, ten yards of calico, seven yards of muslin, ribbons, lace, three reels of cotton thread and a pedal-operated Singer sewing machine, whereby a dozen dresses could be made. Marie-Rose's parents were satisfied; so too was she, and she moved into the eccentric abode for which the painter had engaged a maid and a cook, for roughly ten francs a month. In 1902 she gave Gauguin a daughter, Tahiatikaomata, who was to leave descendants on the island.

'You could go to his house and sit there smoking and talking for as long as you liked, and he would never show any ill humour,' according to one contemporary witness, Guillaume Le Bronnec. 'He was very fond of women; he would sit among them so as to caress them.' The Maison du Jouir was well named; to the great displeasure of the missionaries and the religious congregation, it smelled far too much of sulphur and depravity. Now with debts to no one, the Inca didn't give a damn. He only had to keep on sending his consignment of canvases to Vollard and he could do as he pleased. He told Monfreid: 'I can live very well on 250 francs without stinting myself, since the cost of living is much lower here than in Tahiti.' Joy flared again like a smouldering fire. Was he really happy? He claimed to be in his letters to his last friends, still shivering back in Europe. Yet, Frébault recounted, at night, alone in the darkness of Atuona, Gauguin played the harmonium just as Captain Nemo played the organ in the fastness of his *Nautilus*. Now he, as Vincent van Gogh had once been, was wrecked by 'inner despairs of great magnitude'.

'Gauguin narrated a different life from the one he led . . . This is the one that he painted and this is the one that helped him to paint,' argued his biographer Leprohon. If his body stayed well, this could be a state of grace. Admittedly, the Marquesas barely resembled the description of them to be found in Max Radiguet's *Derniers Sauvages*, but the Inca was occupied with his work, and what more could he ask? Among the paintings of this period are *And the Gold of Their Bodies*, W584, where women are naked in wild woodlands; *Riders*, W597; *Bathers*, W618; *Marquesan Man in a Red Cape* (also known as *The Enchanter* or *The Sorcerer of Hiva Oa*), W616; *The Offering*, W624. And, in response to his dealer's request, still lives, which were considered to be more commercial: *Still Life with Grapefruit* (W631), begun in Tahiti and much like Cézanne in style; *Sunflower Seeds and Mangoes* (W606), which Gauguin mischievously subverted by giving the petals eyes.

'I feel myself to be right where art is concerned.' At Atuona he says he is drunk on this light, this land of generous trees and strange rocks. In spite of the priests' edicts and the plundering carried out by the ethnologists (Karl von den Steinem's mission in 1897–8), he was able still to find a few bracelets made of hair, necklaces made of teeth, fan handles and stilt stirrups and jewellery made of tortoiseshell or bone. He met up with witch doctors, and with old men who had been cannibals, and he drew from photographs the wild-eyed tiki of Takaii, the giant of strength and balance. He knew that in the mountains, near the cataracts, now ruined and reclaimed by the jungle, were the places of taboo cults and the *pae pae*, platform dwellings formed from blocks of lava. Their remains were enough; he was here at the world's beginning, in the time of the ancient gods.

He assimilated that art of carving which made infinite variations upon the human figure and its derivations, as decoration for fabrics and utensils, paddles and clubs. 'There seems to be no awareness in Europe that there was a very advanced art of decoration among the Maoris of New Zealand and the Marquesas Islanders ... The basis of this is the human body or face. The face especially. It is astonishing to find a face where you at first only saw a strange geometric figure. It is always the same and yet never the same thing,' he wrote in *Avant et après*. Yes, these motifs are always the same: man. The only answer to the riddle of the Sphinx.

At Hiva Oa, the Inca realised that he could become someone else, or rather that life is multiple, and that on the other side of this exoticism and primitivism which he was going beyond, were the countless facets of an identical reality that he embraced, the beating powers of a world that he captured as a medium. He was no longer engaged in the 'pursuit of appearances' but, like a shaman, he was listening to the potent breath that emanated from everything, including himself. As he said: 'I held the paintbrush and the Maori gods guided my hand.' He became aware of this 'great Diversity', of a sense of Otherness, of a burgeoning. In this permanent state of hypnosis, he came to burn with that 'last fire of enthusiasm' while his friend Haapuani, a sorcerer, told him about legends and about those words of the world's origin that fray and become obliterated with each passing generation. Indeed, it was too late. But his reverie continued and became transformed, since imagination stood in for reality. On the stairs of his *fare* he carved and decorated tikis, walking sticks, plates and spoons with which he ate his *poé*. He was no longer the Gauguin of rue Laffitte, nor the Koké of the Marquesas; he was merely prodigiously and awesomely alive. And mortal. Each second counted amid the flowers that were eyes. In the Maison du Jouir, there is a yes.

CHAPTER 34

At the Hanakee Hotel, the manager, Gatinel, fixed up the evening nicely: he invited the archaeologist Pierre Ottino-Garanger to dinner. The latter was a slim, almost skinny guy, a little Asian in looks, and around forty. He was a researcher at the CNRS, heading an Orstom mission, and since 1981 had been working in collaboration with the department of archaeology in Polynesia. Together with his wife, Marie-Noëlle, he had been involved in a number of projects directed by Professor Leroi-Gourhan.

Ottino-Garanger had made enormous strides with only a tiny budget, working on the different sites in the Marquesas. And there were a great many, even on Hiva Oa alone. The most renowned of these is still Oipona, on the north coast, because of its monumental tikis, one of which is the Takaii, which rises to a height of nearly nine feet. It is made of *keetu*, red volcanic tufa stone, and represents a warrior chief. As Bob Putigny explained in his book *Le Mana*, 'the tiki is an anthropomorphic or non-figurative representation of a god, a spirit, an ancestor or a dead hero', and: 'These were endowed with a sacred force, a *mana* which was powerful to one degree or other. They functioned as accumulators of supernatural energy.' Their power works through a kind of capture and containment, and should be treated with extreme circumspection since it can turn back on anyone who stands in its way. By means of rituals, channels and sacrifices, they were recharged like batteries. It was the role of the tikis to intercede between men and the gods who invested these stone images with the power to communicate with the priest, the *tau'a*. Thus inspired, the priest would speak in their name. A trembling of leaves, the flight of a tern or a tropic bird, a shifting sky, the sound of something stirring among the banyan trees, all crystallised the divine presence, and on the *meae*, the sacred space, every support, every feather, every wooden framework and woven fibre irradiated. Now on the sites which are still *tapu*, magic places, the majority of these totems are inert. It is said of a tiki that it is empty or alert. In the latter case, people say, columns of ants avoid it.

I could have talked to Ottino for hours; the subject fascinates me. Let's say, in short, that I believe in it. As night falls on Mount Feani, I go on bombarding him with questions. Most of all I want to know about the significance of the grimacing face of these stone foetuses.

'The narrow-eyed gaze expresses supernatural power that is knowing and transcendent; the nose expresses energy and powerful breath; the mouth the force of challenge. We can judge this "grimace" to be the expression of their certainty of winning, the mark of their superiority.'

From his bag Ottino takes some large sheets of tracing paper then rolls them out in front of us. These are his most recent finds: thickly pencilled markings that produced a reverse image of the surface outlines of these monsters. I then talk to him about the petroglyphs at Tehueto, which I had gone to see that very morning in the valley of Faakua before it got too hot. They made quite an impression on me: lizard-men, lobster-men, half-birds, half-monkeys, who seemed to drift through the air, their arms raised to the sky; kites made of flesh or shell, magic tracings running across the basalt rocks, suspended in this seam of stone for all eternity.

'We know very little about them. There are various hypotheses.'

We take our seats at a round table and Serge Gatinel has our glasses filled from a frosted bottle of Sylvaner. Reus and his Spanish woman friend have joined us. Nathalie wears a clingy black dress and looks shy; she must be twenty-five or twenty-six. She is fine-boned and has melancholy velvety eyes. The dinner promises to be a pleasant one.

'Do you have a job in Atuona?'

'I work with Joe,' she replies quietly. 'We do handpainting on silk — T-shirts and scarves for the tourists.'

She seems wary. Is it my charm or the reason for my visit to Hiva Oa? She has observed that I know as much about the Inca as her companion. To thank him for his guided tour I have given him a copy of the Gauguin catalogue by O'Reilly and Artur published at Papeari in 1965. She is touched by this gesture.

'Which magazine do you write for? And why Gauguin?' she ventures.

'This isn't for a piece of journalism; I'm writing a book, and the trip is my own project.'

'A book about him?'

'It's a kind of personal account. Well, we could call it a voyage through Gauguin. A man and his own geography.'

'Are you interested in his paintings?'

'As much as in what he did with his life.'

'He's not a very likeable character, as far as I understand.'

'By any rational criteria, no, he wasn't. But can he be judged in those terms? He was of quite a different stamp. He was Paul Gauguin and he knew it.'

'Joe told me that it was really important to you to see the things from the well.'

'They are relics. Let's say that I believe in . . . their *mana!*'

Reus cut in.

'You won't need to go trekking all over the island! The day after tomorrow I'll show them to you all together. Each of us wanted to keep what we found, that's to be expected. It's all destined for the museum.'

Together with our hosts, we heartily tuck into the *mahi-mahi* with vanilla. Outside the bay windows of the dining room, the balmy darkness circles us, filled with the boom of the sea; it is scored by only a few electric lights. A loose shutter flaps. Gusts of wind are boomeranged back from one mountain peak to another. On Hiva Oa there is a sense of being naked and exposed, as if we were cast adrift on a raft of sand and tufa stone. There is always something oppressive in the palm trees, the plants, the shrillness of the insects, and the depth. It is emptiness, emptiness and wind. A hollow presence.

'Did you know that Marquesans think they're turning their back on the future and facing the past? This makes their lives a walk backwards,' explains Ottino-Garanger.

'Hence the force of the present, a relish for the moment.'

In the penumbra, on the path up to the hotel, a face glimmers in a splash of lamplight, and is blotted out at once.

CHAPTER 35

Unlike me, Koké never saw the tikis of Hiva Oa. He didn't get to the other side of the island, where they are, and made do with photographs. His ankle ruled him and he had increased his intake of wine, rum and morphine. His thighs were riddled with needle tracks. To try and come off the drug he would leave his supplies and syringes at Varney's, but the pain was so excruciating that after three hours of it his neighbour would have to give them back. In the daytime, he alternated between absinthe and laudanum, a derivative of opium, in a solution of water. When the pain became unbearable he would inject himself, over and over if necessary. Then he played the harmonium 'so that his music would make you weep', or prowled around looking at the obscene postcards he had bought in Port Said and pinned up in his bedroom. 'The animal nature in us is not something to be derided ...'

It was twilight over Hiva Oa. The enthusiasm of his early months there had lapsed. His output slowed down; there were fourteen paintings in 1901, and barely double that in 1902. This is a long way from his fertile years in Brittany, when in the course of twelve months between 1888 and 1889 he lined up more than seventy canvases. Skirmishes with the small-scale colonial set-up took a toll on his energies, and after January 1902 these multiplied. Ever ready to quibble, he encouraged school truancy, denounced the sergeants in the gendarmerie for shady dealings, allowed himself the luxury of exposing the vices of the priest, Monsignor Martin, refused to pay his taxes and exhorted Governor Petit to think things through more clearly. Why on earth did Petit imagine he should bring in a hundred families from the French West Indies, who would be given a plot of land, in order to repopulate the archipelago? And when would there be a replacement for *La Croix du Sud*, which had foundered on a reef? And what justification was there for making the Marquesans carry out forced labour on public works for ten days every year? He was threatened with fines, seizure of goods, prosecution; he only laughed scornfully and shook his fist.

To the colony he soon became an evil influence, 'an individual of the lowest kind'. He wrote vitriolic letters, his quixotic invective quickly turning to accusation and denunciation. He wrote to the inspectors. He made combative threats, standing up for his friends the Marquesans. 'Here, the gendarme carries out every kind of office: he is a notary, a special assistant tax collector, a bailiff, a harbourmaster. He fulfils all of these functions with the coarseness of a gendarme – and entirely without any guarantee of discreet silence or of honesty,' he charged. 'Here, in the Marquesas, besides being cruelly racked with pain because of illness, I have to wage a terrible struggle against the administration and the gendarmerie ... Monstrous things are happening here,' he protested.

Happiness had been glimpsed, unhappiness drunk to the very last drop.

Koké pronounced himself incurable. He only ever went out with his legs bandaged like a mummy who had escaped from his sarcophagus. At the end of his tether, he dreamed of returning to Europe and settling in Spain so as to 'seek out fresh visual elements' and find one last emotional jolt. 'Bulls, Spanish women with their hair plastered with lard – these things have been done, over and over again; but it's funny, I picture them differently,' he wrote to Monfreid, sounding him out, in August 1902. The latter dissuaded him; Gauguin was already a myth. 'Either consciously or unwittingly, your reputation is being given momentum. Vollard himself is working on it little by little. He has already caught a whiff of how widespread and undisputed your fame is,' Monfreid wrote, his encouragement well judged. 'You are the unprecedented, legendary artist who sends his disconcerting and inimitable works, works that are definitive, from far-flung Oceania.' Gauguin insisted, pathetically, in February 1903: 'I shall merely pass through Paris, on my way to Spain, where I shall work for a few years. No one else will know, apart from my friends.' Had he done so, it was a period when (as the historian Françoise Cachin fondly imagined) he might well have run into Pablo Picasso, who was born in 1881 and arrived in Paris from Spain in 1904.

Among his sufferings, Gauguin did not however include home-sickness. For what home? He had burnt his bridges – his family, his career, his position and moral standing – and could not go back. He was a traitor, his crime part rupture, part metamorphosis. He was the outcome of a miracle. Exiled on the far side of the world, he had again become the Inca of his childhood, a primordial Indian, the king of an imaginary land, one becoming ever more ripely seasoned. Yet, as the rain trickled down on the woven thatch of his *fare*, and the Pacific beat like a gong against the beach, in front of the photo of his Danish children, stiff as bodkins in their winter coats, he found one insuperable lesson: 'If I am famous after I die, people will say: Gauguin had a large family, he was a patriarch. What bitter scorn.'

If his destiny was sublime, his daily life was ghastly. Everything was fast going from bad to worse, wounds were suppurating. At the Bay of Tahauku, cut off from the rest of the world, the humidity made everything stagnant. Did he still have the strength to paint? Sometimes he did, at least until halfway through 1902. There would be only two more packages for Ambroise Vollard: twenty canvases in April 1902, and fourteen in April 1903, padded out with a batch of transfer drawings, using a procedure elaborated from inked leaves. 'Will he be displeased with the last things I sent? They may not be masterpieces, but all in all they are worth the price he is paying for them.' Gauguin would go from creative periods to total despondency. 'It will be said that I am doomed to fall, rise up, and fall again ... With each day, all my old energy leaves me.' He insisted: 'You have long known what I have wanted to establish: the right to go as far as is possible.'

His eyes were weakening. 'I am not getting better, and I am doubled up with pain.' He sent interminable letters, composed protean manu-scripts, including his *Racontars d'un rapin*, and *Avant et après*, and threw himself into quarrels that wore him out, in an attempt to defend 'this dying race'. 'We, defenceless natives, declared by you as French citizens,' he protested, and drove home his point: 'Let us return to Marquesan art. It is an art which has disappeared thanks to the missionaries, who took the view that sculpture and decoration were fetishism, an offence to the God of the Christians. That's what it comes down to, and the poor wretches submitted to it.'

Powerless, Gauguin was witness to a calamity. The world of Oceania was giving way and giving up. Unprotected, without any immunity against diseases, whole populations were perishing, losing their cultural distinctness, going into exile, dying or allowing themselves to die out. In the thirty years between 1842 and 1872, according to the figures given in the *Bulletin de la Societé d'études océaniennes*, Nuku Hiva's population fell from 8000 to 980, Hiva Oa's from 6000 to 2161, and Fatu Hiva's from 1500 to 639. Even if the censuses are not precise, it is clear that these people were being wiped out. Twenty years later, one traveller gave this account: 'Marquesas Islanders no longer have any interest in the country's affairs, they are no longer the masters, and no longer exist as a free people; since they are no longer engaged in those expeditions of warfare carried out in the past, nor in their work of old, they fritter away their time and energy in sundry meaningless activities, and little by little they lose their dignity and their originality; they are a people languishing and dying out ...' On his way through the Marquesas in 1888, Robert Louis Stevenson already observed that: 'depopulation works both ways, the doors of death being set wide open, and the door of birth almost closed' (*In the South Seas*). In the 1930s, across the six islands of the group, a total of only 2500 Marquesas Islanders would be left.

In addition to the epidemics of tuberculosis, influenza and smallpox, alcoholism also took its toll. Moralistic sermons and rules about proper conduct in a modern society led to other kinds of breakdown. There were to be no more rituals and dances, no more free love or nudity, no more tattoos. Who would now know how to build a *fare*, hollow out a pirogue or a *pahu* (a drum), or uncover the secrets of plants? 'If a young girl picks flowers and artistically fashions a pretty diadem with them, and sets it on her head, Monsignor gets angry!' Everything was prohibited by the civiliser. On contact with the whalers, the soldiers, settlers, functionaries and traders, in the face of a normative society which exploited the country, the Maoris lost their bearings and their reflexes. 'Soon the Marquesas Islanders will be incapable of climbing a coconut palm ... Always clothed (for the

sake of decency), their bodies will become frail and incapable of
enduring a night in the mountains. Soon they will all be wearing
shoes, and their feet, no longer tough, will not let them run over
rugged paths, or carry them across the stepping stones of rushing
streams . . .' If this people dies out, there will be no one left to dance,
no one left to hand on its history, no one left to speak its language.
'They sing in an incomprehensible French,' said Gauguin, deploring
the fate of a people doomed to the role of speaking pidgin. Why
should this link with memory and nature be broken? Who would
know how to talk to the gods on the maraes? Why should these
beliefs be ridiculed? And where are the garments made of bark and
embossed with tutelary figures, the divinities of stone and of bone?
Stolen. Plundered. 'The gendarmerie took it all away and sold it off
to collectors, and yet the administration has given not a single thought
to what would have been so easy: to make a museum in Tahiti of all
Oceanian art,' Gauguin noted with anxiety for the future. 'They want
to incriminate me for being the defender of poor defenceless wretches!
And yet there is even a society for the protection of animals.'

'What a vile sham your laws are . . .' Koké took up the cause of
this world being swallowed up, the world of the first human beings
in harmony with themselves, hunter-gatherers in balance with their
drives, their instincts and their gods. As for Koké himself, 'each day
becoming more of a savage', an outcast-seer made a pariah by this
micro-society, he stated: 'Art therefore encloses within itself the link
between the conscious and unconscious.' He was a prophet of a new
art of 'savage strangeness', whereby he allowed the free flow of his
inner dreams and visions, his deep, inchoate voices. 'As in Edgar Allan
Poe's *The Purloined Letter*, our modern minds cannot see anything
that is too simple and too visible.' The issue was no longer one of
satisfying the bourgeois order, or Vollard the speculator, or some
potential market. 'First of all the awareness and the good opinion of
certain people the aristocrats who understand; beyond that there is
nothing . . .' His art of the rebel and outsider was an offering, a
splitting; thanks to it, through it, he was a witness and medium,
receiving and giving. In this, 'colour is music'.

The more he went forward, the more he simplified, was with, was
inside, was stripped bare. His final canvases are children's drawings,

graceful and clumsy: *The Invocation* (W635), *Women and White Horse* (W636), *Landscape with Dog* (W638), or transfer drawings, touched-up watercolours, successive overlays traced from reality, toying with his disquiet. Among the cassias, Gauguin brushes in hasty suspended outlines. 'Suddenly, I am on earth and in the midst of strange animals, I see creatures who could well be men . . .' Apparitions of this supreme current that impels, irrigates, fertilises and prevails. The Inca no longer composes: awakened, he sings the mysterious beauty of the Living Being. He himself is the score; a tiki of flesh and blood.

CHAPTER 36

Peperu is also called Rogatien. Like the majority of people here, he has a Polynesian name, a French name, and a nickname. He is a giant, he drives around in a gleaming, air-conditioned Toyota four-wheel drive, and he follows an extremely strict diet. By drinking infusions of boiled periwinkle leaves, he has managed to go down from a weight of 377 pounds to 313 pounds.

'I used to crush my wife whenever we had sex,' he confided guiltily, checking to make sure he had his machete under the seat.

He is regarded as the best guide on the island, and he knows everyone in the isolated hamlets of Hannapaaoa, Anahi, Motuua, Eiaone and Hekeani – including Gauguin's descendants. So, according to what I have managed to work out, and what Reus and Peperu have confirmed for me, Marie Rose, Gauguin's companion, gave birth to Marie Antoinette, also called Tahiatikaomata, in September 1902. She in turn had two children in the 1920s: Tehautiaha Alfred and Toho Appoline Huhina, born in 1923, who is said to have Paul Gauguin's features. The former became the father of ten children, the latter the father of three daughters: Teupoovahi Suzanne, Namau Marie Louise, and Tahiatohuani Irène. These three are the painter's great-granddaughters, and they still live in the family village.

'We can meet up with them over there, if you like. But they aren't too fond of talking about that stuff...'

'I'd also like to see that sewing machine I've heard about. It would have belonged to Marie Rose.'

We're on the way to Puamau! It hasn't rained overnight and the track is dry, extremely dry. So much the better. You have to allow three hours to storm the ridge that forms the island's backbone and

239

get down the other side with its volcanic twists and turns. There is no alternative, just this tortuous, unsurfaced blood-red road round the steep mountainside. Other vehicles we encounter are few and far between: the truck that operates the school bus service; a farmer in his pickup with bunches of bananas in the back; two Public Works vans behind a bulldozer, off to repair a stretch of road. When it rains, this track turns into a horrendous skidpan. Everything grinds to a halt then. Hiva Oa is cut in two lengthwise, and the northern valleys rediscover the isolation of the old days. In the Marquesas people never joke about the weather. Two years ago a deluge wrecked the aerodrome for several months. Sometimes, cyclones lash these basalt teeth for a few hours before resuming their headlong course in a straight line for four, five or six thousand miles over the raging ocean.

In January 1903, at the height of the storm, Gauguin almost lost everything in the flooding of the Makemake. 'I came out of my bedroom to see what was happening, and to my great astonishment I stepped into the water up to my waist,' he wrote after his plot of land was submerged. Atuona had been flattened in a single night. 'The huge trees ... snapped in different places and fell to the ground with a thud ... The gale ripped at the light roof of thatched coconut palm, and blew in all around, so that I couldn't keep the lamp lit.' He concluded this account with a 'God, whom I have often offended, spared me this time ...'

'These are what's left of the villages round here.' Peperu pointed to the left side of the road.

Behind this swirling mist, between the rock faces smothered in tree ferns, the clans and tribes once dug in, rivalrous and jealous of each other's fruit trees and their *mape*, a variety of giant chestnut. They did not venture far outside their own territories; it was easy to get lost, and they risked abduction by enemy warriors. The ridge remained a frontier. In the maze of peaks and ravines the occasional clearings scored with rushing streams as cold as ice were the haunts of spirits, the *tupapau*.

'It's a two-hour walk to see the painted caves. If you want to go there ...'

It meant plunging into this mass of vegetation through which, here and there, black rocks poke out; then heading deeper in until you reach the dark of night, under the vault of tangled foliage, inside cathedrals of vegetation, humid tunnels; penetrating the secret of Hiva Oa.

'Another time, perhaps. Do you know the local legends?'

Peperu's great paw-like hands steered expertly as he spoke; he relished every word.

'There is the one about the white woman,' he began, his voice half in earnest, half in fun, as he watched me out of the corner of his eye. 'At dusk she looms up at a bend in the road – I'll show you which one ... She's famous! She stands there, staring at you, as if she was waiting for a lift, and she watches you go past ... In fact, there's no one there. She's dead. If I see her, I accelerate, even if it's raining!'

On the north coast at Hannapaaoa Bay, there is also a rock that juts out into the void, a place where virgins would throw themselves into the sea, as tribute to an enormous shark.

'Up until the eighteenth century this kind of offering was made every year. The sacrificing of women increased the *mana* of their families. For the ceremony, first the shark was lured with blood. There was drumming and chanting and prayers, then when the creature was there, his great fin slicing in and out of the reefs, the victim would move away from the priests surrounding her and jump into the void.'

'Of her own free will?'

'It was an honour. She was sacrificing herself for her clan, her family, her valley. For us it's a horrible thing, but you have to look at it in a different way: the clan's survival was guaranteed by these offerings. They were all convinced of that. It was how their society worked: by sacrificing one of its members, the whole community was saved. One death gave life.'

An hour later, Peperu pulled up his Toyota by the side of the cliff road. This was it. The grass was short, stubbly, the landscape had been slashed, and this spot had a mock air of coastal Brittany about it. Looking at the foam-lashed rocks, and the ocean swell smashing against the jagged shoreline, I could see the green waves Gauguin painted for the *Ondines* at Le Pouldu. There was no amniotic lagoon, no beaches of Polynesian sand; just the empty ocean breaking against the land, fashioned as he liked it, as in Finistère, on the Crozon Peninsula, at the foot of the manor house of Saint-Pol Roux, that other exile.

A lighter coloured path winds round the rocks and ends in front of the high stone we have to climb. We must be more than six hundred feet above the creeks. Repressing my incipient vertigo, I too raised myself up onto the sacrificial rock, balanced at the end of the natural diving board. Below, the sea hits the bottom of the abyss; the Pacific, drawing like a magnet, a convex shape, filling out space and vision in every direction. A blue wall that merges with the sky. A sensation of infinity, of nothingness.

'There's a story about one young girl who was saved by a bird. It caught her just as she went crashing down and flew off with her between its wings, seized from the jaws of the monster.'

We continue on our way, driving at something like twelve miles an hour. The roadway is full of ruts, puddles of water with upside-down reflections of the clouds; the car skids on the bends. At the end of this so-called road, the coast's jugular vein, are hamlets where life is slow, its rhythms those of fishing, copra, and *noni*, a miracle plant that is bought up by American laboratories; along with a little livestock, or hunting wild goats. There are forty people living here, some in *fares* that are permanent structures, others in MTRs, prefabricated constructions publicly financed for cyclone victims; sixty more are tucked away in a river bend, around a co-operative shed in the glare of the sun. Some of the houses are new and have solar panels, with a mini-generator alongside, but the majority are makeshift, patched together with boards and tin sheeting, with no anti-cyclone roofs and only a hosepipe for showering. Each of these hamlets looks deserted. Work is run down; the islands produce very little and the distances involved multiply costs.

'Tourists are still unusual, they don't bring in enough. What people dream about here is having a civil service job with a salary at the end of the month, and nothing to worry about!'

A dog is sleeping, stretched out full-length across the middle of the road, its ears quivering and twitching. What does a Maori dog dream about on the Puamau road, its belly warmed by the earth?

On a terrace, hung up by the tail, three dead-eyed tuna fish attract the flies. A shout rises through the air like a newborn bird. We keep going. Along the road Peperu greets two or three mates. Motionless, a little girl with an alamanda flower at her ear watches us from behind some thin banana trees and grapefruit trees whose branches sag with the weight of the fruit. The sun lurks under the foliage, but at the first turning it can pounce on you like a wild animal; then the windscreen blazes.

'This is Thor Heyerdahl's area!' Peperu told me, lowering his window.

After a catastrophic stay à la Robinson Crusoe on Fatu Hiva in the late 1930s, the adventurer Heyerdahl and his wife, Lis, had come to Hiva Oa to recover. Here, they had struck up a friendship with another exile from the north, Henry Lie, a Norwegian. He had shown them the tikis of Puamau, which somewhat resemble others in Peru. On the basis of Lie's work, their fevered discussions on the subject led them to put together the idea of a Maori settlement originating not in Asia but in South America, in other words from an east-west direction.

'Heyerdahl had Gauguin's rifle, you know. The rifle butt was carved and decorated. But since he didn't have a licence to carry firearms, the gendarme gave him a hard time. Thor got out of it by handing in the rusty gun barrel and keeping the butt.'

Mango trees, lemon trees, pistachio trees, mandarin trees ... a square of drooping coconut palms; a mixture of abandonment and civilisation, sweltering heat and tranquillity. Half-naked children play football in the unshadowed light. A man drowses in a hammock, both his arms tattooed with geometric patterns. Everywhere there are remnants of *pae pae*, the large stones used in building religious sites, and those indifferent horses panting in the shade of the guava trees.

In Puamau, Peperu stops at the shop owned by Orens, who is half Chinese. He is barefoot and wears Adidas shorts and a collarless shirt. Behind his low wire-meshed cupboards, in the warm gloom that smells of soap and fried rice, since 1963 Orens has been selling cans of Soupline, tinned sardines, Arnott's sugar, mosquito coils, gas tubing and Flodor crimped potato chips. His oil-run refrigerator means he can also offer bottles of Coca-Cola and Hinano beer, as well as Baron Romero Spanish wine, bottled and in cartons. This is one of only a few shops on the north coast. Because everything is imported by cargo ship, once every seventeen days, the prices are prohibitive.

Orens' shop is reminiscent of Varney's, where Gauguin got his provisions.

Orens has turned off his radio and is counting out the change from my shopping: two bottles of water, some PK sweets and a packet of biscuits. I try to spin out this encounter. I talk to him, asking him prices.

Peperu has got out of his Toyota and come in search of me. He tells me: 'Orens is married to Irène, one of Gauguin's descendants. His sister-in-law has just turned up.'

'Where?'

'Outside, come on.'

I go outside with him at once and greet the lady who has taken a seat on a bench at the door to the shop. Her feet are hurting. Peperu speaks to her in Marquesan, telling her what I am doing. She shakes her head without looking at me, embarrassed. This is indeed Suzanne-Teupoovahi, one of the painter's great-grandchildren. She is around sixty, and has strongly Polynesian features. She is rather stout, has her hair in a bun, wears a floral print dress and has a beauty spot on the wing of her nose. There is no trace of Gauguin in her face. In one of the biographies, a photograph showed her with her sisters around their great-grandfather's grave. It was 1958, and she would have been sixteen or seventeen. Her bushy hair fell down in a mass over her shoulders, straying across her breasts.

'She's happy to talk to you,' Peperu told me, introducing me as a writer and playing the intermediary.

I sit down next her and offer her my biscuits. Then, feverishly, I ask her a few questions, to which I get evasive answers. My guide has warned me: people in Puamau are fed up with this business of the painter on the other side of the world. They are at home; for them, the other side of the world is us. They've already had a photographer clicking his camera like mad at them, a spread in a magazine, but he sent them nothing. Here people lead a quiet life, and they have no wish to be hunted down like game every time there's a sailing boat in the bay, or a four-wheel-drive on the road. They have nothing to tell, nothing to show. Since I don't have a tape recorder or a camera, and just take notes, the conversation is made a bit easier.

'Do you feel proud of being part of the painter's family?' I venture.

'Yes,' she replies, without any conviction, her eyes drooping.

'Do you sometimes talk about him among yourselves? I mean, in your family?'

'No, not very much.'

'Will you go to Atuona for the centenary, will you take part in some way?'

'I don't know yet. It's the mayor who'll decide. I think so.'

From what Peperu has told me, there was an earlier commemoration when a number of descendants had a reunion in Atuona. Some came from Puamau; others were from the Danish branch of the family, and came from Europe and then from Tahiti on the *Aranui*. The Marquesans had been flattered to be included. They belonged to this big family.

'Are there still things from his day?'

'Not any more. It's hard to tell. But you can still see the sewing machine at Marie Antoinette's house, at the inn.'

Dragging her feet in the heat, Suzanne gets up to go and buy potato chips.

'Excuse me . . .'

The interview was over. I thank her for having answered my questions, albeit briefly, and wish her a good day.

She says quietly: 'It's quite all right, you know.'

We set off again. On the road, in the shade of the coconut palms, a group of five or six women are sitting cross-legged on a mat picking over beans. Their conversation is animated with laughter. Among them is Tahiatohuani-Irène. Peperu stops the car and they exchange greetings.

'She's descended from Gauguin too. Take a good look at her face . . . That's Koké! She's got his hooked nose, and her skin is very light. Would you like to get out?'

The woman does indeed have European features, and she has her great-grandfather's profile. I decide to forego a repeat performance.

'Drive on!'

Oipona is regarded as one of the great sites of pre-European Marquesan civilisation. It is set out over two wide main terraces covering an area of 5000 square metres, edged with mango trees and coconut palms. The site was restored by the Ottino-Garangers in

1991. Its paved platforms are adorned with tikis hoisted up on them. Around it the forest forms a dense screen whose silence seems palpable. One enters this space as if penetrating a pocket of suspended time. There are no birds, not a sound over the squares of lava, just the rustling of leaves as they fall, the whining of mosquitoes, the quivering of ferns roasted by the heat.

The minute we get out of the car, our shirts stick to the skin. I have trouble breathing among this overexposed greenery, this deep, burned blackness, this humidity that lies in stagnant layers beneath the mass of vegetation like tongues of mist. At times the site is so oppressive. It is on a north-south axis, with the Toea peak to the west, and the Ahonu stream to the east. Its ground-level arrangement and lava architecture channel waves and fluxes, and, through a system of bouncing and bottlenecks, it drains energy flows, concentrating them into beams.

Oipona was a religious sanctuary. It was a magic place, a *tapu*, which reverberated with the hypnotic rolling of drums, and chants that wove 'the braid of words' to infinity. A horizontal, roofless cathedral where, among the sacred banyans, shamans immolated their captives, the 'fish of the gods', by sinking a large hook into their throats. *Tuku a! Tuku a! Tuku a! E Tama! E Tama! E Tama! Hapai! Hapai! Hapai!* (He has been given! The child! Raise him up!) The liberated soul of victims who were cast into the oven, then partly devoured, later went to the gods in a final offering.

In the shade, a bored-looking pair of custodians sweep the volcanic flagstones whose surface is alveolar and bubbly. Hundreds of these were hollowed out to hold potions, drugs and tattooing inks.

'Aren't those two afraid to linger in these places of sacrifice?'

'Yes, they are. At night they're off. There is no way they would stay.'

One of the men gives us a long yellow stem which Peperu pulls into strips, and this mini-whip serves to keep off the mosquitoes that have made a meal of us in no time. We proceed by means of self-flagellation.

There are five big tikis: Manuiotaa, in grey tufa stone; Takaii, the one that interested Gauguin; Te Tovae E Noho; Fau Poe, the wife of Takaii; and Maki Taua Pepe, or 'Tiki lying', who is giving birth and sticking out her tongue, half in rage, half defiant. Takaii has the most beauty: flaring nostrils, wide-open eyes that are almost mocking. He is set on huge legs, has solid shoulders and a massive head, square, a solid block, like a wrestler poised and ready to spring. His moss-eaten eyes seem defiant and waiting. Laughing at you, through you, beyond you.

I take my time and make drawings of each one of the idols in my notebook. Like Peperu, there is no way I would lay a hand on the tikis. Out of respect, as if in a church, I keep my distance. I believe in their power, in the possibility of that crackling electric current imprisoned in these natural boundaries. If Gauguin had been fit, he would have been able to come here, leave his belongings with a neighbour and go around the site with his gouaches and his sculptor's chisels. What picture would he have painted then? What idol would he have copied? The further you climb towards the mountain, the twisting hollows of the valley, the more levels there are. At the edge of the first platforms, pebbles, blocks of tufa and small heads of decapitated tikis have been gathered together by the custodians.

We get back in the car to go and have lunch at Marie Antoinette's *auberge*. It's just a house with a garage fitted out as the dining room. A garden flowering with hibiscus, a well. Nearby is the grave of a local princess who, it is said, was buried with her bicycle.

Peperu is at my table. He has a serious appetite. We put away a salad of octopus, pork with pumpkin, raw fish with coconut milk and *uru* fries, and mangoes. Since he is so fat, to sit down he has had to double up two plastic chairs on top of one another, otherwise his chair would collapse. We talk about this and that, and in particular about a man from Puamau who is supposed to have *mana*.

After dessert, I am finally allowed to see the sewing machine. An old treadle-operated Singer, it sits imposingly on the concrete veranda, surrounded by scraps of coloured thread. It has lost its original sheen and gilded lettering and has a reddish colour where the rust has been scraped off. Though the wooden tabletop has been replaced, the four wrought-iron feet are original, as is the openwork treadle with its ornamentation. One of Marie Antoinette's nieces reluctantly gets up from the machine, where she was putting the finishing touches to the hem of a pink dress she will wear to go dancing on Saturday. A bobbin of thread still sits balanced on top. With a touch of my foot on the treadle, I make the needle jog up and down.

'It's such a simple mechanism.'

We stand either side of the machine as the kindly and matronly Marie Antoinette, hands on her hips, tells me about her proud possession.

'It had been left behind under the stilts of a neighbour's *fare*. I bought it in 1956 for 200 Pacific francs. People say it's Gauguin's machine; it has always been in the valley.'

'Will you give it to the museum?'

'No, because it's a family memento. And it's also in good working order!'

Something about this story clearly doesn't quite fit, and I went back to the records of Gauguin's estate. It's true that a machine was given to Marie Rose on her 'marriage' to Gauguin, in 1901. When she was pregnant, she came home again to the valley of Hekeani for the confinement, in June 1902. Did she bring her belongings with her then? The answer is yes if their break-up had already taken place, and no if she intended to return to Atuona, since why would she encumber herself with such a heavy object that would be waiting for her when she went back?

It is claimed that Marie Rose feared her lover would send their newborn to Europe, hence her definitive move back to her family with the baby, Tahiatikaomata. She was probably also beginning to tire of living with the painter. Whatever the case, she never returned to Atuona. Then why is a sewing machine listed as No 29 on the meticulous inventory of Gauguin's *fare* drawn up after his death, in the statement of 27 May 1903, signed by Claverie and Frébault? Moreover, the machine was shipped on the *Durance* to Papeete, listed as box 15, lot 117, and sold at auction for 80 francs to another Polynesian, Tematahi.

It is unlikely that the Singer would have travelled in the opposite direction, from Tahiti to the Marquesas. Was it then a second sewing machine that the painter had bought? There is no reference to it in his statement of accounts with the Societé commerciale de l'Océanie. But that doesn't mean anything. Or else the first one, the one Marie Antoinette is showing me, is false. That's what Louis Frébault, Emile

Frébault's descendant, had given me to understand on the telephone, indicating that there was another machine on the island, that belonged to his family, 'somewhere on Hiva Oa'. A truer, more genuine one than the machine in Puamau!

In other words, there were at least three sewing machines in the picture, two of which would have no historical value. Or one, at any rate, if Gauguin had bought a second machine after Marie Rose's departure, or if he already had one before, for his own use, to stitch his canvases, brought with him from Tahiti. What a dizzying prospect!

All that is known with certainty is what is detailed in the records of the estate. According to this, in the weeks following Gauguin's death, two sales took place. The first, with Sergeant Claverie as intermediary, was held on the spot, on 20 July 1903, to dispose of 'goods and chattels likely to find a buyer on the spot at advantageous prices', namely furniture, food and drink, clothes, lamps, saucepans, a Buffalo rifle, a Japanese sabre, the whole fetching a price of 1077.15 francs. A compass, a set of plates, Gauguin's green beret, a plane, an umbrella, a mosquito net, and a spanner to tighten the wheels of his trap, were purchased by settlers on Hiva Oa. Finally, in Papeete, on 2 September, came the sale where Victor Segalen, authorised from France, brought back 'paintings, sketches, drawings, curios, books, weapons, tubes of paint, palettes, paintbrushes.' In the view of the local administrator, 'the pictures by the deceased, a decadent painter, had little likelihood of finding a buyer.' The Singer is also referred to in the statement of 5 September, as are the trap, the harmonium, and the sculpture implements, which were sold at the time. When these two sale operations were concluded, a total of 171 and 142 lots, the Maison du Jouir, 'emptied by the liquidators like a coconut shell by earth crabs', was dismantled plank by plank. A clean sweep.

After a dreadful coffee with vanilla and the onset of a migraine, I continue on my way, muddled by these contradictions, this multiplication of trails. Why are the details so pointless, and so compelling? What's the good of these signs, scattered like tiny pebbles, which lead nowhere except to what is already evident? Disappearance, a black hole. We leave nothing behind us, only children who do not remember, feelings that dissolve, a dreamed vision of the world, a mirage, a momentary tremor. Any legacy will be whittled away, ground down in advance by the passage of the days. Our lives hang by a mere thread. Countless times the thread is cut; light turns to darkness. And wandering through this dark are our *tupapau*, our final regrets, the only ones that are plausible. At least, the more they are kindled in us, the more we remember, the less we die to ourselves. What haunts us is what has given us our foundation.

At the shoreline, under the casuarina trees, surfers venture into the indigo blue water. A minibus has deposited half a dozen tourists in baggy shorts and shirts brightly patterned with flowers and shells who dip a toe into the waves that extend to infinity, unremittingly. I take a walk on the sand. Peperu has turned on the radio. A kid takes a kick at a fruit-coloured ball that shoots up into the sky and seems never to come back down again. Gauguin said that the human life 'is less than a second'.

The Toyota moves away, then a few yards further on comes to an abrupt halt on the slope of the one and only street. Peperu lowers his window and begins a conversation with a guy of around forty, bare-chested and built like an athlete, who has just emerged from a reviving nap among the tough-leaved banana trees. With him he has his dog, a mangy-looking animal, eaten up by parasites.

Peperu introduces me. I reach out to shake the fellow's hand. But it is his hand, like a branch, heavy, solid and muscular, that stretches inside towards mine, right in front of Peperu, who draws back.

He whispers to me: 'It's the man with the *mana*.'

His hand is suddenly a treasure in mine. I would like to hold onto it longer. He withdraws it. The conversation continues and Peperu translates snatches of it for me.

'You only have to go and see him and he will treat you. Free.'

'How did he come by this power?'

'His father passed it on to him and taught him how to use it. He got it from his father, and it went a long way back, that's how. He puts his hand on the place where you have pain and it goes away. Because of the *mana*.'

'Ask him if it is something that he loses if he doesn't use it.'

Peperu does this. It's obvious that the guy speaks French but he confines himself to Marquesan. 'No, he always has it.'

'Does he need to concentrate a lot?'

'No, he doesn't. He puts his hand on you.'

We say goodbye and head off for the ascent towards the ridges, which are getting drenched. The splashes on the track make it look like a leopard skin. The windscreen wipers rise and fall slowly, then faster. I had the feeling that the man with the *mana* hadn't seen me, or rather that his opaque gaze had been reflecting me back to myself all the time. I am not from here, I am only a weird *Popaa*, a white man in a Toyota on whom the rain is beating down. But I'll come back.

CHAPTER 37

'This is why one should not advise solitude for everyone, for you have to be strong enough to endure it and act alone.' It is May 1903. In his boxes, he has only four canvases. In this last year he will have completed only six works, from W633 to W638. Landscapes with a dog or a pig. Riders on the beach. Whatever he sees from home, from his *fare*. Whatever he remembers. The easiest and most obvious things, because any physical effort makes him spit up blood. He can scarcely move about. He is riddled with eczema, his legs are raw, he overdoses on morphine to the point where it is his oxygen. 'There is one thing to be feared, that I might go blind . . .'

In March he lost his case and was convicted of 'slandering a gendarme in the exercise of his duty'. The sentence was a fine of five hundred francs and three months in prison. 'I have just been the victim of a ghastly trap. It means that my health will be ruined and completely destroyed . . . After certain scandalous events in the Marquesas, I wrote to the administration to request that an inquiry be carried out about them. It didn't occur to me that the gendarmes are all in cahoots, and that the Administrator is on the side of the Governor, etc.' He plans to appeal in Tahiti, to move heaven and earth so that he doesn't end up rotting in a jail. 'The trip there, living expenses, and above all paying for a lawyer. How much is that going to cost me?' Nonetheless, he is confident; all he did was proclaim the truth, his truth. 'I want to tell you that I am going to Tahiti to make my defence and that my defending lawyer will have a lot to say . . . and that even if I am sentenced to prison, which I regard as something that will dishonour me, I shall always walk with my head held high.' He got in touch with a lawyer and rallied his friends in Paris, Morice and Monfreid. But the business that he set in motion by reporting the smuggling activities of a gendarme at Tahuaua and 'the scoundrels who disturb our most remote archipelagoes by their bad example', rebounded against him. It was the catalyst for a good deal of resentment towards him. They were making him pay for being a libertine, a man without religion, an outsider, an artist 'absinthe-sodden, morphine-ridden, out of breath and with a bad heart...'

'At my window here, in the Marquesas, everything is darkening, the dances are over, the sweet melodies are stilled. But this is not silence.' Yet it was very like it. Marie Rose had gone and not come back. Mail seldom arrived. Except for Ky Dong and Tioka, his friends had distanced themselves from the old man, now dangerous, like a wounded animal. The gendarme, all-powerful on the archipelago, had become a personal enemy. The vice was tightening around the man accused of 'anarchist intrigues'. He wrote: 'It is true: I am a savage.'

Two months earlier, the cyclone over the Marquesas had very nearly devastated the Maison du Jouir. Since Tioka's house had been more affected than his, Gauguin offered him a quarter of his plot. It was certainly a magnanimous gesture, but from then on he was haunted by the thought that Vollard would cut off his allowance now that he was no longer producing work. He had neither the desire nor the strength to hold a brush. How would he manage if the dealer blocked his credit? At the beginning of April, he had word sent to Vernier: 'Would I be taking advantage if I asked you for a consultation, now that my faculties are becoming quite inadequate? I am ill and I can no longer walk.' He summed up his situation to Monfreid: 'All these worries are killing me.'

'The work a man produces is the explanation of that man ...' His work was accomplished, the human machine was running out. On the easel in his studio, the painting *Breton Village in the Snow*, W525, remained unfinished. This was a cluster of *pen-ty* shrouded in snow, a blue-and-white canvas dating from 1894 and showing winter in Europe. Outside, on Hiva Oa, it was thirty-eight degrees in the shade.

Gauguin took up his syringe, emptied a phial into it and injected himself. The *fare* was in a shameful state. Everything was strewn about: a handsaw, planes, a guitar, a gilded tiki, a Mexican saddle, one hundred and nineteen tins of food, a dry palette. The cook and the maid had decamped. This was the end. Stretched out on his mattress in a half-gloom where specks of dust and pollen drifted in the air, under the photographs of his Danish children and the reproductions of Puvis de Chavannes, Gauguin lay dying like a beached shark.

The pastor, Vernier, described Gauguin's final moments to Charles Morice: 'On 8 May 1903, early in the morning, he sent Tioka for me. He was complaining about acute pains in his body. He asked me whether it was morning or evening, day or night. He told me he had had two blackouts. He talked to me about *Salammbô*.' After comforting Gauguin and talking to him a little, he left him 'calm and rested'. Later that morning however, Gauguin died of a heart attack, alone, on the first floor of his *fare*. One leg hung out of the bed, an empty medicine bottle had rolled on the floor beside him: Had he taken an overdose? Tioka, the first to discover him, tried to bring him back to life by shaking him, then slapping him, then, as was the Marquesan custom, by biting his head. Since the painter no longer moved, Tioka tore down the stairs and went out into the stifling heat of the garden shouting: 'We are lost!'

Vernier came running and found Tioka and Frébault there. He attempted artificial respiration and cardiac massage. It was no use. Gauguin's heart had stopped, a worn-out mooring. He had died in the midst of his fetishes, his photographs from Port Said, his folios dedicated by Saint-Pol Roux and Mallarmé. His thighs were riddled with needle tracks, his hands stained with old paint, his shaved head blueish and shining in the burning light.

In Atuona there was helpless astonishment, confined to the *maiore* crowding the road. 'The man is gone!' This cry echoed all the way to the rocky slopes of Mount Temetiu.

Paul Gauguin was dead. It was 11 o'clock in the morning. He would soon have turned fifty-five. 'There is nothing of any note here except the death of a sorry individual by the name of Gauguin, a well-known artist, an enemy of God and of everything that is decent,' one of the fathers of the congregation observed in his report.

Most people didn't give a damn.

CHAPTER 38

When she saw me driving up, the Spanish woman at Atuona gave me a nod in greeting then ducked back into the shade of the bungalow like a crab taking cover under the coral.

'She's working,' Reus told me, sympathetically.

I went into their living room with its veranda opening onto a small humid garden overrun with rattan chairs and flowering plants in pots. Reus sat me down at a table covered with oilcloth and we exchanged some small talk – about the heat, yesterday's rain, the impending arrival of the *Aranui*. Then he brought the mango crates in which the objects had been packed in layers, wrapped first in newspaper, blackened pages of *La Dépêche de Tahiti*.

'There it is. We brought up a lot of things and I've put them in order according to the depth where they were lying. We're not saying anything definite, but you'll see for yourself.'

One by one, Reus unwraps them and lines them up in front of me. When five or six items have been laid in a row he begins another row, parallel but following some slightly different sideways alignment visible to his eyes alone. Each find is a link in an unfamiliar ideogram, horizontal, slightly oblique, set out on the table for me to decipher its meaning. Each time Reus picks up an object, he opens out the shell of newspaper, placing it on his right, then briefly shows me what kind of object it is before lining it up.

With extreme care, and size permitting, I trace its contour in my notebook so that I am left with an outline, then I immediately put it back. The next object is shown to me only after its predecessor has taken its original place again.

It all resembles a ceremony and a game. A kind of jigsaw.

'Since it was muddy, the heaviest things slid to the bottom. No one took any notice of this well. It was forgotten, closed off and buried beneath the undergrowth. There was drinking water elsewhere.'

The Maison du Jouir was demolished in order for its component materials to be sold off. The plot was left fallow and belonged to a series of different companies. We can surmise that when the *fare* was dismantled in 1903, what got thrown in the well was whatever could not be taken away or burned, or was already broken, unusable and unsaleable. Likewise, whatever had been deemed shameful by the good missionaries who saw the Maison du Jouir as the Devil's own lair – hadn't the fiendish Koké planted a grimacing totem in his garden representing the Bishop of the diocese, Monsignor Martin, well known for his sexual liaison with his maid?

Here, then, is what had been brought up from the well:

- Some metal rings from barrels, pieces of corroded iron pitted with rust.
- Springs from a trap – Gauguin was the only one in Atuona at the time to possess a horse-drawn vehicle.
- Ten or so solidified blocks of paint; these are yellow, red, white and ochre, and they smell of linseed oil; some of them have the shape of a bottle end. Who else out of Hiva Oa's five hundred inhabitants was painting with professional materials?
- Rusty, moss-covered carpenter's nails.
- Broken-off, demijohn-sized bottlenecks – as shown in the records of his account with the Societé commerciale, this was how Gauguin, a heavy drinker, bought his wine.
- Four broken pieces from a plate and a bowl bearing the mark of the Quimper pottery manufacturer Henriot, probably a memento from Pont-Aven. These fragments are decorated with blue and green symbolic motifs: hatchings, circles, a flower, rushes. We know that Gauguin arrived in Atuona with his crockery and that there is every likelihood of it having been bought in the Quimper area, or at any rate in Brittany.
- A glass tube with two teeth in a brown liquid – his?
- Broken absinthe bottles – the kind that Gauguin, from what he described in one of his letters, would hang at the end of a fishing

rod to dip it in the well. It's easy to imagine that through some clumsy movement one of two of them might have got broken against the wall of the well and fallen to the bottom. The accounts show that it cost seven francs a litre bottle. Gauguin bought his 'green fairy' at Varney's, drank it chilled and had a heavy intake.

- An intact bottle of vinegar, the glass having an old–fashioned shape.
- Part of an oil lamp.
- A phial with 'Sloan's Liniment' printed on it.
- Several brown medicine bottles, marked with measures, having contained Chinese and American products, one for the stomach and intestines, giving the details of manufacture as Warner's Safe Kidney & Liver Remedy, Rochester, NY. Some of these are broken, others are intact. Since the archipelago was closer to the west coast of the USA than to Europe, various American and Chinese products were imported. Moreover, the Asian communities were a significant commercial presence.
- Two empty ampoules made of transparent faceted glass, some 4 inches by 1¼ – according to the senior doctor at the health centre, these would have contained morphine.
- An old-style glass syringe with a plunger mechanism and a rusty needle – Gauguin's syringe, it would seem, probably thrown into the well because it was considered dangerous 'to local people'. When he died it might well have rolled under his bed with the empty morphine phial. Since he depended upon it, he took great care of it.
- A woman's half-comb made of horn, with six teeth and inscribed with the date 1851.

'We're still delving down and hoping to find more things. But at more than twelve feet down, the water's rising. Of course, we can't be sure, anyway . . .'

'Speaking for myself, I find the coincidences quite uncanny. The Quimper pottery, the solidified paint, the morphine, even the syringe . . . It all fits with his story, with his life!'

'I'd really like to come up with something else.'

Reus clams up. He knows that a significant find would be worth a huge amount of money and would have media fallout. What is more, because of the need for prudence as well as the question of fairness, these objects are ordinarily in the shared keeping of the four 'discoverers'.

What else is there to be found? That phallic walking stick that gendarme Claverie broke up with a hammer then threw away? Licentious canvases and drawings, and the pornographic photographs, those 'evil images', were burned in a summary *auto da fé* by the good priests. It would be a miracle if an intact carving or sculpture preserved in the mud were to be brought up from such a depth. In any case, the wood would have rotted, the earthenware would have crumbled.

Reus wraps up these miraculous objects again in their crumpled newspaper casing. We don't exchange another word. What is there to add to this pleasure which is like a kind of helplessness? It's all there; there is nothing there. We are like police doctors looking at an extraordinary corpse whose personality needs to be reassembled on the basis of a few bones, and which we are carrying away packed flat in layers in a mango crate-cum-sarcophagus. The corpse of Gauguin himself extracted from a hole. His pitiful and sublime life, his human life. 'A man's life is such a small thing and yet in it there is time to do great things, pieces of our shared creation,' he wrote in *Avant et après*.

At the back of the bungalow, Nathalie lurks smiling like a shadow. She is listening to the Rolling Stones.

CHAPTER 39

A steep path climbs the 1200 or so feet up to the cemetery that overlooks the Bay of Traitors. This is the hill of Hueakihi. Inside the coffin of plain boards lies the already decomposing body of Paul Gauguin, decorated with red and yellow flowers and anointed by his friend Tioka with *monoï*, the oil made from gardenias and coconut.

On 9 May he was buried in haste, near that high cross of the Catholic mission which happened to be painted in the background of his final pictures, *The Invocation*, W635, and *Women and White Horse*, W636. Brother Mahé noted in his private journal: 'The ceremony was an extremely sad one: six men were paid to carry him, the priest was in the simplest of vestments, two brothers saying the rosary preceded the small cortège of Messieurs Frébault, Hamon, Cham, two Germans, two natives and the Mother Superior . . .' Cham was Ky Dong and one of the two natives was Tioka. The Germans were from the Societé Commerciale. The priest was father Victorin Saltel, who had arrived on Hiva Oa three months earlier. He had no quarrel with the artist.

The Catholic brother went on: 'As soon as the priest had thrown some holy water on his grave the six paid men set about the task of covering it up because already the odour it gave off was not a fragrant one.' He added: 'Everything was cut extremely short. There was no oration and very few prayers; the only ones who prayed for his soul were those he had fought against since his arrival. There was not a word of regret.'

The ceremony was carried out in the early afternoon, at a mere half-hour's notice. When Pastor Vernier got to the Maison du Jouir

261

just before 2 p.m., so as to be present for the funeral, he learned that Gauguin had already been taken away. It was too late. Was this deliberate? A kind of takeover? Or was it a fundamental duty for these men of God not to abandon a baptised Catholic without the Christian sacrament?

At the instigation of Sergeant Claverie, Frébault, 'friend of the deceased, trader', and Tioka, 'neighbour of the deceased, farmer', were the signatories to the death certificate. Emile Frébault saw fit to add in the margin: 'It is known that he is married and has children but we do not know the name of his wife.' No one in Europe knew of the artist's death until much later. Oddly, Monfreid had meanwhile written him three anxious letters in which, moved by some premonition, he asked: 'If you or I were to die, what should be done? ... Should I send everything I have of yours to your wife in Denmark? And let her take from Vollard any pictures not yet paid for or any monies due to you? Would you not prefer to make a beneficiary of someone out there who perhaps means more to you?'

Monfreid was informed of the death only four months later, on 23 August 1903. Devoted to the end, he had a card printed and sent out, told the newspapers, wound up the accounts, took receipt of the money from the auction and the balance in the Société Commerciale account, this being a total of four thousand francs, and finally assembled a consignment of paintings to send it all to Mette, the legal heir. 'My poor Paul died in particularly sad circumstances,' Gauguin's wife wrote in answer. She herself would die in 1920, having witnessed an exponential growth in the craze for the work of her Tahitian exile, after the 1906 retrospective of the Salon d'automne at the Petit Palais. She paid a high price for this heroic status, sacrificing her life as a wife and mother. She never forgave him this waste, and the Danish 'clan', foremost among them her son Pola, confirmed it to have been a profound betrayal. Emil, the eldest, who became an engineer in the USA, regarded his illustrious paternity 'as a curse'.

What a strange and so decisive destiny, undergone as much as it was impelled, desired as much as it was hated, arranged and recomposed countless times, simultaneously transcended and felt ... Paul Gauguin. In this systematic wandering across the globe, this essential flight, should we see a lesson for living? He was at once cowardly and brave, resolute and calculating, intransigent and opportunistic, more generous in his art than in his life. And yet to the last he remained a man who desired without end, obstinately himself, to the ultimate essence, striving to get closer to the 'mysterious crux of thought'. With him, as the historian René Huyghe put it: 'there is a wholly conscious fulfilment of that search for reality and appearances which Western art had never abandoned, ever since the thirteenth century.' Indeed. But behind this search, which renewed his faith in primitivism, there is a mystic quest, a piercing petition addressed to God himself, whether this God be Inca, Christian or Maori: 'Where do we come from? What are we? Where are we going?'

The grave is under a frangipani tree, at the eastern end of Atuona's small cemetery, which rises in terraces. Red stones pointed with grey cement. At its foot is a necklace of white shells left by an admirer, in front of it a round stone with an inscription. On the left there stands a darkish brown statue fixed like some immemorial tiki: a reproduction of Oviri (savage), an enigmatic figure who is half-foetus, half-Diana the huntress, 'Buddha born in a Maori land', in Segalen's words; it clasps a wolf cub against its hip. Gauguin had asked to have it by his side for all eternity. On the right the frangipani branch casts a gentle shadow and leaves a starry seedbed of withered yellow-centred gardenias upon the volcanic stone.

The day I am there is 8 May, at dawn, with a few hibiscus flowers I have gathered in the thickets, my shirt sticking to me with sweat. The temperature is sizzling behind the fringe of trees blurred by the shimmer of the heat. 'In front of me I have coconut palms and banana trees, and everything is green ... What am I to say to all these coconut palms?'

The waves beat all the way to the horizon. The whole of nature is singing breathlessly. A crucified Christ watches over the site from a height of some fifteen feet. And this god made of metal, mass-produced in some French foundry, would be lugubrious amid this saturated lushness were there not a great swarm of bees lodged in the folds of his sagging loincloth, a buzzing hive hooked on to him like some obscene excrescence of foliage. Insects who shear through the air from grave to grove, magnetised by juices and pistils, vibrant atoms of life renewed.

Apprehending this dawn of the 8 May for which I had travelled more than twelve thousand miles, I promised myself to say something, to read some poems for instance, to make a tracing of the round tufa stone rock which bore the curving three-line inscription in clumsy letters:

PAUL

GAUGUIN

1903

And then, as I looked at it, in its simplicity and sobriety, here in this tropical Finisterre, I saw no point, I no longer had any need of intercession, of filters, echoes and words. Gauguin was in his last setting. For me. Without me. And I placed my hand upon this rough grave as one might stroke a sublime and complicated musical instrument. A cordial hand upon this life, that of a friend, a hand upon you, my dear old Gauguin, anointed with *monoï*, adorned with flowers in your box of rotting wood.

EPILOGUE

During his travels in the Marquesas Archipelago in August 1903, Victor Segalen, a navy doctor aged twenty-five, embarked on the sloop *La Durance*, had as yet no idea of the extent of his discovery, the importance of his role in this inventory, or of the myth that he would set in motion. On Hiva Oa, in a few days' time, he was to become the first inheritor of the savage work, the witness and the herald of an artistic colossus. Nor did he imagine that his own destiny as a writer would be sealed, his own ambition and aesthetic, through the Inca of the South Seas.

The young Segalen was 'enlightened'. The few paintings by Gauguin that he saw, but above all the events of his life, made 'an overpowering and thundering impression' upon him. He told Monfreid: 'I can say that I saw nothing of the Maori lands and people before I perused and well-nigh experienced Gauguin's sketches.'

Like an investigative reporter, he met Tioka, Ky Dong, Frébault, Reiner and Claverie; he talked to Pastor Vernier, and collected every bit of information he could, as he reconnoitred Gauguin's territory. He describes it: 'I am on a pious peregrination to Gauguin's studio, an ordinary longhouse which is now stripped quite bare.' He said of Gauguin, whose very last disciple he had become: 'He was loved by the natives, whom he defended against the gendarmes, the missionaries and all the "stuff" of murderous civilisation ... He was in a way the last upholder of the ancient cults.'

Over the next few months Segalen submitted a text on Gauguin to the *Mercure de France*, drafted his novel *Les Immémoriaux*, a homage to the people of Oceania, and laid the foundations for his *Essai sur l'exotisme*, which is haunted by the theme of the double and the Other.

On 2 September 1903, after following the directives of the estate trustee and bringing all of Gauguin's possessions back to Papeete, Segalen bought paintings, drawings, objects and pieces of wood. Opposite the governor's residence in the Place du Marché, in an auction room where the crowd veered between indifference and mockery, he recovered as much as he could of the 'holy relics': seven of the ten paintings, one being *Breton Village in the Snow*, which the auctioneer presented upside-down with the title *Niagara Falls*; drawings; the carved wood that had framed the entrance of the Maison du Jouir, which he intended for Saint-Pol Roux manor house in Finistère; a dictionary, books, albums, a notebook, various engravings, pencil sketches; the artist's palette; and lastly several lots of images, photographs and papers.

The auction was derisory. 'The buyers numbered traders and functionaries; a few naval officers; the governor in office at the time; gawpers and one teacher of drawing.' By a strange irony, Judge Horville, who had sentenced Gauguin, picked up a tiki for fifty centimes (lot number 32), and Governor Petit bought two or three lots, which included some paintbrushes. The sewing machine fetched eighty francs, the harmonium one hundred and five francs, and the trap one hundred and seventy-one francs, but all the 'artistic things' went for shameful prices. The two easels were knocked down to fifty centimes apiece, the sculpture tools for twelve francs, the carved walking sticks for between one and fifteen francs, the paintbox for four francs.

Segalen spent more than half of his budget, a total of 188.95 francs, on acquiring twenty-four lots. 'Bidding in the thick of the auction, I bought whatever the opportunity allowed me.' For the seven paintings he paid between seven and thirty-five francs, and sixteen francs for four of the five large wood carvings, 'the ornamental pediment and metopes of the Jouir', which he gave to Saint-Pol Roux; he got the palette for a mere two francs, and paid four francs for a printing plate. Among his purchases, besides the print of Mallarmé's portrait, monotypes and a variety of engravings, there was also a 'jumble of drawings, some of them squared off for enlargement'. He also picked up 'a lot of miscellaneous papers' (No 82) for sixteen francs, and 'a lot of albums' at eleven francs (No 119), and for one franc each, two 'lots of images' (Nos 132 and 133). Others, as well as Governor Petit, notably two buyers named Cochin and Nouveau, bought 'images and papers' for between one and seven francs (lots 95, 99, 100, 101, 129, 130–134, and 136). What did these consist of? Seemingly, documents including portraits, reproductions of paintings, photographs of relatives, friends and people close to him, Marquesan warriors, and monuments, his personal gallery and museum of what mattered, which was with him to the end, pinned to the walls of his *fare*.

Years later, in the course of a sale at auction, the photograph of Helena Suhas reappeared. Was it among those lots of images, the painter's last 'dear little friends' in his Maori exile? I would like to believe so. 'An original photograph, pre-1900, period print on sepia paper, in very good condition ...' An ordinary photo stuck on cardboard, for a few hundred francs: a bare-headed *vahine*, solemn in her muslin missionary dress, a gardenia flower at her ear, a silver bracelet on her wrist ... The mother of a child painted by Gauguin in 1892 while he was distraught with loneliness, turning back towards Papeete with his dream at an end. Helena Suhas, Atiti with his eyes shut; Aristide, the child asleep on his painted pillow in a Dutch museum, the child who is dead, the magic mummy, the bait for this story, where a witness passed through. The spark that moved me to begin.

Paris, Hiva Oa.
1998–2001.

BIBLIOGRAPHY

BIOGRAPHIES, MONOGRAPHIC STUDIES AND CATALOGUES

Jean Dorsenne, *La Vie sentimentale de Paul Gauguin*, L'Artisan du Livre, Paris, 1927.

Pola Gauguin, *Paul Gauguin, mon père*, trans. Georges Sautreau, Editions de France, Paris, 1938.

Jean Leymarie and René Huyghe, *Gauguin*, Catalogue of the Centenary Exhibition, Musée de l'Orangerie, Editions des musées nationaux, Paris, 1949.

Dossier de la succession Paul Gauguin, Société des études océaniennes, Papeete-Paris, 1957.

René Huyghe, *Gauguin*, Flammarion, Paris, 1959.

René Huyghe et al, *Gauguin*, Collection Génies et Réalités, Hachette, Paris, 1960.

Catalogue Wildenstein, Fondation Wildenstein and Editions des Beaux-Arts, Paris 1964.

Charles Chassé, *Gauguin sans légendes*, L'Oeil du temps, Paris, 1965.

Gauguin, Catalogue of the Musée Gauguin, Papeari, 1965.

Bengt Danielsson, *Gauguin à Tahiti et aux îles Marquises*, Editions du Pacifique, 1975; English translation, *Gauguin in the South Seas*, trans. Reginald Spink, Allen & Unwin, London, 1965.

Pierre Leprohon, *Paul Gauguin*, Gründ, Paris, 1975.

Victor Segalen, *Gauguin dans son dernier décor et autres textes de Tahiti*, Fata Morgana, Fontfroide-le-haut, 1975.

Jean-Marie Dallet, *Je, Gauguin*, Robert Laffont, Paris, 1981.

G. M. Sugana, *Tout l'oeuvre peint de Gauguin*, Flammarion, Paris, 1981.

José Pierre, *Gauguin aux Marquises*, Flammarion, Paris, 1982.

Maurice Malingue, *La Vie prodigieuse de Gauguin*, Buchet-Chastel, Paris, 1987.

Paul Gauguin vu par les photographes, Edita, Lausanne, 1988.

Françoise Cachin, *Gauguin*, Hachette, Paris, 1989; English translation, *Gauguin, The Quest for Paradise*, Thames & Hudson, London, 1992.

Gauguin et l'Ecole de Pont-Aven, catalogue, Bibliothèque nationale, 1989.

Gauguin and the Pont-Aven School, catalogue, Tate Gallery, London, 1966.

Gauguin, catalogue, Galeries nationales du Grand Palais, Editions de la Réunion des musées nationaux, Paris, 1988–9.

Rencontres Gauguin à Tahiti, conference proceedings, 1989.

Ky Dong, *Les Amours d'un vieux peintre aux Marquises*, A Tempera, 1989.

David Sweetman, *Paul Gauguin, A Complete Life*, Hodder & Stoughton, London, 1995.

Belinda Thomson, *Gauguin*, Thames & Hudson, London, 1995.

Paul Gauguin, exhibition catalogue, Hiva Oa, Marquesas, 1996.

Gauguin, catalogue, Fondation Gianadda, Martigny, 1998.

Bulletin de la Société des Etudes océaniennes, 'Gauguin' special issue, Nos. 279–80, Papeete, 1998.

Armand Seguin, *Paul Gauguin*, Baudouin, 1999.

Michel Butor, *Quant au livre, triptyque en l'honneur de Gauguin, Conférences del Duca*, Bibliothèque nationale de France, 2000.

CORRESPONDENCE AND PRINCIPAL TEXTS

Annie Joly-Segalen (ed.), *Lettres de Gauguin à Georges Daniel de Monfreid*, Plon, Paris, 1930.

Cahier pour Aline, facsimile edition, with commentary by Suzanne Damiron, Fonds Jacques Doucet, Paris, 1963.

Daniel Guérin (ed.), *Oviri ou les écrits d'un sauvage*, Folio-Gallimard, Paris, 1974.

Victor Merlhès (ed.), *Correspondance de Paul Gauguin, documents, témoignages*, Fondation Singer-Polignac, Paris, 1984.

Victor Merlhès (ed.), *Lettres Gauguin-Van Gogh*, Avant et après, Papeete, 1989.

Racontars d'un rapin, Taravao, Tahiti, 1994.

Maurice Malingue (ed.), *Lettres de Gauguin à sa femme et à ses amis*, Grasset, Paris, 1946, 1992; English translation, *Paul Gauguin: Letters to His Wife and Friends*, trans. H. Stenning, Saturn, London, 1948.

Noa Noa, Gilles Artur, Jean-Pierre Fourcade, Jean-Pierre Zingg, musée Paul Gauguin, Tahiti, 1987.

Paul Gauguin: Lettres à Octave Mirbeau, A l'Ecart, 1992.

Noa Noa, Editions Assouline, Paris, 1995.

Noa Noa, Abbeville Press, New York, 1995.

Avant et après, Editions de l'Après-midi, 1996.

OTHER TAHITIAN SOURCES

Jean Dorsenne, *Un fils de cannibales*, Editions Nouvelle Revue critique, 1927.

Jean Dorsenne, *Polynésie*, Emile Paul, 1929.

William Somerset Maugham, *The Moon and Sixpence*, 1919, Mandarin, London, 1990; French translation, *L'Envoûté*, Editions de France, Paris, 1928.

William Somerset Maugham, *Purely for My Pleasure*, William Heineman, London, 1962.

Jean Reverzy, *Le Passage*, Flammarion, Paris, 1977.

Fleurs et plantes de Tahiti, Editions du Pacifique, Papeete, 1978.

Bob Putigny, *Le Mana*, Editions de l'Après-midi, 1987.

Christian Buchet, *La Découverte de Tahiti*, Tallandier, Paris, 1993.

Paul Theroux, *The Happy Isles of Oceania*, Penguin, Harmondsworth, 1992; French translation, *Les Iles heureuses d'Océanie*, Grasset, Paris, 1993.

Alain Gerbault, *Un paradis se meurt*, Hoëbeke, Paris, 1994.

Marc Chadourne, *Vasco*, La Table Ronde, 1994.

Aiu Boullaire-Deschamps, *Une vie d'exception aux Tuamotu*, Barthélemy, 1997.

Dominique Agniel, *Aux Marquises*, L'Harmattan, Paris, 1998.

Eve Sivadjian et al., *Iles Marquises, archipel de mémoire*, Autrement, Paris, 2000.

Max Radiguet, *Les Derniers Sauvages*, Phébus, Paris, 2001.

ADDITIONAL SOURCES AND REFERENCES

Gauguin: Lettres à Emile Bernard, Editions Nouvelle Revue Belgique, 1942.

Théophile Briant, *Saint-Pol Roux*, Seghers, Paris, 1952.

Jean-Louis Bédouin, *Victor Segalen*, Seghers, Paris, 1963.

Correspondance Saint-Pol Roux-Segalen, Rougerie, Mortemart, 1975.

Robert Louis Stevenson, *In the South Seas*, Chatto & Windus, London, 1900.

Robert Louis Stevenson, *Veillées des îles, Le Creux de la vague* and *Dans les mers du Sud*, UGE, Paris, 1977.

Viviane Forrester, *Van Gogh ou l'Enterrement dans les blés*, Le Seuil, Paris, 1983.

Patrick O'Reilly, *Victor Segalen et l'Océanie*, Editions du Pacifique, Papeete, 1985.

Catherine Puget, *Gauguin et ses amis à Pont-Aven*, Editions Le Chasse-Marée/Armen, Douarnenez, 1989.

A. S. Hartrick, *A Painter's Pilgrimage through Fifty Years*, Cambridge University Press, Cambridge, 1939.

Alfred Thornton, *Diary of an Art Student*, Isaac Pitman, London, 1938.

Pierre Loti, *Romans*, Editions Omnibus, Paris, 1989.

Gilles Manceron, *Victor Segalen*, Jean-Claude Lattès, Paris, 1991.

Pierre Loti, *Voyages*, 'Bouquins', Robert Laffont, Paris, 1991.

Ambroise Vollard, *En écoutant Cézanne, Degas, Renoir . . .*, Grasset, Paris, 1994.

Alain Quella-Villéger, *Pierre Loti, le pèlerin de la planète*, Aubéron, Bordeaux, 1993.

André Cariou, *Les Peintres de Pont-Aven*, Editions Ouest-France, Rennes, 1994.

Victor Segalen, *Oeuvres complètes*, 'Bouquins', Robert Laffont, Paris, 1995.

Alain Quella-Villéger (ed.), *Polynésie, les archipels du rêve*, an anthology from eight novels, Editions Omnibus, Paris, 1996.

Pierre Loti, *Cette éternelle nostalgie* (Loti's journal), La Table Ronde, 1997.

Herman Melville, *Typee*, Oxford University Press, Oxford, 1996.

Herman Melville, *Taïpi, Omou, Mardi* (Oeuvres complètes, vol. 1), La Pléiade, Paris, 1997.

Vincent Van Gogh, *Dernières Lettres*, Mille et une Nuits, Paris, 1998.

Alain Buisine, *Pierre Loti*, Tallandier, Paris, 1999.

André Cariou, *Impressionistes et néo-impressionistes en Bretagne*, Editions Ouest-France, Rennes, 1999.

François-Bernard Michel, *La Face humaine de Vincent Van Gogh*, Grasset, Paris, 1999.

Jean-Michel Belorgey, *Transfuges, voyages, ruptures et métamorphoses: des Occidentaux en quête d'autres mondes*, Autrement, Paris, 2000.

Alberto Manguel, *Stevenson sous les palmiers*, Actes Sud, Arles, 2001.

INDEX